GRAIN MAINS

GRAIN
MAINS

101 Surprising and Satisfying
WHOLE GRAIN RECIPES *for*
EVERY MEAL OF THE DAY

BRUCE WEINSTEIN *and*
MARK SCARBROUGH

RODALE

Rodale books may be purchased for business or promotional use or for special sales. For information, please write to: Special Markets Department, Rodale Inc., 733 Third Avenue, New York, NY 10017.

Printed in the United States of America

Rodale Inc. makes every effort to use acid-free ♾, recycled paper ♻.

Book design by Christina Gaugler

Photographs by Tina Rupp

Prop styling by Leslie Siegel

KAMUT® is a registered trademark of Kamut International.

Library of Congress Cataloging-in-Publication Data

Weinstein, Bruce.
    Grain mains : 101 surprising and satisfying whole grain recipes for every meal of the day / Bruce Weinstein and Mark Scarbrough.
        p.   cm.
    Includes index.
    ISBN 978–1–60961–306–8   hardcover
    1. Grain.   I. Scarbrough, Mark.   II. Title.
TX557.W45   2012
641.3'31—dc23   2012002301

Distributed to the trade by Macmillan
2   4   6   8   10   9   7   5   3   1   hardcover

We inspire and enable people to improve their lives and the world around them.

rodale.com

I worked for chaff and earning Wheat
Was haughty and betrayed.
What right had Fields to arbitrate
In matters ratified?

I tasted Wheat and hated Chaff
And thanked the ample friend—
Wisdom is more becoming viewed
At distance than at hand.

—Emily Dickinson, poem #1269

CONTENTS

PERIMETER, CLOCKWISE FROM BOTTOM RIGHT: Job's tears; white, black, and red quinoa; rye berries; sorghum; millet; teff; buckwheat groats; wild rice and "cultivated" wild rice; and triticale berries. CENTER FROM TOP: amaranth; oat groats; hull-less and black barley

GOOD NEWS—AND THEN MORE

You probably already know much of the good news about whole grains:

1. **They're terrific at helping you keep the pounds off.**

   Because of all the digestible and indigestible fiber in whole grains, you feel full and content—and are thus encouraged to eat less. All that fiber exits your stomach at a crawl, about four calories per minute. You not only feel sated more quickly; you also feel sated longer. By contrast, sugars leave your stomach at a gallop, about ten calories per minute. That's why a mid-afternoon snack of a bowl of pudding will leave you rummaging again in the pantry for another snack even before you start dinner.

2. **Whole grains can keep your heart in fighting shape.**

   A Wake Forest University analysis of seven studies encompassing 285,000 people found that those who ate 2½ servings of whole grains a day reduced their risk of coronary disease by almost a quarter. And what's a serv-

ing? Not much. Any one of the following counts as one: a slice of whole-grain bread, about ¾ cup of whole-grain cereal, ½ cup of whole wheat pasta, or as little as ¼ cup of cooked whole grains themselves. A single serving of many of the recipes in this book will set you up for the day.

3. **They can cut your risk for type 2 diabetes.**

   Because whole grains exit the stomach slowly and require increased digestive activity, they morph into glucose (a.k.a. brain and muscle food) at a fairly slow rate—and so they give you a long, slow energy burn, not a short, aggressive insulin spike.

And there's still much more! A study published in *The American Journal of Clinical Nutrition* in 2011 found that those who ate a whole-grain cereal in the mornings significantly reduced their risk of hypertension. Whole grains can help lower blood cholesterol levels. They've been shown to fight gum disease. And some of the compounds in some whole grains—lignans and oligosaccharides—

function as "prebiotics," stimulating the growth of good flora in your gut.

Suffice it to say, whole grains are a veritable medicine cabinet on the plate. But believe it or not, there are more reasons why whole grains are nature's wonders. And these are the ones that interest us the most: the culinary reasons. For us—two cookbook writers with 21 titles under our belts in 12 years, not counting the ones ghostwritten for celebrities, and not counting the countless articles and columns we've written for most of the food and health magazines—these reasons may well be the most compelling:

1. Whole grains are incredibly versatile.

We have a good friend who once said, "I'd be a vegetarian if I knew how to cook." When pressed to explain, she mumbled something about boiling a pot of quinoa and getting stuck with it all week. She's not alone. Many of us think cooking a whole grain is nothing more than dumping it in a cauldron and then looking at a forlorn bit of beige in the colander later.

In fact, whole grains are up to the challenge of a world of cheffy techniques and preparations, stir-fries to braises, soups to salads, roasted this to fried that, vegetarian, vegan, or neither. Because of a complex interaction of carbohydrates, they absorb some flavors with nary a change and enhance others by suppressing bitter notes; they provide back-taste notes for blander ingredients and bring

out the sweet or sour notes in more commanding ones.

2. The range of textures and flavors is greater than almost any food group in the supermarket.

We love pork. And beef. And chicken. And rotisseried baby goat. But we'll also confess that there's a fairly small range among protein flavors. No, lamb doesn't taste like goat; however, there's a small continuum of flavors among various cuts from various animals. Of course *smoked* pork doesn't taste like *wine-braised* beef; but as you homogenize and standardize the cooking techniques among various cuts, you reduce the flavor range even more. For example, a broiled pork chop and a broiled flank steak can taste within spitting distance of each other. Sad to say, the taste of lobster isn't that far from that of shrimp. Nor halibut from bass. Yes, subtly different—but on a small continuum.

Not whole grains! The range of textures and flavors is astounding: from the subtle sweetness of amaranth to the in-your-face sour/savory slapdash of spelt berries; from the soft, gentle luxury of teff to the molar-satisfying dankness of hull-less barley; from the nutty earthiness of red rice to the slightly musky, grassy give of brown. Whole grains can hit four of the five flavor nodes without a problem: sweet, sour, bitter, and umami. You can add your own salt.

3. Whole grains are the gourmet ingredient hiding in plain sight.

For us two food writers, this is the big one. Let the backyard boys have their whole pigs in pits. It's been done. Many times. But not black barley. Or Job's tears. Or rye berries. Maybe as side dishes, but rarely as the center of the plate.

You want to pump up your foodie creds? An entire category is hiding in plain sight, right on the shelves of the corner supermarket. You don't need to dig a pit—or go all the way around the world to discover some esoteric ingredient. Whole grains have been here all along, even if some of us have passed them by on our way to the smoked jowls and organic fennel. We should stop and consider the creaminess of whole-grain farro, the spike of triticale, the snap of rye berries.

4. Despite being a gourmet find, whole grains won't break the bank.

A brown rice casserole will put you back a few bucks; a standing rib roast, a chunk of your IRA. And when you buy an affordable bag of millet or buckwheat, you're also stocking up for satisfying meals for the future, not just for tonight.

5. Finally, whole grains are deeply connected to us as humans.

They're "founder crops," some of the first things we learned to cultivate back in the shadows of history. By relishing whole grains, we connect ourselves to our past in a deep and fundamental way. Whole grains led our ancestors to settle in large groups—and thus gave us what we now call "civilization" and even "culture." We grouped together to be near the grain stores; we became social (not just familial) creatures; we began doing things for larger and larger gathered groups—a.k.a. audiences. Voilà, Mozart and Monet.

Given all that, why aren't most of us eating more whole grains?

Yes, there's the 6:15-on-a-Wednesday-night factor. Some whole grains take time to cook, something few of us have in ready supply. But we've developed some ways around that problem, as you'll see. You can make cold salads on a Sunday afternoon when you have more free time, then enjoy them for days: lunch at your desk or a quick dinner when you're back home. What's more, if you do some simple batch-cooking on the weekends, whipping up a bowl of wheat berries or a pot of barley for the fridge, you can have several whole-grain hot meals in the days ahead as you dip into your storehouse, adding grains to soups or casseroles.

We'll also admit that some whole grains are rather esoteric, more aspirational than inspirational. Triticale berries, anyone? But a cook's reach should exceed his grasp. Or hers. With apologies to Robert Browning.

But what else keeps us from eating whole grains? We suspect they're too often shellacked with all those nutritional (and digestive) claims. Sure, it's hard to talk about whole grains without bringing up the power pack of vitamins and fiber that they are.

But let's. In fact, let's never mention your colon again. From here on out, let's think about whole grains from a culinary standpoint, not a nutritional one. Let's assume their pharmacopeia status—and move on.

What's more, whole grains are too often forgotten because of where they're found in the modern grocery store—that is, the middle aisles.

Many of us have swallowed whole that foodie canard about "shopping the perimeter of the supermarket to find real food." In turn, we've missed the red rice, amaranth, barley, buckwheat, and even rye berries.

With whole grains, you can burnish your culinary creds and explore a wide-open category you may have passed by; you can find a new way to think about dinner while also crafting salads for lunch in the days ahead and set-you-up-right breakfasts for the weekends. You can embrace the widest range of flavors in the supermarket *and* the roots of human civilization. All without thinking about your colon. Seems like a win/win to us.

ONE QUIBBLE

Whole is deceptive. To figure out why, we need to look more closely at the seeds we call *grains.* Most have four components:

- the tough, outer, mostly inedible, protective **hull,** which functions like the shell for a mollusk;
- the thin mesh of fibrous, protective **bran,** which seals moisture and nutrients into the seed and provides both the nutty, earthy flavor notes as well as the inherent chew, delicate to dramatic;
- the tiny, dark **germ,** which powers the seed to reproduce but also provides most of the luxurious fat, much of it polyunsaturated, with grassy, savory, and even umami overtones;
- and the large, pale **endosperm,** the center of the seed, which offers most of the luxurious, soft texture and the sometimes floral, always pronounced sweetness in the flavor profile.

So here's the quibble, the deceptive part: Almost no whole grain that you buy is whole. Very few recipes in this book—or in any whole-grain book—call for grains straight out of the field. Most are not yet edible, some are edible in only very small quantities unless you're willing to brave a stomachache, and a few sport grossly bitter chemicals that protect the seeds from anyone who (or anything that) wants to eat them.

More confusing still, white rice and pearled barley are sometimes pointed to as "processed grains," as if "whole grains" themselves are somehow unprocessed. True, brown rice and hull-less barley are not *as* processed as white rice and pearled barley; but they, like almost all whole grains, are indeed processed—in two, three, or even four steps:

1. The chaff or stalks and other flowery bits are removed to reveal the seeds.

2. Their inedible hulls are also usually removed.

3. The naked grains may be washed to remove any of those chemical deterrents to culinary bliss.

4. And the grains are often dried for long storage.

Without their tooth-cracking hulls, most whole grains are not whole, per se. In truth, we should call them *culinary whole grains*. Or perhaps *as-whole-as-is-feasible grains*. But perhaps we're lazy.

You'll also note we keep using qualifying words like "almost all" in this discussion. That's because there are *culinary* whole grains that are not *botanical* grains: buckwheat and quinoa, for example. These have a slightly different structure, although they get lumped with other whole grains in the kitchen because of their epicurean similarities.

And there's one whole grain we can eat raw right out of the field, with almost no processing, or with minimal cooking, and almost always with the hull intact: sweet corn.

In the end, most of the culinary whole grains we'll work with in this book still have three of their four components: the bran, germ, and endosperm. By definition, we've just excluded all white rice, almost all couscous, and most of the farro sold in our supermarkets (both *perlato* and *semi-perlato* farro—more on this in a bit). However, we have not knocked out certain whole-grain flakes (grains that have been steamed and rolled but left with those three essential parts intact): barley flakes, rolled oats, or wheat flakes, for example. Nor have we kicked whole-grain polenta or grits to the curb.

In fact, the key difference for us is the one between a *processed* grain and a *refined* one. In modern agriculture, the processing can go well beyond our three or four steps. The bran or the germ can also be removed. Most of the time, both are.

Because of the abundance of polyunsaturated fats in the germ, grains go rancid in long storage. And because of the abundance of fiber in the bran, grains do require more chewing. To fit our speedier, apparently toothless world, a *refined* grain is stripped down just to the sweet endosperm—a lovely treat, no doubt; but a long way from the dynamic flavor continuum of its whole-grain incarnation. Pearled barley, white rice, all-purpose flour, most cornmeal, white rice flour, *perlato* farro—these are your endosperms done up as pantry staples.

We'll never turn down a layer cake made with all-purpose flour. But that's not our purpose in this book. Not a one of these recipes even centers on grain flours: whole wheat flour, quinoa flour, and the like. While some of the recipes call for those, they also include a whole grain of some sort. And there's not a grain "sneak" in the mix, barley buried in brownies. As you can see, we're serious about whole grains. More so than you might think. We want to take them off the side of the plate and move them to the center.

THE GLUTEN QUESTION

With the rampant rise of celiac disease in Western countries, as well as burgeoning gluten allergies around us, some shills have rushed into the breach to offer whole grains as the answer.

The truth is far more nuanced. Without a doubt, four whole grains contain glutens, sometimes in ample supply: barley, rye, triticale, and wheat in all its forms, from wheat berries to Kamut® to farro. And yes, even spelt, which is a type of wheat. It's not gluten-free.

Other whole grains are void of glutens: amaranth, buckwheat, corn, millet, quinoa, rice, sorghum, teff, and wild rice.

Oats are not in either list. While they do not *appear* to contain glutens—more research is needed—they are often contaminated with glutens because 1) oats are grown near gluten-rich crops and pick up some of the dust, particularly during harvest, or 2) oats are often processed in a plant that also processes gluten-rich grains, thereby offering them the chance to pick up even more of said dust. With those caveats in tow, some celiac support groups say oats may be a gluten-free but only if they are consumed in small quantities and purchased from a manufacturer that guarantees a gluten-free production line. Oat groats—the whole grain itself, not steamed and flattened—may have a lower level of cross-contamination than rolled oats, but the evidence is spotty and too often anecdotal.

In fact, given the predominance of wheat throughout North American grain processing facilities, gluten cross-contamination remains a distinct possibility with many other whole grains. Don't fear; be informed. Consult the individual manufacturers. Some are incredibly forthcoming with studies and certifications. But also consult your personal physician as well as a reliable celiac organization. The more you know, the better you'll eat.

THE LAY OF THE LAND (OR OF THE BOOK, AS THE CASE MAY BE)

The most important thing you need to know is that this is a book of main courses. There's not a side dish here. Even the gratin (page 157) has been pumped up to make it center-of-the-table fare.

Since whole grains are not only nutritional wonders but also culinary ones, and since they are indeed the gourmet ingredient hiding in plain sight, we want to make them the focus of the meal, not an afterthought with a pat of butter. In other words, we want them at the center of the plate. Which means we want to explore and—yes—play around with whole grains as the very ballast of a dish, the way chicken breasts might be in a skillet sauté. In all that follows, a whole grain is the heart of a recipe's flavors, the fulcrum on which the others balance.

That all said, this is not a vegetarian book. We've scattered lots of meat around—although we should also tell you plenty of the recipes swing vegetarian or vegan (or can be so swung with slight emendations). And any meat used is often a "flavoring agent" for the grains themselves.

The recipes are cast in three chapters: *Early, Cold,* and *Warm.* That is, 1) breakfast fare, 2) salads and such that can be made ahead, and 3) hot meals, best for supper or even dinner parties, barley burgers to quinoa crepes, soups to casseroles. Within each chapter, the recipes are collected in like-minded groups: In the breakfast chapter, for example, there are cereals in one section and weekend fare in another.

The recipes themselves have distinct components. At the start of each, you'll always find these:

Serves. A *rough* approximation of how many servings the recipe yields. We're two middle-aged foodies; we can polish off a bowl of salad more quickly than our parents but can't compete with our nieces and nephews.

Active time. The time you'll spend actually doing the work of the recipe: chopping an onion, filling a pot, and grilling the fish.

Total time. The start-to-finish time the recipe takes, including all the times you're lolling about: when the grains are soaking, when the casserole is baking.

The recipe may also include one or more of these:

Make ahead. Tips for how to store the dish for later or how to cook it partially one day and finish it another.

Save time. By and large, how to make the recipe if you already have that pot of cooked wheat berries or quinoa or what have you in the fridge: what steps to skip and how much of the cooked grain to add at the right moment.

Vegetarian/Vegan/Make It Vegetarian/Make It Vegan. A marker for a recipe that fits one of those parameters, always found in the upper left or right corner of the page. To clarify, *vegetarian* means that the recipe has no direct animal products (like meat) but does have ingredients that may have come from a living animal (like milk, butter, cheese, yogurt, eggs, or honey). We have *not* used *vegetarian* to mean *pescatarian* (that is, someone who doesn't eat land animals but does eat fish and shellfish). Therefore, a standard bottling of Worcestershire sauce kicks a recipe out of the vegetarian category because of the sauce's reliance on anchovies. *Vegan* is the strictest term of all, connoting a recipe in which there are no animal products *whatsoever,* including honey or milk. (Note that the *vegan* designation pertains only to the recipe itself, not to whatever else is offered as serving suggestions in the notes.)

If the recipe lends itself to an easy vegetarian or vegan conversion without destroying its flavor profile, we've given you a way to do that.

To the side of the recipe itself, you'll also find one or more tips like these:

Testers' Notes. Tips or tricks that we discovered in making the recipe or that our testers discovered in remaking it. You'll also find some serving suggestions here, as well as information about less-familiar ingredients.

Grain Swaps. Suggestions for other grains that will work with this flavor profile.

Chef It Up! Ways to go whole hog. In truth, there are two of us working on this book. Bruce the chef always tries to push the boundaries of flavors and textures; he loves to fiddle with whatever he's found on his latest shopping trip, even his online shopping excursions. Mark the writer struggles to pare it all back to make it more accessible. Many of these tips are then the ways the recipe was first tested—or further turns Bruce wanted to make in the concept while Mark applied the brakes. They'll no doubt make a more interesting dish; they may also send you on a more extensive shopping trip, probably some of it online for esoteric spices and such.

Make It Easier! Ways to streamline or simplify the recipe. For example, our granola calls for three kinds of whole-grain flakes, but it could also be made with a selection of two. Or a recipe might call for cutting the kernels off ears of corn but we'll give you the equivalent amount of frozen corn kernels to use instead.

WATER, WATER EVERYWHERE: COOKING WHOLE GRAINS

Getting whole grains from the box to the table often involves two if not three steps. All involve water—or on rarer occasions, some other liquid like vegetable broth. The cooking process can be divided into **three steps.** To wit:

1. Water Before the Heat

Believe it or not, it's not necessary to rinse whole grains before cooking them. Yes, many cookbooks, particularly older ones, are nuts for this step. Even newer ones proffer this advice, mostly because recipe-testing has yet to catch up with modern production.

Even a decade ago, grains were often left with saponins or other bitter elements on the bran. Quinoa was particularly notorious, but even some varietals of spelt could knock you out. What's more, shipping methods for some grains like rice included coating them in talc to absorb rot-inducing moisture in a ship's hold. Finally, whole grains were often only found in bulk at health-food stores—and heaven knows where hands had been before they reached into those bins.

These days, rinsing has become essentially unnecessary. You needn't worry too much about residual, bitter compounds. Reputable, large producers thoroughly wash quinoa and other grains before packaging them. If you're buying from some small producer online, ask questions—or rinse away to be safe. Otherwise, you're good to go. These days, talc-coated rice is illegal in almost all developed countries (although you can sometimes find bags of it in discount Chinese supermarkets). And bad stuff from dirty hands will not be cured by water, but maybe by the heat of cooking. Besides, you should be spending your hard-earned money at a market with better sanitary practices.

However, there is still the matter of rinsing and aesthetics. Some cooks insist on rinsing long-grain rice to wash off excess starch so the grains stay separate after cooking. But this is not even an issue with long-grain brown, red, or black rice since the bran coating keeps the starch tucked inside the grains.

That said, there are times when rinsing is advisable—particularly if you're lucky enough to buy whole grains directly from a farmer selling them at a roadside stand or from his online store. In this case, bitter compounds may be present; pesticides may be an issue. Also, certain grain producers package "minimally processed" grains. A rinse can't hurt any of these.

Whether you rinse or not, you still can't turn off the tap. Whole grains are dried for long storage and economic convenience. Along the way, they may have lost copious amounts of moisture, often more than half their weight. So you may need to soak them before they hit the heat.

Soaking

Soaking gives the grains a head start on the water uptake in the pot. Heat and water both work to tenderize the grains, but they don't work at the same rate. Heat actually works more quickly *and* more relentlessly, breaking apart the exterior cells before the inner ones have tenderized, causing inner cells to rupture before they've plumped, and eventually compromising the prized texture (although not much of the flavor). By rehydrating grains, you give the water a leg up on the tyranny of the heat: If you get the innards doped with moisture before the coating has broken apart, you end up with more even cooking—and therefore better texture, more chew without mushy bits.

So to soak or not to soak? We've got a few general guidelines. We'll detail specific cases in the recipes themselves. Some of those suggestions may also contradict these guidelines, for reasons we'll explain on a case-by-case basis. Be that as it may, here's what we suggest:

- Many whole grains can benefit from a soak in advance: any wheat berry, oat groats, rye berries, triticale berries, hull-less barley, and sorghum.

- Some either don't need it at all or aren't particularly enhanced by soaking: amaranth, buckwheat, millet, corn, quinoa, and wild rice.

- Rice is the outlier. You *can* soak whole-grain rice. You will reduce the cooking time by as much as 25 percent. But because of the porous, delicate structure of the bran, we don't find that soaking rice enhances the texture one whit. In fact, we find it can turn the grains mushy. That said, if a reduced cooking time is more important than a pitch-perfect texture, by all means soak whole-grain rice in a big bowl of water during the day while you're at work, for about 8 hours. Dinner will be on the table faster, although not necessarily better.

- You can go overboard with the soaking. We found that 16 hours was the utter limit. After that, the grains can get a tad waterlogged and end up mushy in the pot, the texture definitely compromised. Assuming you're sleeping a fairly average 8 hours or so, figure on soaking the grains overnight if you intend to cook them sometime the next morning. Or soak them while you're at work: Get up, set them to soak, go off for your day, and come home to them ready to go.

- Finally, no grain *must* be soaked. Yes, the texture of many of the harder grains—rye berries, triticale, and such—will be a bit mushier. The larger, harder grains will also take up to 25 percent *longer* to get tender over the heat if they're not soaked. But that trade-off may be worth it in the face of the impending dinner hour. If you find yourself making a recipe that calls for soaking but you've skipped this step, increase the water and the cooking time to compensate. Or try what's often called *the quick-soak method:* Bring them to a boil in a big pot of water, boil for 1 minute, then remove from the heat and set aside, covered, for 45 minutes. Drain and you're ready to start the recipe.

2. Water Over the Heat

Don't cook whole grains in their soaking water. It contains released, dissolved starches and sugars that can affect the grains' texture. If they're not certified organic grains, they may have also leached pesticide residue and such into the water. After their initial soaking on the counter, drain the grains in a colander set in the sink, then fill a saucepan with fresh water before bringing it to a boil over high heat.

And don't cook them in a roiling cauldron over high heat. Instead, once you bring the water up to a boil and add the grains, drop the heat under the pot to low for a gentler bubble, more like a good simmer. This is especially important during the final 10 minutes of cooking to ensure that the grains do not bash each other into mush.

Although whole grains are cooked in water most of the time, they can also be simmered in broth of any stripe, chicken to vegetable. But steer clear of acidic liquids like wine or most fruit juices. Because of complex chemical interactions, the grains will end up squishy rather than tender.

There are two basic methods to cooking whole grains on the stovetop:

The Asian Method. You try to predict the exact amount of water needed for the amount of grain at hand, simmering both together, most often covered, until the water has been fully absorbed. This is how most of us in North America cook rice. We end up with tender, fluffy grains, no draining necessary. The grains also benefit by sitting off the heat, covered, for 10 minutes after the water has been absorbed so they can steam and plump before serving.

The East Indian Method. You swamp the grains with lots of water in a big saucepan, bring it to a boil, and get them tender at a good simmer without necessarily covering the pan; then you pour off the excess liquid by dumping the contents of the saucepan into a colander set in the sink. Note the two most important words in that explanation of the method: "swamp" and "big." You want lots of water in a large saucepan. Even if you're cooking only a cup or so of grains, they need room to dance over the heat. Otherwise, they'll clump at the bottom of the pan and cook unevenly—or worse yet, burn. If you give them enough water and enough room, there's no need to stir at all: Just set the pot to simmering, reduce the heat, and turn the timer on. Many East Indian cooks even make rice this way. In general, this method leads to chewy, dense, hearty grains.

In terms of knowing when the grains are ready, there's only one real solution: taste. Pull a grain out with a spoon, blow on it to cool it down, and test its tenderness. Sure, set the timer to give you a general hint of the amount of time you'll need to cook the grains over the heat. But the proof is in the pudding. Or the grains, as it were.

Because nothing is ever as quite as simple as it seems, we do have three "howevers" to our two methods:

1. All grains can be cooked with the Asian method; a few *cannot* be cooked successfully with the East Indian method: amaranth and buckwheat, the most prominent.

2. If you're batch-cooking lots of whole grains to store and use in recipes during the week, follow the package instructions exactly, particularly if the manufacturer recommends the Asian method (or a method like it without being so-named). Producers dry grains to varying moisture contents or grow varietals that require various timings, factors that become more pronounced when you're working *en masse*.

3. Recipe timings are like traffic lights in New York City: mere suggestions. If you're cooking whole grains with the Asian method, you cannot walk away and leave the pot unattended. You need to check occasionally to make sure the water hasn't boiled away before the grains are tender. If you're using the East Indian method, you have a little more flexibility, given the serious sousing in the pot; but you still need to be a mindful, watchful cook. Scorched grains are nobody's idea of dinner.

3. Water After the Heat

Particularly with the East Indian method, the excess cooking water must be removed—that is, drained off. Even with the Asian method, the grains are sometimes done before the water has been fully absorbed; so it, too, must be poured off to prevent a squishy texture as the grains sit waiting for you to get dinner on the table.

It's not as easy as it sounds. Some grains are tiny. Teff, millet, and even quinoa can slip through the holes of a standard colander. The best solution? Invest in a fine-mesh sieve, preferably a conical one, sometimes called a *chinoise* (French, *cheen-WAHZ*), a throwback to a less-PC time when its shape was said to resemble a Chinese hat.

That said, you can make do with a standard colander by lining it with cheesecloth or paper towels to keep smaller grains inside. Too many layers and the water will not drain off quickly enough and you can overflow the colander; too few, and the paper can collapse or tear, the grains then down the drain. Better to invest in the right tool.

A BIRD'S-EYE VIEW OF OUR WHOLE GRAINS

We will not be working with all the whole grains in the world. Instead, our focus is on those grains readily available in supermarkets or from online suppliers. So no einkorn or mesquite pods for us. But yes, some of these whole grains are indeed readily available but still unknown to some of us, like rye berries and Kamut. You can find these in almost any large supermarket—and because whole grains are made for storage and shipping, a quick online shopping trip will always do the trick.

And one more thing: There's no popcorn in this book, perhaps a glaring omission. But we couldn't figure out how to make popcorn into a main course, other than a bowlful with half a stick of melted butter and bottle of soda to soothe a bad breakup. We assume you can take care of that recipe on your own.

So let's take a look at the whole grains you're going to encounter—their distinct flavors and textures, information about their various cooking techniques, as well as some history and culinary trivia. You'll also find a list of recipes from the book that use each of the stated grains (not as a "swap" or substitution but as the grain called for in the recipe itself).

Amaranth

Although more than 60 varieties are cultivated worldwide, in North America you'll find either beige (very common) or black (very rare) amaranth.

Flavor: Earthy, grassy, even woody, and vaguely herbal. It stands up to hot chiles and acidic tomatoes beautifully, as well as to maple syrup and warming, winterish spices like cinnamon and nutmeg. Black amaranth has a more bitter taste than the standard beige grains.

Texture: Porridgelike, slippery, silky, even gummy. The grains release lots of starch to create a velvety mush with individual crunchy bits in the mix. If you look closely, you'll see the germ haloed around the tiny endosperm of each grain.

Historically: Amaranth is equal to corn as a fundamental crop of the precolonial Americas. The Aztecs used it in small cakes during religious ceremonies. After colonization, the Spanish banned its cultivation because of the resemblance of those cakes to the wafers used in the Mass—and the grain went "underground," cultivated in home plots rather than large farms for the next several centuries. Today, most of the world's commercial production takes place in the United States; most of what is grown in Asia, South America, and Africa is still a subsistence crop for individual families.

Presoak: No.

Preferred cooking method: Asian in a 1 part grain to $1\frac{1}{2}$ parts water ratio for 15 to 20 minutes. A 1 part grain to $2\frac{1}{2}$ parts water ratio will give a thicker porridge.

Yield: 1 cup raw = $2\frac{1}{2}$ cups cooked.

PERIMETER, CLOCKWISE FROM BOTTOM LEFT: soft white wheat berries, hard red wheat berries, Kamut, spelt berries, whole-grain bulgur, and whole-grain wheat flakes. CENTER: Kamut flakes

Also: Amaranth is not truly a cereal grain but the seed of a plant in the goosefoot family, related to spinach and chard. It's lumped in with other whole grains because of its similar culinary and nutritional profile.

Recipes that call for amaranth:

- OAT AND AMARANTH PANCAKES (PAGE 50)
- VEGETABLE AND GRITS POT PIE (PAGE 171)
- SOUTHWESTERN AMARANTH POLENTA (PAGE 204)

Barley

Most of the barley sold in supermarkets is "pearled"—that is, the bran has been scored or even partially removed so the grains cook more quickly. As such, pearled barley is not a whole grain and does not fit the confines of this book. Instead, search out hull-less barley, a modern hybrid with hulls that simply fall off at harvest.

Flavor: Sweet, slightly musky, with earthy and mildly tannic notes.

Texture: Dank and chewy, sort of the grain equivalent to dates, and thus quite a sophisticated gnaw, a great balance to crunchy vegetables in a salad.

Historically: The oldest barley stores have been found in Egypt dating from 6000 BCE. Barley was carried east on ancient trade routes until it was cultivated in China around 2800 BCE. It first spread to North America, thanks to Dutch and British colonists, not as a food source, but for beer production.

Presoak: Yes for hull-less and black barley; no for barley flakes and grits.

Preferred cooking method: East Indian for 50 minutes to 1 hour, depending on the grains' residual moisture content from long storage.

Yield: 1 cup raw = 2⅔ cups cooked.

Also: Recent analysis for minerals and nutrients in the bone fragments of Roman gladiators has concluded that most were vegetarians who ate a diet almost exclusively of barley and beans.

Black barley is a varietal with a deep-purple bran, a gorgeous luxury with a more pronounced flavor and slightly less sticky texture.

Several recipes also call for barley grits (sliced whole-grain barley) or barley flakes (rolled barley, liked rolled oats). Check the package labeling to make sure you've got a brand that's truly a whole grain. Note particularly the fiber content—it should be high.

One recipe even calls for whole-grain barley couscous, a Moroccan specialty that is available at Middle Eastern markets or from online suppliers. Barley couscous is in fact an authentic couscous from North Africa and makes a particularly savory, sophisticated main course with sour and umami hints from the grain itself.

Recipes that call for barley (hull-less barley, black barley, barley flakes, or barley grits):

- MAKE-AHEAD MULTIGRAIN MUESLI (PAGE 37)
- WAY-MORE-THAN-JUST-OATS GRANOLA (PAGE 38)
- GROATS AND GRITS HOT CEREAL WITH HONEY AND ORANGE ZEST (PAGE 42)
- SLOW-COOKER THREE-GRAIN PORRIDGE WITH DATES AND HONEY (PAGE 44)
- CINNAMON-RAISIN BARLEY PUDDING (PAGE 52)
- BARLEY GRITS CASSEROLE WITH APPLES AND SAUSAGE (PAGE 53)
- SPANISH-INSPIRED BLACK BARLEY SALAD WITH CHICKPEAS, DATES, AND ALMONDS (PAGE 113)
- BARLEY AND PECAN BURGERS (PAGE 125)
- MILLET, BARLEY, AND SPLIT PEA SOUP WITH COCONUT AND GINGER (PAGE 147)
- BAKED WHEAT BERRIES, BARLEY, AND CHEESE (PAGE 163)
- BAKED BARLEY, BEANS, AND BACON (PAGE 183)
- MOROCCAN-INSPIRED BARLEY COUSCOUS (PAGE 184)
- BARLEY, MUSHROOMS, AND PEAS (PAGE 201)
- BARLEY RISOTTO WITH MUSHROOMS AND LEEKS (PAGE 202)

Buckwheat

Once the hulls have been removed, buckwheat kernels are called *groats*—from a Dutch word meaning "a thick penny," as opposed to a thin, worthless one. Buckwheat groats are small pyramids with one darkened point and an overall beige color with a pale green tint.

Flavor: If toasted (and thus called *kasha*), a bit-ter, pugnacious kick that has unfortunately put many a child off buckwheat for life; if untoasted, milder and grassier, with honey and floral notes, and a very subtle, sour accent.

Texture: Moist and toothsome, with a slight give in each groat.

Historically: Although buckwheat is probably indigenous to northern Asia, even Siberia, it has long thrived in cold, harsh climates like northern Europe and northern Asia. It's often refined into flour for the likes of pancakes on this continent and soba noodles in Japan. It was brought to North America by German and Dutch settlers and now grows wild through much of the continent.

Presoak: No.

Preferred cooking method: East Indian for 10 to 15 minutes. But because buckwheat soaks up water like a sponge, make sure you use at least twice the water to buckwheat by volume in the pan. That said, you'll find a wide variety of cooking techniques in this book for buckwheat—including toasting the groats before cooking and then coating them in egg.

Yield: 1 cup raw = 2¼ cups cooked.

Also: Another pseudograin like amaranth, buckwheat is actually the seed of a plant related to rhubarb. Because of its sticky texture and rela-tively quick cooking time, untoasted buckwheat groats can be tossed into stews to thicken them slightly—or added to soups and stews in the slow cooker to give them a little more body.

Recipes that call for buckwheat groats:

- GROATS AND GRITS HOT CEREAL WITH HONEY AND ORANGE ZEST (PAGE 42)
- SLOW-COOKER OAT GROAT PORRIDGE (PAGE 43)
- BUCKWHEAT AND CASHEW BURGERS (PAGE 126)
- KASHA VARNISHKES SOUP (PAGE 153)
- BUCKWHEAT HASH (PAGE 195)
- STIR-FRIED BUCKWHEAT (PAGE 197)

Corn

Sweet corn on the cob is the quintessence of summer in North America. But corn's astounding taste and texture can be preserved via freezing—which means it's available as a culinary staple year round. Although almost all of the recipes in this book call for "sweet corn," there are many other varieties, most grown solely for feed or industrial purposes.

Flavor: Sugary sweet, mild, with honey overtones.

Texture: Soft and luxurious. Terrific raw, corn needs minimal cooking—but can in fact stand up to long simmers in soups and stews, thanks largely to the grains' tough but edible hull.

Historically: The colonial Spanish saw corn crops in North America, mistook them for sorghum (which they grew as food for pigs back in Europe), and bypassed the grain entirely. The starving, winter-weary English settlers were the first Europeans to recognize that the Native Americans weren't throwing their corn crops to the animals but were instead cooking and eating the grain.

Presoak: No.

Preferred cooking method: Since corn is edible raw, any cooking should be minimal—at best. Roast, broil, or grill ears with the kernels intact—or cook corn by stirring it into a pot of boiling water, covering, and setting aside off the heat for no more than 10 minutes.

Yield: 2 large ears of corn yields about 1 cup raw corn kernels, which in turn yields about 1 heaping cup boiled corn kernels or a scant 1 cup roasted or grilled corn kernels.

Also: Several recipes call for whole-grain cornmeal or coarse, whole-grain polenta. In all cases, make sure you have the whole-grain version in hand. Read the labels or check the manufacturer's websites for more information. If you need whole-grain corn grits and only have whole-grain polenta on hand, grind it in a food processor fitted with the chopping blade to a coarse meal.

One recipe calls for posole (a.k.a. hominy)—kernels of field or flint corn from which the tough hulls may have been removed by cooking them in an alkali; the dried kernels must then be dealt with in a long, complicated process. Some manufacturers make posole (or hominy) by using lye as their alkali, a none-too-savory process. If you're going to the trouble to make real posole at home, look for a brand that is merely dried field corn without any chemical fandango. Anson Mills dries field corn on the cobs, then cribs it for further dehydration—and leaves you with the perfect stuff for a pot of posole.

Recipes that call for corn (or whole-grain polenta or whole-grain cornmeal):

- GROATS AND GRITS HOT CEREAL WITH HONEY AND ORANGE ZEST (PAGE 42)
- CORNMEAL AND OAT WAFFLE MIX (PAGE 48)
- BREAKFAST POLENTA CAKE WITH KAMUT CRUNCH TOPPING (PAGE 59)
- MILLET SALAD WITH CORN AND PEANUTS (PAGE 103)
- ROASTED CORN AND SHRIMP "CEVICHE" (PAGE 120)
- AVGOLEMONO SOUP WITH CORN GRITS DUMPLINGS (PAGE 140)
- HONEST-TO-GOODNESS POSOLE VERDE (PAGE 150)
- HAM AND CORN PUDDING (PAGE 169)
- THAI-STYLE CORN AND PORK SKEWERS (PAGE 214)
- QUINOA CREPES WITH CORN, AVOCADO, AND MEXICAN CREMA (PAGE 220)

Job's Tears

Called *hato mugi* (鳩麦) in Japanese (which translates as "beauty pearls"—for their ostensible ability to clear the complexion), these hard, puffy, teardrop grains are a favorite in Asian kitchens but are just starting to make an appearance in this country, found mostly at high-end markets and health food stores. Job's tears are sometimes refined, in which case the grains are about the color of uncooked barley. The unrefined grains are dark red and hard as little pebbles. Search for *yuuki hato mugi*—that is dark *hato mugi*—for the most intact bran.

Flavor: Dry, nutty, sort of like a dry chestnut or a savory black-eyed pea.

Texture: Grainy, coarse, dry, but also tender. Job's tears need lots of moisture from surrounding ingredients.

Historically: They have been ground into medicinal teas and floury powders for centuries across Asia. Many Chinese markets sell Job's tears mislabeled as "wild barley" or "Chinese barley."

Presoak: No.

Preferred cooking method: East Indian for somewhere between 1 hour and 1 hour 15 minutes, depending on how dry they got as they sat on the shelf. Dark *hato mugi* can take up to 1 hour 30 minutes to get tender.

Yield: 1 cup raw = 3 cups cooked.

Also: Most of the Job's tears grown in the world go into jewelry production. They are often the lacquered beads of a rosary.

Recipes that call for Job's tears:

- JOB'S TEARS AND EDAMAME IN A CARROT DRESSING (PAGE 109)
- ASIAN PICADILLO WITH JOB'S TEARS (PAGE 110)
- ROASTED RATATOUILLE WITH JOB'S TEARS (PAGE 205)

FROM LEFT: whole-grain polenta, whole-grain cornmeal, posole, and fresh corn

NO PRESOAKING REQUIRED

Presoaking whole grains is often a hindrance to their wider acceptance in the kitchen. "Must I start this recipe the day before?" some might ask. We've already discussed the pros and cons of presoaking (page 10)—and that it doesn't have to be an overnight event. But in any case, fear not: These recipes require no presoaking at all.

- Make-Ahead Multigrain Muesli (page 37)
- Way-More-Than-Just-Oats Granola (page 38)
- Groats and Grits Hot Cereal with Honey and Orange Zest (page 42)
- Slow-Cooker Oat Groat Porridge (page 43)
- Slow-Cooker Three-Grain Porridge with Dates and Honey (page 44)
- Brown Rice Congee (page 45)
- Cornmeal and Oat Waffle Mix (page 48)
- Oat and Amaranth Pancakes (page 50)
- Teff Griddle Cakes (page 51)
- Barley Grits Casserole with Apples and Sausage (page 53)
- Quinoa Cashew Muffins (page 56)
- Quinoa Date Bread (page 58)
- Breakfast Polenta Cake with Kamut Crunch Topping (page 59)
- Wheat Berry Salad with Zucchini, Boiled Lemon, and Almonds (page 67)
- Spicy Brown Rice Salad with Chicken and Peanuts (page 85)

- Brown Rice Salad with Red Peppers and Dried Apricots (page 88)
- Lebanese-Inspired Brown Rice Salad with Chickpeas and Grapes (page 89)
- Red Rice Romesco Salad (page 90)
- Red Rice and Lentils (page 91)
- Wild Rice Salad with Orange Supremes, Shaved Fennel, and Pistachios (page 92)
- Wild Rice Salad with Apples and Bacon (page 94)
- Tabbouleh with Chicken and Pineapple (page 97)
- Curried Carrot and Bulgur Salad (page 98)
- Asian-Inspired Quinoa with Canadian Bacon (page 99)
- Quinoa with Asparagus and Shiitakes (page 101)
- Quinoa with Grilled Shrimp and Peppers (page 102)
- Millet Salad with Corn and Peanuts (page 103)
- Job's Tears and Edamame in a Carrot Dressing (page 109)
- Asian Picadillo with Job's Tears (page 110)
- Tomatoes Stuffed with Black Rice and Shrimp (page 116)

Millet

Millet is one of the tiniest whole grains—but packs one of the most distinct flavors, very sophisticated, in fact elegant. Because so much of the millet grown in this country goes into bird-seed blends, we have a hunch the grain's gotten a bad rap by association—which is really too bad, given how nutritious and flavorful it is. But we do have one caveat: Check the expiration date on the package. Millet can go rancid quite quickly. Best to try to smell inside the package, if possible.

Flavor: Savory, like an earthy version of corn with more grassy notes and white wine overtones.

Texture: Crunchy pops and a dense, dry chew if cooked in a low-liquid environment; thick and gooey if swamped in water as it cooks.

Historically: Most likely the original staple crop of China. The oldest known noodles found in Chinese archeological digs were made from millet flour.

Presoak: No.

Preferred cooking method: Asian in a 1 part millet to 2 parts water ratio for the drier version; 1 part millet to 3 parts water for a more porridgelike consistency—in either case, for 18 to 20 minutes.

Yield: 1 cup raw = 2⅓ cups cooked.

Also: Pliny the Elder attributes the fierce fury of the Mongol hordes to a porridge of millet, mare's milk, and horse blood. No, thanks. We'll stick with millet burgers (page 133).

Recipes that call for millet (or millet grits):

- SLOW-COOKER THREE-GRAIN PORRIDGE WITH DATES AND HONEY (PAGE 44)
- MILLET SALAD WITH CORN AND PEANUTS (PAGE 103)
- MILLET BURGERS WITH OLIVES, SUN-DRIED TOMATOES, AND PECORINO (PAGE 133)
- MILLET, BARLEY, AND SPLIT PEA SOUP WITH COCONUT AND GINGER (PAGE 147)
- JAPANESE-INSPIRED BROWN RICE AND MILLET CASSEROLE (PAGE 156)
- MILLET AND SPINACH CASSEROLE (PAGE 167)
- VEGETABLE AND GRITS POT PIE (PAGE 171)

Oats

Although most of us know oats as a rolled grain eaten at breakfast, many of the recipes here use the *groats*—that is, the grain still intact without its hull. Yes, standard rolled oats are also whole grains; but they've been steamed and flattened for quicker cooking. That processing does knock down the flavor profile a bit. Although we do call for rolled oats in a few recipes, we hope we can encourage you to try the real thing: the oat groats themselves.

Flavor: Sweet and mild with a slightly bitter finish—groats taste like oatmeal squared.

Texture: Very firm with a distinct, chewy give toward the center of each grain.

Historically: Oats are one of the newer grains in human cultivation, although the plants were growing wild in northern Africa and central

Russia by 2500 BCE. The Romans first saw the culinary uses and began adding them to the barley-and-bean diet of the gladiators.

Presoak: Yes for the groats.

Preferred cooking method: East Indian for the groats—and for between 45 minutes and 1 hour 15 minutes.

Yield: 1 cup raw = 2 cups cooked.

Also: Oats store a great deal of their fat in the endosperm, rather than the germ; so they go rancid fairly quickly. To alleviate that problem, almost all oats are toasted at harvest, thereby chemically changing the fat into a more neutral component.

Steel-cut oats are simply the groats sliced into small bits. They take a long time to cook because they're not necessarily steamed and flattened the way rolled oats are.

Recipes that call for oat groats or rolled oats:

- MAKE-AHEAD MULTIGRAIN MUESLI (PAGE 37)
- WAY-MORE-THAN-JUST-OATS GRANOLA (PAGE 38)
- SLOW-COOKER OAT GROAT PORRIDGE (PAGE 43)
- SLOW-COOKER THREE-GRAIN PORRIDGE WITH DATES AND HONEY (PAGE 44)
- CORNMEAL AND OAT WAFFLE MIX (PAGE 48)
- OAT AND AMARANTH PANCAKES (PAGE 50)
- OAT GROAT AND BLACK-EYED PEA SALAD (PAGE 108)
- MILLET, BARLEY, AND SPLIT PEA SOUP WITH COCONUT AND GINGER (PAGE 147)
- OAT GROAT AND POTATO PANCAKES WITH SMOKED SALMON AND CRÈME FRAÎCHE (PAGE 217)

Quinoa

There may be no bigger, modern success story for grains than quinoa. Because it has a mild taste and cooks quickly, it's now a pantry staple and even found in take-out salads at neighborhood supermarkets. The individual seeds sprout little rings as they cook, billions of little Saturns in a bowl. Although white quinoa is the most common varietal in our supermarkets, you can also find red quinoa, originally from the high Andes in modern Bolivia, as well as an intense, gritty hybrid called "black quinoa" that's been crossed with lamb's quarters. Be wary: Some versions of red quinoa are not strictly whole grains. Look for packages specifically labeled as "whole grain."

Flavor: Grassy but mildly so, slightly nutty (more so if first toasted), with a pleasant, earthy overtone, sort of like a light red wine. Red quinoa is drier in texture and black is bigger in flavor.

Texture: A distinct pop with just a faint hint of gumminess, although mostly dry.

Historically: Quinoa was originally a high-altitude plant. It was first cultivated by prehistory Andean tribal groups before these peoples were subsumed into the Incan empire.

Presoak: No.

Preferred cooking method: East Indian for about 12 minutes.

Yield: 1 cup raw = 3½ cups cooked.

FROM TOP: red Cargo rice, black Venere rice, medium-grain brown rice

Also: Quinoa was first introduced to North America in the 1880s, not as a culinary staple, but as a flowering garden plant by avid plant breeder Luther Burbank.

Quinoa is another pseudograin, closely related to amaranth—and thus also to beets and spinach.

Recipes that call for quinoa:

- QUINOA CASHEW MUFFINS (PAGE 56)
- QUINOA DATE BREAD (PAGE 58)
- ASIAN-INSPIRED QUINOA WITH CANADIAN BACON (PAGE 99)
- QUINOA WITH ASPARAGUS AND SHIITAKES (PAGE 101)
- QUINOA WITH GRILLED SHRIMP AND PEPPERS (PAGE 102)
- ITALIAN-STYLE BLACK QUINOA AND SPINACH SUMMER ROLLS (PAGE 118)
- BLACK QUINOA AND BLACK BEAN BURGERS (PAGE 128)
- PUMPKIN-QUINOA SOUFFLÉ (PAGE 207)
- QUINOA CREPES WITH CORN, AVOCADO, AND MEXICAN CREMA (PAGE 220)

Rice

With wheat, rice has been a dietary grain staple since at least the time of ancient Rome and, along with corn, certainly is so now. Although most of us know the overly sweet, refined white rice that's a side dish for many a meal, whole-grain brown, red, and black rice bear it no resemblance, especially with their bolder flavors, distinct nuttiness, and more pronounced chew—all of which means they're better suited for the center of the plate.

White rice is a neutral palette; whole-grain rice is a bruiser than needs balancing by other, complex, forceful flavors.

Rice varietals come in three forms: long-, medium-, and short-grain. The differences are, yes, the length of the grains, but more importantly, the ratio of two sticky starches: tough, firm amylose and sticky, soft amylopectin. The less amylose—the grains are "short" in amylose—the stickier the rice. In truth, some medium-grain rice kernels are shorter than many short-grain ones. Long-grain rice is dry, almost flaky; medium, stickier and chewier; short, quite glutinous and moist.

Flavor: Nutty and intense, with a slightly bitter nose and spiky notes of asparagus, turnips, and sweet potatoes. Black rice adds many more sweet accents to the mix.

Texture: Chewy and dense, sometimes very dry (especially red rice), although short-grain brown rice can be quite sticky.

Historically: Although global production has surpassed 200 billion tons a year, rice remains one of the hardest crops on the land. Because rice is grown in water, the land slowly silts, suffocating under repeated harvests. Plus, the methane release from rice crops is astounding, the stalks acting as little drinking straws that allow the decaying muck underwater to bubble the gas into the atmosphere. As we'll see, there are farmers who are meeting this challenge head-on.

Presoak: No (although you can—see page 10).

Preferred cooking method: Asian for this book—although plenty of East Indians, Italians, and Spaniards would disagree. Check the package instructions or the specific recipes for the various ratios and timings among various sorts of brown, red, and black rices.

Yield: 1 cup raw long-grain brown rice = 3⅓ cups cooked.

1 cup raw medium-grain brown rice = 2¾ cups cooked.

1 cup raw short-grain brown rice = 2⅔ cups cooked.

1 cup raw red rice = 3½ cups cooked.

1 cup raw black rice = 3 cups cooked.

Also: Although black rice is grown across the world—particularly in Southeast Asia where it's used in a variety of sweet and savory dishes—the only varietals called for in this book are the various Italian ones, often lumped together as *venere* rice (that is, "from Venus"). This black rice is nutty but very moist, almost damp, with a pronounced sweetness.

Half of the over 20 million tons of rice grown in the United States each year is exported. In fact, China consumes over 150 million tons of rice a year—and needs all the help it can get to meet the demand. Of the rice that remains in the United States, 16 percent goes into beer and liquor production; 10 percent into pet food.

Recipes that call for rice:

- BROWN RICE CONGEE (PAGE 45)
- SPICY BROWN RICE SALAD WITH CHICKEN AND PEANUTS (PAGE 85)
- BROWN RICE SALAD WITH RED PEPPERS AND DRIED APRICOTS (PAGE 88)
- LEBANESE-INSPIRED BROWN RICE SALAD WITH CHICKPEAS AND GRAPES (PAGE 89)
- RED RICE ROMESCO SALAD (PAGE 90)
- RED RICE AND LENTILS (PAGE 91)
- TOMATOES STUFFED WITH BLACK RICE AND SHRIMP (PAGE 116)
- JAPANESE-INSPIRED BROWN RICE AND MILLET CASSEROLE (PAGE 156)
- BAKED RED RICE CASSEROLE WITH AN EGG-AND-CHEESE CRUST (PAGE 162)
- BROWN RICE AND BEANS (PAGE 178)
- BIZEH B'JURAH (SYRIAN-STYLE RICE AND SHORT RIBS) (PAGE 179)
- BROWN RICE-STUFFED CABBAGE (PAGE 180)
- BLACK RICE PAELLA (PAGE 210)
- SEARED TUNA AND BROWN RICE CHIRASHI (PAGE 212)

Rye Berries

Most of us know rye from the flour used in the slightly fermented bread: a big hit of flavor, often balanced with molasses (in central European traditions) or honey (in Scandinavian ones). However, rye berries themselves are a different culinary animal altogether—and a surprising find for the whole-grain kitchen. The grains themselves can range in color from pale green to pale brown, a hard little seed that offers a surprisingly complex taste.

Flavor: Sweet, with mildly sour marks, vaguely reminiscent of chocolate without any of the bitter notes.

Texture: Very chewy, quite dense, always *al dente* even after long cooking.

Historically: A European crop, rye was cultivated fairly late in the game, probably first in the early Middle Ages but still not very much until its introduction to England in the 500s CE when it was found to contain ample sugars for distilling.

Presoak: Yes.

Preferred cooking method: East Indian for about 1 hour.

Yield: 1 cup raw = 2⅔ cups cooked.

Also: In the early 19th century, rye was the most cultivated grain crop in the United States. Blame the new republic's distilleries.

Recipes that call for rye berries:

- REUBEN SALAD (PAGE 104)
- RYE BERRIES AND GOAT CHEESE IN A DIJON VINAIGRETTE (PAGE 106)
- RYE BERRIES STEWED WITH SAUERKRAUT AND PORK (PAGE 190)

Sorghum

Drought-resistant sorghum has long functioned as an African staple, a gorgeously starchy and toothsome addition to stews and curries.

Flavor: Fairly bland, like a duller form of millet with slight, earthy notes and a faint sweetness that nonetheless refuses to be masked, even under lots of chiles.

Texture: Dry and even a little crunchy after long cooking, sort of like red rice, but firmer—and thus often paired with creamy dairy products or added to stews.

Historically: First cultivated in Egypt and other parts of northeastern Africa by 2200 BCE, sorghum became food for slaves in the West Indies where it was known as guinea corn. There was a huge push during the 1930s to get US farmers to grow sorghum because of its drought resistance (the Dust Bowl was winding down) and its high yield (World War II was gearing up). Despite much hoopla, crop plantings fell to almost nil when the war effort ended.

Presoak: Yes.

Preferred cooking method: East Indian for between 45 minutes and 1 hour, even a little longer if the grains are very dry from long storage.

Yield: 1 cup raw = 2 cups cooked.

Also: Until the late 1950s, sorghum was the third most cultivated grain on the planet, behind wheat and rice. It is now grown extensively in China in areas too dry for rice—and is used there in the production of a type of wine.

Sorghum syrup is a delicacy in the American South. However, it is made from the sweet juice of a species related to but separate from our whole-grain plant.

Recipes that call for sorghum:

- SORGHUM SOUP WITH CHILES AND SWEET POTATOES (PAGE 146)
- CELERY ROOT AND SORGHUM GRATIN (PAGE 157)

Teff

Botanically, teff is a form of millet. In the kitchen, however, the two are quite different, seemingly unrelated. Teff is available in ivory and brown varietals—which are interchangeable for the purposes of this book, although ivory teff is a bit milder than brown (and much rarer in our supermarkets). If you've ever eaten the flatbread called *injera* in an Ethiopian restaurant, you've had teff flour.

Flavor: A sweet/sour balance unmatched in any other grain with slight, savory, even umami notes.

Texture: Wet and moist, with just a slight amount of give, mostly the result of the way teff even absorbs moisture in the mouth as it is chewed.

Historically: Teff is associated almost exclusively with modern Ethiopia, since it's been grown there since at least 4000 BCE. Ethiopian long-distance runners attribute their amazing stamina to teff.

Presoak: No.

Preferred cooking method: Asian in a 1 part teff to 1½ parts water ratio for distinct, individual grains; or a 1 part teff to 2½ parts water ratio for a richer porridge; or a 1 part teff to 3 parts water ratio for a thick paste. For each, plan on 10 to 15 minutes, as the recipe indicates.

Yield: 1 cup raw = 3 cups cooked.

Also: Teff is a moisture sponge, even more so than millet; baked goods can turn dry and tough overnight. Without larding them up with too much fat to compensate, the only answer is to consume teff dishes when they're made.

Recipes that call for teff:

- TEFF GRIDDLE CAKES (PAGE 51)
- TEFF GNOCCHI IN A CHEDDAR SAUCE (PAGE 164)
- FRIED TEFF AND CRAB BALLS WITH YELLOW PEPPER RELISH (PAGE 215)

Triticale

Pronounced *tri-teh-KAY-lee*, this grain is a modern hybrid, first developed in Scotland in 1875, a cross between wheat (Latin, *triticum*) and rye (Latin, *secale*). The culinary whole grain is sometimes called "triticale berries."

Flavor: Grassy, definitely herbal, even a little pungent, with umami notes among the sour overtones.

Texture: Dense and resistant, just what you'd expect from a cross between wheat berries and rye berries.

Historically: The original plants were developed in Scotland by dusting wheat blooms with rye pollen; the subsequent generations, however, proved sterile. A decade later, a German researcher noticed that a few of the seeds were fertile; he did some research to discover that triticale would only reproduce if its chromosomes were doubled. No process was found to make this occur on a consistent basis until the 1930s when the grain plants were inoculated with an alkaloid from crocus plants.

Presoak: Yes.

Preferred cooking method: East Indian for 45 minutes to 1 hour.

Yield: 1 cup raw = 2⅔ cups cooked.

Also: Triticale made its closest run at fame with the original *Star Trek*. In the famous episode "The Trouble with Tribbles," Mr. Spock explains that this grain is part of the ongoing genetic experimentation of food sources: "A high-yield grain, a four-lobed hybrid of wheat and rye . . . a perennial, also, if I'm not mistaken . . . ancestry all the way back to 20th century Canada." Apparently Mr. Spock didn't know his agricultural history too well.

Recipes that use triticale:

- TRITICALE WITH SMOKED TROUT AND ARTICHOKES IN A LEMON TAHINI DRESSING (PAGE 107)

- LAMB AND TRITCALE TAGINE (PAGE 192)

- TRITICALE WITH OLIVE OIL, GARLIC, AND ANCHOVIES (PAGE 200)

Wheat Berries

By far our largest category, wheat berries offer such a range of tastes and textures—from soft white wheat berries to spelt berries—as to defy simple description. Given this spectrum and the satisfaction you can derive from its meals, wheat berries can be said to form the core of this book. You'll encounter these:

- **Hard red wheat berries.** The biggest chew of any whole grain used, hard red wheat berries are decidedly wheaty, like bread, only chewy. They are sometimes called "hard winter wheat berries" or simply "winter wheat berries" since the crops are planted late in the season, up until December in some regions. Hard red wheat berries take a long time to get tender and offer a beautiful texture contrast to softer ingredients like tomatoes or cheese.

- **Soft white wheat berries.** Strains of wheat come in hard and soft varietals, usually blended to make various flours. Soft wheat is most often ground into pastry flours—like whole wheat pastry flour. While not "soft" in the sense of pudding, these wheat berries have much less chew with a nuttier, sweeter finish than their hard red cousins. They are also sometimes called "spring white wheat berries" or "spring wheat berries," again to indicate the season when the grain is sown.

- **Whole-grain farro.** Most of this Italian staple—also called "emmer wheat"—is pearled like barley, the bran either scored (*semi-perlato* in Italian parlance) or removed altogether (*perlato*). However, there are whole-grain varieties available—and these are the only ones called for in this book. You may have to do an Internet search to turn up producers. Whole-grain farro has an intense, nutty flavor, a decided snap to the chew with a creamy center.

Spelt berries. The basis, of course, of spelt flour, spelt berries are larger than hard or soft wheat berries. They have a red-tinged bran than can darken to a gorgeous, pale brown as it cooks. Spelt berries are decidedly sweet, although they have a sour muskiness back in the afternotes, often brought to the foreground by vinegars or acids.

THE SPEEDIEST RECIPES FOR WHOLE GRAINS

Not every whole grain recipe takes a long time. You can get these gourmet powerhouses on your table in a surprisingly short time with these recipes, every one with a total time of less than 1 hour—and a fairly short active time as well.

- Make-Ahead Multigrain Muesli (page 37)
- Groats and Grits Hot Cereal with Honey and Orange Zest (page 42)
- Cornmeal and Oat Waffle Mix (page 48)
- Oat and Amaranth Pancakes (page 50)
- Quinoa Cashew Muffins (page 56)
- Brown Rice Salad with Red Peppers and Dried Apricots (page 88)
- Lebanese-Inspired Brown Rice Salad with Chickpeas and Grapes (page 89)
- Red Rice and Lentils (page 91)
- Asian-Inspired Quinoa with Canadian Bacon (page 99)
- Quinoa with Asparagus and Shiitakes (page 101)
- Quinoa with Grilled Shrimp and Peppers (page 102)

- Millet Salad with Corn and Peanuts (page 103)
- Tomatoes Stuffed with Black Rice and Shrimp (page 116)
- Italian-Style Black Quinoa and Spinach Summer Rolls (page 118)
- Roasted Corn and Shrimp "Ceviche" (page 120)
- Buckwheat and Cashew Burgers (pagwe 126)
- Black Quinoa and Black Bean Burgers (page 128)
- Millet Burgers with Olives, Sun-Dried Tomatoes, and Pecorino (page 133)
- Turkish Red Lentil and Bulgur Soup (page 149)
- Stir-Fried Buckwheat (page 197)
- Pumpkin-Quinoa Soufflé (page 207)
- Thai-Style Corn and Pork Skewers (page 214)

- **Kamut.** Actually, this is a brand name, like Coke or Kleenex. Bob Quinn, founder of Kamut International, wanted to assure the quality of an organic, heirloom strain of khorasan wheat. With his guidance, Kamut was trademarked—and will never be genetically altered or modified. Kamut has the most intense pop of any grain in this book, with a lovely, sweet finish, minimal grassy notes, and a slight umami backtaste.

- **Whole-grain, quick-cooking bulgur.** This is made from parboiled wheat berries that are dried and ground. Standard bulgur is not a whole-grain product—much of the bran and germ are removed by processing. Standard bulgur also comes in a wide variety of grinds (usually identified by a number on the package, #1 being the finest). Make sure you have whole-grain bulgur, not its more processed, branless, refined kindred. Whole-grain bulgur is usually *not* labeled by the intensity of the grind on the package (#1 and so forth); instead, whole-grain bulgur is usually fairly coarse, a standard to ensure the bran and germ stay intact during its processing.

Historically: Although we think of wheat as a distinctly Western grain, it was actually first cultivated in southwestern Asia around Iran. Wheat was one of the world's first cultivated crops, if not *the* first, a staple that went with the goats, the world's first animal domesticated for human consumption. Even back then, most wheat was ground for flour production.

Presoak: Yes for wheat berries of all stripes, farro, spelt berries, and Kamut; no for whole-grain bulgur and wheat flakes.

Preferred cooking method: East Indian for between 45 minutes to 1 hour, depending on the wheat berry varietal.

Whole-grain, quick-cooking bulgur needs to be doused with boiling water and set aside to soak for 1 hour, until the water has been absorbed. The amount of water used for soaking whole-grain bulgur varies by the final texture that the recipe requires. That is, more water for a softer finish.

Yield: 1 cup raw hard red winter wheat berries = 2¾ cups cooked.

1 cup raw soft spring white wheat berries = 2⅔ cups cooked.

1 cup raw whole-grain farro = 2⅓ cups cooked.

1 cup raw spelt berries = 2⅔ cups cooked.

1 cup raw Kamut = 2¾ cups cooked.

1 cup raw whole-grain, quick-cooking bulgur = 2½ cups soaked.

Also: Unlike corn, wheat has shown itself resistant to hybridization. Wheat flowers are complete and self-pollinating—think of the trouble the scientists had working with them and rye pollen to create triticale. In general, while various strains are in constant production in the modern world, they are quite closely related to the ancient strains of these grasses.

Recipes that use various kinds of wheat berries (or wheat flakes or whole-grain bulgur):

- MAKE-AHEAD MULTIGRAIN MUESLI (PAGE 37)
- WAY-MORE-THAN-JUST-OATS GRANOLA (PAGE 38)
- SYRIAN SLIHA (PAGE 41)
- BREAKFAST POLENTA CAKE WITH KAMUT CRUNCH TOPPING (PAGE 59)
- WHEAT BERRY SALAD WITH ZUCCHINI, BOILED LEMON, AND ALMONDS (PAGE 67)
- SICILIAN-INSPIRED WHEAT BERRY AND TUNA SALAD (PAGE 68)
- WHEAT BERRIES WITH FETA AND OLIVES (PAGE 69)
- GAZPACHO-STYLE WHEAT BERRY SALAD (PAGE 71)
- WHEAT BERRIES WITH OVEN-ROASTED TOMATOES AND FAVA BEANS (PAGE 72)
- FARRO NIÇOISE (PAGE 73)
- FARRO WITH NECTARINES, BASIL, AND TOASTED PINE NUTS (PAGE 74)
- FARRO AND SMOKED CHICKEN SALAD WITH CARDAMOM AND CHUTNEY (PAGE 76)
- CREAMY FARRO POTATO SALAD (PAGE 77)
- KAMUT SALAD WITH CAULIFLOWER, OLIVES, AND RAISINS (PAGE 79)
- DECONSTRUCTED KAMUT CAESAR SALAD (PAGE 80)
- SPELT BERRY SALAD WITH WHITE BEANS, SAGE, AND HAM (PAGE 81)
- SPELT BERRY SALAD WITH CHERRY TOMATOES, PECANS, AND BASIL (PAGE 82)
- TABBOULEH WITH CHICKEN AND PINEAPPLE (PAGE 97)
- CURRIED CARROT AND BULGUR SALAD (PAGE 98)
- SANDWICH WRAP WITH WHEAT BERRY SPREAD (PAGE 117)
- KAMUT BURGERS WITH SHALLOTS, PECANS, AND LEMON ZEST (PAGE 129)
- FALAFEL BURGERS WITH ALMOND HARISSA (PAGE 130)
- KAMUT AND BEEF CHILI (PAGE 142)
- VEAL AND FARRO STEW (PAGE 144)
- TURKISH RED LENTIL AND BULGUR SOUP (PAGE 149)
- BAKED WHEAT BERRIES, BARLEY, AND CHEESE (PAGE 163)
- TURKEY KIBBEH LOAF WITH TZATZIKI SAUCE (PAGE 186)
- LOUISIANA-INSPIRED RED BEANS AND KAMUT (PAGE 188)

Wild Rice

Like rice, wild rice is indeed the seed of an aquatic grass—but rice and wild rice are only tangentially related in the botanical scheme of things. And because of the way the grains form on the stalks and their physical makeup, wild rice is not truly a cereal grain but actually one of our four pretenders, along with amaranth, buckwheat, and quinoa.

Flavor: Pecan and herbal notes, combined with sweet backtastes, sort of reminiscent of a freshly mowed lawn, or cooked corn without the cloying sweetness.

Texture: Tender and luxurious.

Historically: Wild rice is one of the very few grains indigenous to North America. Until quite recently, it was not a cultivated crop but rather a gathered one from lakes near the Boundary Waters on the US and Canadian border in upper Minnesota. The rice was harvested by hand, sometimes in a two-person, labor-intensive process: One person would direct a canoe into the stalks and the other would bend them into the boat with the use of sticks called "knockers," tapping the stalks and thereby filling the canoe with the tiny grains as it glided over the lake. The plants were repeatedly harvested over weeks, mature seeds continuing to loosen along the stalks as the season progressed.

Presoak: No.

Preferred cooking method: East Indian for between 30 minutes and 1 hour 15 minutes, depending on the varietal you have in hand. Check the package for more information.

Yield: 1 cup raw = 3½ cups cooked.

Also: These days, there are two forms of wild rice in our supermarkets: the rice that is still hand-gathered from canoes in Minnesota and Wisconsin, and the more prolific crops grown in California and Oregon, which are modified, hybridized, black grains that are of a uniform height and weight to make them easier to harvest with industrial machines. Both sorts can be certified organic. In general, hand-gathered wild rice is more savory than its combine-harvested cousin.

Recipes that call for wild rice:

- WILD RICE SALAD WITH ORANGE SUPREMES, SHAVED FENNEL, AND PISTACHIOS (PAGE 92)

- WILD RICE SALAD WITH APPLES AND BACON (PAGE 94)

- WILD RICE AND VEGETABLE BIRYANI (PAGE 160)

- SPANISH-INSPIRED WILD RICE, CHICKEN, AND CHORIZO CASSEROLE (PAGE 173)

- TROUT STUFFED WITH WILD RICE (PAGE 209)

1

EARLY

Chances are, if we're going to eat a whole grain at all, we do so in the morning: cereal out of a box, oatmeal from a package, or a bran muffin of some whole-ish pedigree. Why are whole grains so associated with our first meal of the day? Partly because they're an easily prepared food.

Say, what? you might be thinking. *I soak a batch of wheat berries overnight and cook them for 55 minutes and you have the nerve to call that an "easily prepared food"?*

Not now. Not with a zillion-hour work week and college prep for kids starting in the crib. (*Is he learning Mandarin yet? Is he? Is he?*)

Instead, we have to go back in human history. Whole grains were crucial crops, not only for satisfying hungry clans, but also for getting those same clans to live near one another in the first place. Cultivated grains shaped our settlement patterns: the Fertile Crescent, the Nile delta, and the interior mountain coast of modern-day Mexico, as well as the Indus and Yangtze River ecosystems. We can locate our relationship with grains in our bones.

Quite literally. Bone density and trace elements scans from human remains at archeological sites worldwide confirm the increasing importance of grains to human settlement. People tented together; they started eating grains—which left chemical markers in their bones.

Their teeth, too, showed the effects of the change in diet. The dental wear patterns for the maize-growing human communities of Central America were gentler and less pitted than those for clans still practicing a nomadic lifestyle and eating tough shoots, roots, and jerkylike dried meat. The grain-eaters exhibited the angular, sloped wear of modern teeth, rather than the flat, even, sawed-off look of hunter-gatherers.

In short, grains were the earliest convenience foods, not the complicated preparations of joints and braises over the fire, not something you had to go out and hunt, kill, bleed, gut, butcher, hang, and dry, but just a big pot of water (or broth or milk) put to a boil with handfuls of the dried seeds from the harvest.

Indeed, grains may have put an end to our wandering around. Although causal connections are cloudy in prehistory, grains might not have been an outgrowth of human settlement but the very reason for it. Our ancestors not only wanted to live near the storehouses to keep from starving; they also couldn't very well transport those stores on horseback across the steppes or plains.

What's more, despite the goat culture that developed in the Middle East in the Bronze Age and the pig culture that developed in Europe after the collapse of the Roman Empire, there was a dearth of animal protein available to a growing, global population. In the Americas, amaranth and corn filled out the bill of fare; in Africa, sorghum and rice; in the Middle East, barley and wheat; and in Asia, buckwheat and millet—and much later rice.

These days, our brains may have thought up smart phones and Twitter, but our bodies are still in the tents. We developed biologically, socially, *and* gustatorially to require what grains provide. We thus connect them to what may be our most elemental meal: milk and carbs in the morning. And more elaborate fare as well—as you'll see in the recipes ahead.

THE WEEKDAY CEREALS

Our tour of grain mains starts simply, almost modestly—with granola and muesli, long-standing favorites in our home. The former is perfect for warm mornings. In our part of New England, that's from July 10 to 15. The latter is for cooler mornings when the pops in the radiators wake us before the alarm clock does.

Either dish is a make-ahead. Make-weeks-ahead, in fact. In keeping with the origins of whole grain storage and human settlements, they're breakfasts from the storehouse of your pantry! But do invest in a couple of sturdy, airtight, sealable containers. You don't want to stumble down to breakfast only to find that ambient humidity has ruined your hard work by turning the grains soggy—or worse, rancid.

After those recipes, we turn to the first of many Middle Eastern dishes in this book: Syrian Sliha. It's a mixture of nuts, wheat berries, and fruit that has become something of a make-ahead staple in our home when guests are on the way up from New York for a weekend in the country. It'll keep about a week in the fridge, if well covered. We bet you'll find it both new and comforting, an odd combo for a simple breakfast but one of the reasons you might turn to it again and again. It's also terrific for Christmas morning with green pistachios and red pomegranate seeds.

We finish off this first section with several hot, whole-grain cereals—the last three are either made in a slow cooker or with a slow-cooker variation. That way, they can be thrown together the night before, no more than a quick stir before heading off to bed. And once the slow cooker clicks to "warm," they can be kept covered in the appliance on the counter for a couple of hours, a good way to accommodate the varying schedules of a household. We find that the long, slow, even heat of the slow cooker mellows almost any whole grain into a lovely porridge, deeply satisfying in that way that only whole grains can be.

Among these recipes, you'll find congee, the Chinese classic, a staple of workers on their way to their jobs at restaurants across this country's many Chinatowns. Unlike the other fare in this section, it's a savory breakfast—and so unusual by whole grain breakfast standards (or certainly by North American standards). Although congee is usually made with white rice, ours is (of course) made with brown. It's made stovetop, but we also give you the directions for making it overnight in the slow cooker.

Try any one of these cereals and you'll soon see why whole grains were pantry staples for millennia. They're so satisfying, you might even find yourself out of bed before the radiator pops—or the air conditioner kicks in for the day. You might also be surprised when lunchtime rolls around without a hunger pang in sight. We can't think of better morning news than that!

THE CEREALS

MAKE-AHEAD MULTIGRAIN MUESLI

Active time: 10 minutes

Total time: 10 minutes

Make ahead: Store in an airtight container at room temperature for up to 2 months.

Make It Vegan: Instead of using milk or yogurt when preparing the muesli, use soy- or nut-based milk.

MAKE IT EASIER!

▪ Omit the soybean flakes and use 1½ cups barley flakes.

CHEF IT UP!

▪ Substitute chopped dried blueberries, dried raspberries, or even dried strawberries for the raisins.

TESTERS' NOTES

▪ This muesli is not sweetened with anything except the dried fruit. If you want it sweeter, stir in up to 1 tablespoon maple syrup per serving when you set it to soak overnight, after the hot cereal has gone into bowls, or after you've added the milk to the cold version.

▪ It's also chewier that many versions of muesli, most hot cereals, or just plain oatmeal, thanks to the whole-grain flakes in the mix. They won't turn to mush, even if soaked overnight in yogurt.

2 cups old-fashioned rolled oats (do not use quick-cooking or steel-cut)

1 cup wheat flakes

1 cup barley flakes

½ cup soybean flakes

½ cup chopped raisins

½ cup unsweetened shredded coconut

2 tablespoons sesame seeds

16 dried apricots, chopped

Mix everything in a big bowl. Dump it all into a big zip-closed plastic bag or an airtight container. Store it in the pantry for up to 2 months.

NOW WHAT?

There are several ways you can prepare this muesli for breakfast:

▪ The I-remember-my-Swiss-grandmother way: For a single serving, stir ½ cup muesli and ¾ cup plain yogurt (whole-milk, low-fat, or nonfat) in a small bowl. Cover and refrigerate overnight.

▪ The I'm-freezing-this-morning way: For a single serving, stir ½ cup muesli into 1 cup whole, 2%, 1%, or fat-free milk in a small saucepan; bring to a low simmer over medium heat. Cover, reduce the heat to very low, and simmer very slowly for a few minutes, until the milk has mostly been absorbed into the cereal.

▪ The I-overslept way: Pour it into a bowl and add milk or yogurt, like any other cereal.

WAY-MORE-THAN-JUST-OATS GRANOLA

⅔ cup almond oil

⅔ cup honey

1 tablespoon vanilla extract

3 cups old-fashioned rolled oats (do not use quick-cooking or steel-cut oats)

1 cup Kamut flakes

1 cup wheat flakes

1 cup barley flakes

1 cup sliced almonds

¾ cup instant nonfat dry milk

½ cup packed dark brown sugar

½ cup toasted wheat germ

1 tablespoon ground cinnamon

1½ teaspoons salt

1. Position the racks at the top and bottom third of the oven (or do the best you can dividing your oven into thirds) and preheat to 350°F.

2. Stir the oil, honey, and vanilla in a small saucepan over medium-low heat until the honey dissolves. Continue heating, stirring a few times, just until a few whiffs of steam come off the top. Set aside off the heat.

3. Mix the rolled oats, Kamut flakes, wheat flakes, barley flakes, almonds, dry milk, brown sugar, wheat germ, cinnamon, and salt in a big bowl. Pour in the oil mixture. Stir until everything's moist. Spread the mixture into even layers on 2 large rimmed baking sheets.

4. Bake until crunchy and irresistible, about 20 minutes, stirring once halfway through baking. Cool on the sheets set on a rack for at least 1 hour, maybe 2. Don't mess with it as it cools. It'll harden to a great crunch. Then break the granola into bits, chips, and flakes for storage.

SERVES 16

Active time: 15 minutes
Total time: 1 hour 50 minutes

Make ahead: Store in a sealed, airtight container at room temperature for up to 1 month.

MAKE IT EASIER!

■ Cut down on the number of different flakes. Use the rolled oats as they are, but use 1½ cups wheat flakes or Kamut flakes and 1½ cups barley flakes.

TESTERS' NOTES

■ Most nut and seed oils are available in toasted and so-called "untoasted" varieties. If toasted (that is, the nuts were toasted before the oil was extracted), the can or bottle will be so labeled. In this book, we call for *untoasted* nut and seed oils unless otherwise stated. For the best flavor, do not use a refined oil but rather one marked "unrefined" or (even better) expeller-pressed or cold-pressed. Because nut oils do not move quickly off supermarket shelves, always smell the oil before you use it. Once opened, reseal the can or cap the bottle and store the oil in the fridge.

■ Whole-grain flakes give this granola an irresistible crunch. You can find them at gourmet supermarkets, in health food stores, or from suppliers online. Do not substitute grain flake cereals.

■ Feel free to swap out the nut-and-nut-oil combo to create your own version: walnuts and walnut oil, pecans and pecan oil, hazelnuts and hazelnut oil.

SERVES 12

Active time: 15 minutes

Total time: 1 hour, plus soaking the wheat berries for at least 8 hours

Make ahead: Store, covered, in the fridge for up to 1 week.

CHEF IT UP!

▦ Add ½ teaspoon rose water with the cinnamon and salt.

GRAIN SWAPS

▦ Substitute 1 cup Kamut for the wheat berries.

TESTERS' NOTES

▦ Syrian Jews in Damascus make this pomegranate, grain, and nut mixture to celebrate a baby's first teething—probably to remind the grown-ups of why they have teeth in the first place! Still and all, it makes a perfect breakfast. Spoon it into bowls on its own—or serve it with a little garnish of plain yogurt. It can be eaten at room temperature or cold from the fridge.

▦ Because the wheat berries are cooked with the fennel seeds, there's no real way to save time by using precooked grains. That said, you can cook the wheat berries with the fennel seeds up to 2 days in advance and store them in a zip-closed plastic bag in the fridge.

SYRIAN SLIHA

1 cup wheat berries, preferably soft white wheat berries

2 tablespoons fennel seeds

1 cup shelled, unsalted pistachios

1 cup pine nuts

1 cup chopped walnuts (in about ½-inch bits to match the pistachios)

¼ cup sugar

¼ cup pomegranate seeds

¼ cup unsweetened shredded coconut

½ teaspoon ground cinnamon

½ teaspoon salt

1. Soak the wheat berries in a big bowl of cool water for at least 8 hours and up to 16 hours.

2. Drain the wheat berries in a fine-mesh sieve or a small-holed colander set in the sink. Dump the grains into a medium saucepan with the fennel seeds and fill the saucepan two-thirds of the way with water. Bring to a boil over high heat. Reduce the heat to low and simmer until the grains are tender, about 50 minutes. Drain again in that sieve or colander; if you're using a standard colander with larger holes, line it with cheesecloth or paper towels so you don't lose the fennel seeds.

3. As the wheat berries cook, scatter the pistachios, pine nuts, and walnuts in a large dry skillet and set it over medium-low heat. Toast, stirring once in a while, until the nuts are lightly browned, maybe 5 or 6 minutes. Spread them out on a large cutting board and cool for a few minutes; then chop them into small pieces, about the size of the wheat berries themselves.

4. Scrape the wheat berries and fennel seeds into a big bowl. Mix in everything else: the chopped nuts, sugar, pomegranate seeds, coconut, cinnamon, and salt. Cool to room temperature before serving, or store in a sealed container in the refrigerator for breakfasts (or snacks) in the week to come.

GROATS AND GRITS HOT CEREAL WITH HONEY AND ORANGE ZEST

6 cups water

½ cup coarse, whole-grain polenta (sometimes called rustic polenta)

½ cup millet grits (see page 172)

½ cup buckwheat groats

½ cup whole-grain barley grits

3 tablespoons honey

1 teaspoon finely grated orange zest

½ teaspoon ground cinnamon

½ teaspoon salt

1. Bring the water to a simmer in a large saucepan, a small Dutch oven, or a small cast iron casserole set over high heat. Stirring all the while, pour in the polenta, millet, buckwheat groats, and barley grits.

2. Drop the heat to very low and stir in the honey, orange zest, cinnamon, and salt. Cover and simmer until the mixture has thickened and the grains are tender but with some tooth, stirring once or twice, about 15 minutes.

SERVES 8

Active time: 10 minutes
Total time: 25 minutes

CHEF IT UP!

▥ Add some finely chopped nuts and/or dried fruit once the cereal has cooked. Set it aside, covered, to infuse the flavors from them for 5 minutes before serving.

TESTERS' NOTES

▥ Although this recipe makes a lot—probably best for a holiday weekend with guests—you can halve it for a more run-of-the-mill breakfast. If so, use a medium saucepan.

▥ Barley grits are simply barley that's been cut and sliced into small, uneven bits. Search out whole-grain barley grits for the real deal, not just pearled barley that's been turned into grits.

▥ Although the flavors are big enough that you don't have to add anything else, you can add a pat of butter to the bowls—or even a splash of warmed whole, 2%, or 1% milk. You might also consider a drizzle of maple syrup.

SERVES 6

Active time: 10 minutes
Total time: 8 hours 10 minutes

CHEF IT UP!

▓ Substitute chopped dried blueberries, dried apricots, or dried pineapple for the dried cranberries.

TESTERS' NOTES

▓ This is the real oat-y deal: a hearty porridge made with oat groats, not rolled oats or even steel-cut oats.

▓ Because of the bran's tight embrace, the groats won't release enough of their ample starch to thicken the cereal. So we've added some buckwheat groats to thicken it up a bit—and also to balance the oat groats' more assertive flavor.

▓ Don't dare use anything but real maple syrup for recipes like these. Although labeled by various ratings based on state and national systems, choose a dark amber syrup of the best or first grade—or failing that, the far darker second grade or B-grade syrup. Whole grains need the more insistent taste of a more fully flavored syrup, not the wispy lightness of a light amber variety.

SLOW-COOKER OAT GROAT PORRIDGE

4 cups water

2 ripe pears, peeled, cored, and chopped

1 cup oat groats

½ cup buckwheat groats

½ cup dried cranberries, chopped

2 tablespoons maple syrup

½ teaspoon ground cinnamon

½ teaspoon salt

Mix everything in a 5- to 6-quart slow cooker. Cover and cook on low for 8 hours. Stir well before serving.

SLOW-COOKER THREE-GRAIN PORRIDGE WITH DATES AND HONEY

SERVES 6

Active time: 10 minutes
Total time: 9 hours 10 minutes

3 cups water

3 cups milk (whole, 2%, 1%, or fat-free)

1 cup oat groats

½ cup hull-less barley

¼ cup millet

6 Medjool dates, pitted and chopped

2½ tablespoons honey

One 2-inch cinnamon stick

Stir everything together in a 5- to 6-quart slow cooker. Cover and cook on low for 9 to 10 hours. Stir well before serving.

CHEF IT UP!

- Honey is not one thing but a multitude. There are so many varietals besides the standard "wildflower" or "clover." To complement the cereal, search out a dark, rich honey like buckwheat or oak.

TESTERS' NOTES

- A 2-inch cinnamon stick is shorter than the standard ones found in the jars from the spice aisle. Break one of those longer sticks into a segment that's about this length so the spice won't overpower the porridge.

- It's hard to imagine this spirited, sweet but earthy porridge without a slice of whole-grain toast on the side. Seems like that toast would require apple butter, too.

Active time: 35 minutes
Total time: 2 hours 15 minutes

MAKE IT EASIER!

▦ Make the congee overnight in a slow cooker. Decrease the water (or a water/broth combo) to 8 cups. Cook covered on low for 10 to 12 hours.

CHEF IT UP!

▦ Use 6 cups water and 6 cups reduced-sodium vegetable broth.

TESTERS' NOTES

▦ Congee is usually served with a bunch of savory stir-ins, sometimes spread around the table in little bowls. Even at breakfast, try sliced scallions, minced cooked boneless skinless chicken from a rotisserie bird, minced cooked shrimp, diced tofu, and/or thinly sliced shiitake mushroom caps. You can also fry sliced garlic in a little oil in a small skillet over medium-low heat until brown and frizzled. Or you can make it more of an American affair with toasted nuts, a pat of butter, and maple syrup.

BROWN RICE CONGEE

12 cups water

1 cup medium-grain brown rice, such as brown Arborio rice

1 tablespoon minced fresh ginger

1. Mix all the ingredients in a large saucepan or Dutch oven; bring to a simmer over medium-high heat, stirring occasionally. Reduce the heat to very low, just so the water percolates slowly enough that you can count the bubbles as they form. Cook uncovered for 1½ hours, stirring once in a while.

2. Cover and continue cooking until thick and porridgelike, about 30 more minutes, stirring often now to prevent sticking as the congee thickens.

THE WEEKENDERS

Now we turn to more elaborate breakfasts. True, some aren't too involved—like the whole-grain waffle mix you can have in the pantry and whip up anytime. Still, the sun doesn't rise and shine on make-aheads. Some of these recipes are probably best for a weekend morning, like the Cinnamon-Raisin Barley Pudding or the Quinoa Date Bread. But who could argue with Oat and Amaranth Pancakes just about any morning? Or evening? And you just have to try the Breakfast Polenta Cake!

As we've said, whole grains are so foundational to who we are as humans, they've become standard morning fare, probably the one chance some of us have to eat a whole grain in our rush-rush world. Unfortunately, almost any whole grain has an Achilles heel. The germ is loaded with polyunsaturated fats, a prime candidate for going rancid. The bran is stocked with fiber, which then locks rot-inducing moisture right against the germ. It's a recipe for trouble—or spoilage.

To solve the problem, industrial processing gives the germ and bran a Mafia whack. Remove only the hull and the grains can stick around a year. That fit the bill for our ancestors who were trying to get through one winter at a time. But remove the germ and bran as well and it can last a lot longer.

Although there are nutritional issues involved with removing the bran and the germ, let's focus on the culinary ones. By leaving just the endosperm, we simplify a whole grain's complex flavor palette until it's little more than baldly saccharine. We then don't experience the earthiness, the inherent savoriness, the complex but subtle balance of flavors, sophisticatedly pure but with a coarse, rustic streak as well.

Given that grains are a part of our morning routines, we're left with a start-the-day impulse for them without its proper fulfillment. We pull out boxes of grain-based cereals, few of which offer whole grains themselves—or even taste like grains at all. We reach for that cinnamon-raisin Danish in the morning, partly because of the sugar that jolts us awake, but also because we have always woken up to grains, albeit now depressingly monochromatic in their refined forms.

Face it: Humans eat a lot. Several times a day. We're trying to stoke the fire in our heads—that is, our brains. To run those complex machines up top, we need to give them a steady supply of ready energy. We don't do our best work when we're hungry.

But we can't stoke the fire before we build it. Our palates need to wake up, even before our brains. Our mouths lead to our guts, which lead to our heads. And here's where grains play a gustatory role. They're not a big whap up side the head first thing in the morning, like a roasted pork shoulder or a braise of oxtails. Instead, they're gentler, subtler, more in keeping with the morning hours. More *Ellen* than *True Blood*.

Yes, we've gone too far. We've taken those delicate, muted cues of what were the foundation crops for human civilization, refined the grains to last even longer, and so morphed the flavors until they're no more than a slick of sweet on the tongue. But behind it all, we know that real taste, the whole-grain taste: the gentle balance of earthy and sweet, the perfect way to start the day.

We've always known it, since the dawn of human history. Sometimes it's great to have that reminder in the form of a simple make-ahead granola or muesli. But other times, it's important to give whole grains the full treatment, more culinary folderol—like this Barley Grits Breakfast Casserole with Apples and Sausage or these muffins stocked with quinoa and cashews. They are celebrations of whole grains. And some of the best reasons to get out of bed.

THE WEEKENDERS

CORNMEAL AND OAT
WAFFLE MIX

4 cups coarse, whole-grain,
    yellow cornmeal

2 cups whole wheat flour

1¾ cups spelt flour

1 cup old-fashioned rolled oats
    (do not use quick-cooking or
    steel-cut oats)

¾ cup sugar

¼ cup baking powder

4 teaspoons salt

1 teaspoon ground cinnamon

Whisk all the ingredients in a large bowl, taking care that the baking powder is evenly distributed throughout. Spoon or pour the whole kit and caboodle into a large container and seal tightly. Store up to 3 months in a dark, cool pantry.

NOW WHAT?

To make 3 waffles, scoop 1 cup plus 3 tablespoons of the mix into a bowl. Whisk in 1 large egg, ½ cup plus 1 tablespoon milk (whole, 2%, 1%, or even fat-free), ½ teaspoon vanilla extract, and 2 tablespoons nut oil (walnut, hazelnut, or pecan) or 2½ tablespoons melted and cooled unsalted butter. Mix well and set aside for 10 minutes while the waffle iron heats. Then make the waffles in the iron according to the manufacturer's instructions.

SERVES ABOUT 24,
with a heaping 9½ cups of mix

Active time: 15 minutes
Total time: 15 minutes

Make ahead: Store in a sealed, airtight container at room temperature for up to 3 months.

CHEF IT UP!

▥ Although butter and maple syrup are the standard condiments, you might want to try sorghum syrup, a Southern favorite.

TESTERS' NOTES

▥ A whole-grain mix you can make ahead and have on hand for when you're ready for waffles? Sounds like heaven to us!

▥ If you want to turn this mix into pancake batter, thin it out with about ¼ cup additional milk—or maybe even a little more, depending on how dry the flours have gotten as they've sat on the shelf.

▥ Make sure you buy coarse, whole-grain cornmeal. While the mix can be made with more standard yellow cornmeal—and is still a whole-grain recipe because of the rolled oats—the coarse cornmeal will make every forkful more toothsome.

▥ Can't find whole-grain cornmeal? Grind coarse, whole-grain polenta in a large blender or food processor until it's the consistency of coarse cornmeal.

OAT AND AMARANTH PANCAKES

1½ cups whole wheat pastry flour

2 tablespoons packed light brown sugar

1 tablespoon baking powder

½ teaspoon salt

1½ cups old-fashioned rolled oats (do not use quick-cooking or steel-cut oats)

¼ cup amaranth

2 large eggs, at room temperature

1⅓ cups milk (whole, 2%, 1%, or fat-free)

3 tablespoons toasted nut oil of any stripe (pecan, walnut, etc.), plus more for the griddle

1 teaspoon vanilla extract

1. Whisk the whole wheat pastry flour, brown sugar, baking powder, and salt in a small bowl until the brown sugar is well mixed throughout the other ingredients. If the brown sugar is clumpy, crumble it into grains between your fingers.

2. Dump the oats and amaranth in a large blender and blend until the mixture has the consistency of a grainy but fine meal, a little finer than standard cornmeal, 2 or 3 minutes.

3. Plop the eggs, milk, oil, and vanilla in the blender; whir until well combined. Don't wimp out too soon. You want a thick, rich batter. About 2 minutes should do it.

4. Dump in the flour mixture; pulse a few times, just until combined, scraping down the inside of the canister to make sure there are no pockets of dry flour anywhere.

5. Lightly grease a large nonstick griddle or skillet with some nut oil dabbed on a paper towel, then set it over medium heat—or melt a bit of butter in the pan over medium heat. Pour about ¼ cup of the batter into the griddle or skillet; make 2 or 3 more similar pancakes without crowding. Cook until permanent bubbles form across the surface of the raw batter and the bottom has browned, about 2 minutes. Flip the cakes with a flat spatula, then cook another 2 minutes or so, until browned and set. Transfer these pancakes to plates and continue making more, regreasing or rebuttering the skillet as needed to prevent sticking.

SERVES 4 to 6, with 16 pancakes

Active time: 20 minutes

Total time: 20 minutes

Make ahead: Do steps 1 and 2 the night before.

CHEF IT UP!

■ Although maple syrup is the go-to condiment for pancakes, you might consider birch syrup, something of an Alaskan treasure. It's quite sophisticated, like burnt-sugar caramels, intense and complex. You can find lots of suppliers online.

TESTERS' NOTES

■ Because amaranth will sap all the available moisture out of batters, these pancakes are best if you make them as soon as the dry ingredients have been blended with the liquids. Also, eat the pancakes while they're still hot off the griddle.

■ Don't overblend the mixture once the flour and other dry ingredients get added. You'll stretch the glutens and end up with tough pancakes. Just moisten the flour and get it even throughout.

TEFF GRIDDLE CAKES

SERVES 4, with 2 pancakes each

Active time: 15 minutes
Total time: 1 hour 15 minutes

Make ahead: Bake the sweet potatoes up to 3 days in advance; wrap and store in the fridge.

CHEF IT UP!

▦ Although syrup seems a natural, these cakes are even better with apple or pear butter.

TESTERS' NOTES

▦ These griddle cakes are not terribly sweet. They're also a tad wet inside—not battery, just moist, which is good because teff sucks up all available moisture. For that reason, they're best eaten within a few minutes of their coming off the griddle.

▦ Be careful not to confuse whole wheat flour and whole wheat pastry flour. The former is more coarse, often with plenty of hard wheat in the mix; the latter, much finer, made with mostly (if not all) soft wheat. The former offers heft; the latter, a more ethereal finish—which is just what baked goods like these griddle cakes need!

2 sweet potatoes (7 ounces each)

2 cups water

⅔ cup teff, preferably brown teff

1 cup whole wheat flour

½ cup milk (whole, 2%, 1%, or fat-free)

¼ cup packed brown sugar, preferably dark brown sugar

2 teaspoons baking powder

2 teaspoons vanilla extract

Up to 1 teaspoon salt

½ teaspoon ground cinnamon

Nut oil or unsalted butter, for greasing the skillet or griddle

1. Preheat the oven to 350°F. Set the sweet potatoes on a baking sheet and bake until soft, about 1 hour. Cool on the baking sheet until you can handle them.

2. Meanwhile, mix the water and teff in a medium saucepan; bring to a boil over medium-high heat, stirring fairly often. Cover, reduce the heat to low, and cook until all the water has been absorbed and the teff is about the consistency of cream of wheat, about 10 minutes. Scrape the teff into a large bowl; cool for 10 minutes.

3. Peel the sweet potatoes and scrape the flesh into the bowl with the teff. Stir in everything else: the flour, milk, brown sugar, baking powder, vanilla, salt, and cinnamon. The batter should be stiff, thick, even a little sticky, but with no pockets of unmoistened flour remaining.

4. Heat a little oil in a nonstick griddle or skillet set over medium heat—or melt a little butter in it. Spoon about ¼ cup of the batter into the pan; spread it to a circle about 3½ inches in diameter and slightly more than ¼ inch thick. Add more cakes, taking care not to crowd the pan. Cook until browned and a little crisp, 2 to 3 minutes. Flip the cakes and continue cooking until brown and set, 2 to 3 more minutes. Transfer to plates and continue making more until you've used up all the batter.

CINNAMON-RAISIN BARLEY PUDDING

½ cup hull-less barley

3 cups milk (whole, 2%, or 1%)

⅓ cup sugar

¼ teaspoon ground cinnamon

¼ teaspoon grated nutmeg

¼ teaspoon salt

2 large eggs plus 1 large egg yolk, at room temperature

½ cup chopped raisins, dried cranberries, or blueberries

2 teaspoons vanilla extract

1. Soak the barley in a big bowl of cool water for at least 8 hours and up to 16 hours. Drain the barley in a fine-mesh sieve or small-holed colander set in the sink. Scrape the barley into a medium saucepan, fill it about two-thirds of the way with water, and bring to a boil over high heat. Reduce the heat to low and simmer until the barley is tender, about 55 minutes. Drain again in that sieve or colander.

2. Pour the cooked barley back into a large saucepan; stir in the milk, sugar, spices, and salt. Bring the mixture to a full simmer over medium heat, stirring occasionally. It's important to keep the heat fairly low from here on out because the barley can stick. Once everything's simmering, reduce the heat to low and cook until somewhat thick, sort of like a pudding, about 5 minutes, maybe less depending on the residual moisture content in the barley.

3. Whisk the eggs, egg yolk, dried fruit, and vanilla in a medium bowl. Whisk half the barley porridge into this egg mixture, then whisk this combined concoction back into the remaining barley porridge in the saucepan over the heat. Cook on low, whisking constantly, just until thickened, no more than 2 minutes. Serve warm.

SERVES 4

Active time: 15 minutes

Total time: 1 hour 10 minutes, plus soaking the hull-less barley for at least 8 hours

Make ahead: Once cooled, store covered in the fridge for up to 3 days. Microwave individual servings for 30 seconds or so to warm them up.

Save time: Use 1⅓ cups cooked hull-less barley and omit soaking and cooking the raw grains.

MAKE IT EASIER!

▪ Skip the dried fruit in the recipe—and the necessary chopping. Serve the hot pudding with some jam or preserves to top each bowlful.

TESTERS' NOTE

▪ Say bye-bye to rice pudding. Barley is way more luxurious: chewy, rich, and satisfying. You might even save some of this breakfast for dessert!

Active time: 20 minutes

Total time: 1 hour 30 minutes

Make ahead: Store, covered, in the fridge for up to 2 days. Reheat, covered with foil, in a preheated 350°F oven for 15 minutes. Or cut into individual wedges, seal in plastic wrap, and freeze for up to 3 months.

Make It Vegetarian: Use sausage-flavored textured soy protein; heat it in the skillet for a minute or two before adding the other ingredients. Also omit the Worcestershire sauce altogether—or substitute a vegan Worcestershire sauce.

BARLEY GRITS CASSEROLE WITH APPLES AND SAUSAGE

2½ cups water

1 cup barley grits

1 pound turkey breakfast sausage, any casings removed, the filling broken into 1-inch clumps

2 tart apples (such as Granny Smith, Empire, or Northern Spy), peeled, cored, and chopped into ½-inch pieces

8 scallions, thinly sliced

2 garlic cloves, minced

1 tablespoon Worcestershire sauce

1 tablespoon fresh thyme leaves or 2 teaspoons dried thyme

5 ounces Gruyère, shredded through the large holes of a box grater

2 large eggs, at room temperature, separated

1½ tablespoons unsalted butter, plus more for greasing the baking pan

1. Position the rack in the center of the oven and crank it up to 475°F. Grease a 6-cup oval gratin dish or 9-inch square baking pan with a little butter on a wadded-up paper towel or piece of wax paper.

2. Mix the water and barley grits in a medium saucepan; bring to a boil over high heat. Reduce the heat to low, cover, and simmer until most of the water has been absorbed, about 5 minutes, stirring a few times. Set aside off the heat, covered, to steam for 5 minutes. Transfer to a large bowl and cool for 10 minutes.

3. Meanwhile, fry the sausage clumps in a dry skillet set over medium heat until nicely browned, about 5 minutes, stirring occasionally. Stir in the apples, scallions, and garlic; cook, stirring, until the apple and scallions begin to soften, about 2 minutes. Stir in the Worcestershire sauce and thyme. Scrape the contents of the skillet into the bowl with the grits. Mix together, then cool for 5 minutes, before stirring in the cheese and egg yolks until there's no trace of any egg in the mixture.

(continued)

4. Use an electric mixer at high speed to beat the egg whites in a separate bowl until light, foamy, droopy peaks can be made off the beaters when they're turned off and dipped back into the egg whites.

5. Use a rubber spatula to fold the beaten egg whites into the barley grits mixture, taking care to use gentle, long strokes to keep as much of the air and fluff in the egg whites as possible. Spoon and spread this mixture into the prepared dish or pan. Dot the top with the butter.

6. Bake until puffed, browned, and set, about 40 minutes. Cool for 5 minutes before scooping up big spoon-fuls into bowls.

TESTERS' NOTES

▥ This is a hearty, filling dish, probably best for a holiday morning when dinner will be mid-afternoon. Make sure you use only barley grits, not just stone-ground barley (and certainly not barley couscous).

▥ Some supermarkets sell breakfast sausage filling not yet in its casings, sometimes called "bulk sausage," to be formed into patties at home. If you buy this sausage filling, you'll need to form it into small, 1-inch clumps before using it in the casserole.

▥ We like turkey breakfast sausage best in this casserole. Pork sausages can lard it up with a bit too much fat. While we're usually all for such larding, in this case we felt that the lower-fat turkey sausage let the other flavors come through unmasked, particularly those of the earthy barley grits.

QUINOA CASHEW MUFFINS

6 tablespoons quinoa, preferably white quinoa

1½ cups whole wheat pastry flour (page 51)

½ cup quinoa flour

1 tablespoon baking powder

½ teaspoon ground cinnamon

½ teaspoon salt

⅔ cup packed dark brown sugar

6 tablespoons unsalted butter, plus more for greasing the muffin tin

¾ cup cashew butter

2 large eggs, at room temperature, separated

2 teaspoons vanilla extract

1 cup milk (whole, 2%, 1%, or fat-free)

SERVES 18

Active time: 15 minutes
Total time: 45 minutes

Make ahead: Once cooled, wrap the muffins individually in plastic wrap and freeze, then set as many as you need on the counter overnight to thaw for the morning.

Save time: Use ¾ cup cooked quinoa and omit cooking the raw grains.

CHEF IT UP!

- Substitute ground cardamom for the ground cinnamon.

1. Place the quinoa in a small saucepan, submerge in lots of water, and bring to a boil over high heat. Reduce the heat to medium and cook, uncovered, until the grains are tender and have sprouted their characteristic halos, about 10 minutes. Drain in a fine-mesh sieve or a lined colander set in the sink. Refresh with cool water to bring the quinoa back to room temperature. Drain thoroughly.

2. Meanwhile, position the rack in the center of the oven and pre-heat to 400°F. Grease the cups of a muffin tin with a little butter on a wadded-up paper towel or piece of wax paper. The recipe will make 18 muffins; you can make this in one batch with two 12-cup muffin tins or in multiple batches with the same tin, pro-vided you regrease it after the first baking.

3. Mix the whole wheat pastry flour, quinoa flour, baking powder, cinnamon, and salt in a medium bowl.

4. Use an electric mixer to beat the sugar and butter in a large bowl until creamy and fluffy, about 5 minutes, scraping down the inside of the bowl as necessary with a rubber spatula to make sure the sugar is slowly being dissolved in the fat. Beat in the cashew butter, egg yolks, and vanilla until smooth and creamy.

5. Beat in half the milk, then add half the flour mixture and beat at low speed just until combined. Beat in the remaining milk until smooth, then scrape down and remove the beaters. Add the remaining flour mixture and the cooked quinoa. Stir with a rubber spatula just until there are no pockets of dry flour in the bowl.

6. Clean and dry the beaters. Put the egg whites in a clean and dry bowl. Beat at high speed until soft, foamy peaks form when you turn off the beaters and dip them back into the egg whites. Use a rubber spatula to fold these into the batter, taking care not to deflate them but working in wide, steady arcs. Don't worry if there are white streaks left in the batter.

7. Spoon the batter into the muffin cups, filling each about three-quarters full. Bake until puffed and brown and a toothpick inserted into the center of a muffin comes out clean, about 15 minutes. Cool in the tin a couple of minutes before turning the muffins out onto a rack to cool completely. Once cool, they can be stored in a sealed container at room temperature for a day or two—or wrapped individually to store in the freezer for several months.

TESTERS' NOTES

▨ Make sure you allow 15 minutes for your oven to preheat. Muffins get a good, crunchy top when the batter is suddenly put right into the inferno.

▨ The best egg separator is your clean, dry hand. Crack the egg into the cup of your palm, then let the white drip through your fingers while the yolk stays put in your palm. Of course, you'll get messy; but what's the point of cooking otherwise? (Oh, right, the food made.)

▨ Don't worry about that blather about filling extra, unused cups in a muffin tin with water before baking. It's simply not true. Bake away, even with unfilled cups!

QUINOA DATE BREAD

½ cup quinoa, preferably white quinoa

1 cup all-purpose flour

1 teaspoon baking powder

½ teaspoon baking soda

½ teaspoon garam masala

½ teaspoon ground cinnamon

½ teaspoon salt

½ cup packed dark brown sugar

6 tablespoons unsalted butter, plus more for greasing the loaf pan

⅓ cup granulated sugar

10 ounces Medjool dates, pitted and chopped

2 large eggs, at room temperature

½ cup plain yogurt (whole milk, low-fat, or nonfat)

1 tablespoon vanilla extract

1. Put the quinoa in a small saucepan and cover with plenty of water. Bring to a boil over high heat. Reduce the heat to medium and simmer until the grains are tender and have sprouted their halos, about 10 minutes. Drain in a fine-mesh sieve or a lined colander set in the sink, then run cool water over the quinoa to stop it from cooking.

2. Position the rack in the center of the oven and preheat to 350°F. Grease a 5 × 9-inch loaf pan with a little butter on a wadded-up paper towel or piece of wax paper.

3. Whisk the flour, baking powder, baking soda, garam masala, cinnamon, and salt in a small bowl.

4. Use an electric mixer to beat the brown sugar, butter, and granulated sugar in a large bowl until creamy and light, about 5 minutes, scraping down the sides of the bowl occasionally.

5. Beat in the dates, then the eggs. Continue beating until fairly smooth and creamy. Beat in the yogurt and vanilla, then scrape down and remove the beaters.

6. Stir in the cooked quinoa and the flour mixture with a rubber spatula just until there are no dry pockets of flour throughout the batter. Scrape and spread the batter into the prepared loaf pan.

7. Bake until the loaf is browned, cracked a little in the center, firm to the touch, and until a toothpick inserted into its center comes out clean, about 55 minutes. Cool in the pan on a rack for 10 minutes before turning the loaf out onto the rack to cool completely.

SERVES 8

Active time: 20 minutes
Total time: 1 hour 30 minutes

Make ahead: Seal the cooled loaf in plastic wrap and store at room temperature for up to 3 days or in the freezer for up to 3 months.

Save time: Use 1¾ cups cooked quinoa and omit soaking and cooking the raw grains.

TESTERS' NOTES

- Remember old-fashioned date breads? When we were kids, they were even made in empty coffee cans! This is our whole-grain take on that classic, moist and delicious. It cries out for a cup of hot tea, especially when the bread is still warm. Oh, and cream cheese, too.

- This quick bread has a great crumb, just dense enough to hold the quinoa in place. However, it can get a little stiff by the third day on the counter. If so, toast slices on a baking sheet about 4 to 6 inches from a preheated broiler for a few minutes, just until lightly browned and crunchy.

- Avoid the boxes of prechopped date pieces for baking. Instead, use soft, fragrant whole dates that you then pit and chop. They'll almost dissolve into the mix, like bananas in banana bread.

Active time: 20 minutes
Total time: 1 hour

Make ahead: Store under a cake saver at room temperature for up to 2 days. Or, when cooled, wrap individual slices in plastic wrap and store them in the freezer for up to 4 months.

CHEF IT UP!

▌ Turn a wedge of cake on its side on a plate and spoon a dollop of strawberry or apricot preserves over the slice. And go ahead, add a little crème fraîche.

BREAKFAST POLENTA CAKE WITH KAMUT CRUNCH TOPPING

Cake

1¼ cups whole wheat pastry flour (page 51)

1 cup coarse, whole-grain polenta

2 teaspoons baking powder

1 teaspoon salt

4 large eggs, at room temperature

¾ cup granulated sugar

1 tablespoon finely grated orange zest

1 teaspoon vanilla extract

8 tablespoons unsalted butter, melted and cooled, plus more for greasing the baking pan

Topping

½ cup Kamut flakes

¼ cup whole wheat pastry flour

3 tablespoons packed light brown sugar

2 tablespoons unsalted butter, melted and cooled

1 tablespoon maple syrup

½ teaspoon ground cinnamon

¼ teaspoon salt

1. Position the rack in the center of the oven and preheat to 350°F. Lightly grease a 9-inch round springform pan with a little butter on a wadded-up paper towel or piece of wax paper.

2. To make the cake: Whisk the whole wheat pastry flour, polenta, baking powder, and salt in a medium bowl.

3. Use an electric mixer at medium speed to beat the eggs and granulated sugar in a large bowl until creamy, light, and pale yellow, about 5 minutes. Seriously. The stuff has to double in volume.

4. Beat in the orange zest and vanilla. Scrape down and remove the beaters, dump in the flour mixture, and stir with a rubber spatula or a wooden spoon just until there are no pockets of dry flour in the batter. Pour in the melted butter and stir until incorporated. Spread the batter in the prepared pan.

(continued)

5. To make the topping: Mix all the ingredients in a medium bowl—the Kamut flakes, whole wheat pastry flour, brown sugar, melted butter, maple syrup, cinnamon, and salt. Sprinkle and crumble this mixture all over the top of the batter.

6. Bake until a toothpick inserted into the cake comes out with a couple of moist crumbs attached to it, about 30 minutes. Cool in the pan on a rack for 15 minutes, then unlatch and remove the sides of the springform pan. Slice some warm wedges—or continue cooling the cake to room temperature.

TESTERS' NOTES

▪ This cake has a coarse, grainy crumb. Remember: It's not a cornmeal cake but a polenta cake, ever so much more satisfying in the morning.

▪ This cake tastes better with a topping made from grade A dark amber maple syrup—or even grade B maple syrup.

▪ We used Kamut flakes in the topping because we liked their intense chewiness against the cake's crumb. However, you could use wheat or spelt flakes, if you prefer.

▪ Individual wedges freeze beautifully if wrapped tightly in plastic wrap and sealed in a plastic bag. Set the frozen wedges out on the counter the night before to enjoy them the next morning.

Quinoa Cashew Muffins, page 56, and
Breakfast Polenta Cake with Kamut Crunch Topping

2

COLD

This is a chapter of mostly whole-grain salads, plus a few other items that you can keep in the fridge for days at a stretch. Most are probably best for lunch, although it's hard to argue with a grain salad and some creamy hummus for a dinner without much fuss in the warmer months. Still, most of these dishes can be made on the weekend, saved in the fridge in sealable containers, and relished throughout the week for midday meals.

And that's a great thing—because lunch all too frequently gets squeezed by all sorts of constraints, some of your own making, some not. You end up with a subpar sandwich on the run or a wilted salad at your desk. There's little to savor in any of that.

Too bad. Eating is not only about sustenance. It's fundamentally about pleasure. Yes, when we taste something wonderful, we sense the saliva in our mouths and the gurgle in our stomachs. But we might not know about other, less familiar reactions: chemicals in the brain that set us up for anticipation and fulfillment from our mouths to our stomachs.

Did you know you have as many neurons lining your digestive track as exist up in your head? Things don't just taste good. They *feel* good—because of the release of a powerful neurotransmitter from your head to your stomach: dopamine, common across a huge spectrum of life, vertebrates to invertebrates. Among other things, it stimulates voluntary movement. See a fly, swat it, and thank dopamine. But it also sets up a reward-based pleasure principle in the digestive track—and all the way back up to the brain.

And how does this feel-good, warm-and-fuzzy dopamine make its appearance? First, it gets triggered by our personal, culinary histories. When we taste something delicious, we ping the brain's hippocampus, our memory center. If we find tastes that match or are analogous to previously pleasurable ones, that ping sets off the Rube Goldberg cascade of chemicals that finally leads to dopamine all the way down the body.

Second, dopamine is triggered by chewing. Moving our jaws, we signal the vagus nerve to start firing. (It's pronounced *VAY-gus*, as in Las

Vegas.) That nerve is the single link between those up-top neurons and the ones in our digestive tracks. By chewing, we give the vagus nerve permission to release more of the pleasurable stuff.

Put simply, we eat because food feels good. If we ever intend to solve our overeating dilemmas in the modern world, it's because we'll embrace the very root of tasting and eating—that is, pleasure—and not run away from it. And here's where whole grains play a crucial role: They offer big tastes and lots of chew in every spoonful. What's more, every bite is laying down a good memory of better food for the years to come.

Still it's sometimes hard to say "no" to that gummy, takeout sandwich—especially since our work week has expanded so dramatically. According to the Bureau of Labor Statistics, the average US blue-collar worker now puts in 47.1 hours per week and the average white-collar worker 53.2 hours. Those are 10-hour days—and that's on average, with many reporting not-uncommon 70-hour work weeks. While other developed countries—France, Great Britain, Canada—lag behind the United States, they're catching up, the pace ever increasing globally and locally at once.

No wonder the average amount of time Americans spent cooking fell so dramatically throughout the 20th century. In the 1930s, Americans spent almost 2½ hours a day preparing food at home. By the June Cleaver '50s, we were down to an hour. Just at the turn of the millennium, the average American spent around 30 minutes a day preparing (or just unwrapping) all the food he, she, or the family consumed: breakfast, lunch, dinner, *and* snacks. Voilà: the gummy sandwich.

Not very long ago, some design experts were predicting that the kitchen would become a relic of the past, remodeled and fancified into uselessness, like the parlor that had morphed into the formal living room to be used only on the holidays.

How wrong they were! There's been a startling reversal in the early years of the 21st century. Stats show that people are cooking at home again. And mostly on the weekends, rather than during the week. Time was, people ate out on Saturdays, called in on Sunday evenings, and used their kitchens the rest of the week. These days, our kitchens stay idle most of the week and go through a workout on the weekends.

So this chapter fuses what we need to eat with how we're cooking—all in the service of hearty, tasty lunches or quick dinners from the fridge when time is short. Every dish here can be made in advance and squirreled away for several days: whole wheat salads with the likes of white beans, olives, sage, and tomatoes in the mix; rice salads that run from brown to wild; salads that use unusual grains like Job's tears or black barley as well as the more familiar whole-grain bulgur wheat or quinoa. There are even a few dishes that aren't salads at all: stuffed tomatoes, summer rolls, and the like.

Whole grains take to these preparations. The nuanced flavors don't degrade when stored in the fridge the way those in other dishes can. Face it: Roast chicken is not so stellar 2 days later. The flavors have dulled; the skin, gone squishy. But grains hold up because they were designed to.

So whip up a couple of tasty salads when you've got some time. You'll have meals all week. Sure, you may still eat it at your desk, but at least you won't need to stop for that always-tempting-but-in-the-end-rarely-good slice of soft, mushy, cheese pizza. You'll have chewed well and savored well. It'll feel good all over your body.

WHEAT BERRY SALADS

In many ways, wheat is the backbone of this book. There are more recipes using wheat berries than recipes for any other grain; there are also more "Grain Swaps" that call for wheat berries than any other grain. And none of that counts the recipes for other wheat products like wheat flakes or whole-grain bulgur, some of which we've already seen in breakfast dishes and others we'll get to in subsequent sections.

Wheat's importance to this project is sort of strange, given that it's actually the third most produced grain on the plant, just behind runner-up rice and far behind our champ, corn. You'd think one of those other grains would get top billing.

Then again, wheat's dominance in our book is not so strange, given that the fates of humans and wheat have been linked for millennia. Some archeologists and prehistorians claim that wheat was the first thing humans ever domesticated—and that it in turn domesticated us, allowing us to give up the roam-and-kill lifestyle for the benefits of city living.

It's a two-way street. Wheat is now dependent on us. These days, it bears no resemblance to its undomesticated kin, wild einkorn and wild emmer. These were scrawny competitors in the plant world, usually driven into poor clay soils on the edges of scrub-oak forests by far more aggressive weeds. Tasty but relatively wimpy, wheat saw its one chance with us, a species that finds not just sustenance but actual pleasure in its food.

So modern wheat—of the sort that gives us the full range of wheat berries, spelt to Kamut—evolved to depend on humans as much as we depend on it. Cultivated wheat cannot regenerate on its own. It needs us to gather its seeds and plant them. When a wheat farmer abandons his or her field, it does not continue to yield a crop. Left to its own devices, a wheat field will fall fallow, go to weeds, and eventually morph into a prairie or a new-growth forest. Modern wheat's only method of reproduction is us, among the strongest competitors on the planet. Consider it a rare, healthy codependency. We call it the staff of life, both supporting us in bad times and becoming a symbol of the good times in those waving fields of amber grain. In turn, wheat needs us to survive into the next generation. No wonder wheat berries get the biggest share of these recipes.

In developing them, we put wheat berries on this continuum from most assertive to fairly mild: spelt berries—whole-grain farro—hard red winter wheat berries—Kamut—soft white spring wheat berries. If you want to morph our recipes by using one wheat berry in place of another, you might consider a similar continuum, adding bolder flavors to balance a more commanding grain, or taking the flavors down a notch so they don't mask a milder choice.

Wheat's predominance took over not only our recipe *testing* but our recipe *tasting,* too. We host a variety of groups in our New England home: lunches for book groups and the like. We live in a resort area, the Berkshires. Half the houses are owned by weekenders. Believe us, these people will show up whenever they hear

there's free food. Even for a discussion of Virginia Woolf! Which is how, on the Friday before Labor Day last year, we ended with double the usual contingent milling about our house. It was like a family reunion in Arkansas. We had to walk around asking, "Are you sure you're supposed to be here?"

We were right in the middle of testing recipes for this chapter. We had bowls of wheat salads on the counter: spelt berries with tomatoes and white beans, Kamut with cauliflower and olives, a gazpacho-style wheat berry salad. Fortunately, in the face of throngs, we also had bowls of cooked, unadorned wheat berries in the fridge. In a flurry of mincing and dicing, we whipped these up into more choices. There's something comforting about a bowl of cooked farro or spelt berries that you can toss into a hearty salad when crowds drop by. Let the good times roll!

There's also something so summery, so satisfying about wheat berries of all stripes. No matter the season, their savory nuttiness pairs beautifully with bright, fresh flavors. You can celebrate the summer *or* perk up the winter.

You, too, can have such abundance with simple salads like these. Seal them in a container and they'll keep in the fridge for days. And that's pretty much the essence of this staff of life. And a great reason to celebrate our codependent relationship with this grain.

WHEAT BERRY SALADS

SERVES 4

Active time: 20 minutes
Total time: 1 hour 50 minutes

Make ahead: Refrigerate, covered, for up to 4 days.

Save time: Use 2 cups cooked soft white wheat berries and omit soaking and cooking the raw grains.

TESTERS' NOTES

▪ For this one bright, fairly light salad, we preferred the texture when the berries were not presoaked. They got a little softer in the long cooking, offering a luxurious bite, more in keeping with the shredded zucchini.

▪ This salad can weep moisture like mad as it sits, partly because of the salt on the zucchini. If you're storing it for meals ahead, consider omitting the salt and adding a pinch to individual servings.

WHEAT BERRY SALAD WITH ZUCCHINI, BOILED LEMON, AND ALMONDS

¾ cup wheat berries, preferably soft white wheat berries

1 lemon plus ¼ cup fresh lemon juice

½ cup sliced almonds

2 zucchini

3 tablespoons olive oil

2 ounces Parmigiano-Reggiano, finely grated

½ teaspoon salt

½ teaspoon ground black pepper

1. Dump the wheat berries into a large saucepan. Fill it with water until they're submerged by several inches. Bring to a boil over high heat; reduce the heat to medium-low and simmer, uncovered, until the wheat berries are tender, about 1 hour 15 minutes. Drain in a fine-mesh sieve or small-holed colander set in the sink. Run cool water over the grains to stop their cooking.

2. While the wheat berries are simmering, place the whole lemon in a medium saucepan, cover it with water, and bring to a boil over high heat. Cover, reduce the heat to medium-low, and simmer until the lemon is soft and tender, almost squishy, about 20 minutes. Drain in a colander set in the sink, then run cool water over the lemon until you can handle it. Halve it, then scrape out and discard the mushy inside. Mince the softened rind and transfer it to a serving bowl.

3. Toast the sliced almonds in a dry skillet set over medium-low heat, stirring often, until lightly browned and fragrant, about 4 minutes. Scrape them into the bowl with the lemon rind.

4. Grate the zucchini through the large holes of a box grater. Pick up handfuls of the threads and squeeze over the sink to remove excess moisture.

5. Stir the zucchini threads into the bowl with the lemon rind and almonds. Stir in the cooked wheat berries. Finally, stir in the lemon juice, olive oil, cheese, salt, and pepper.

SICILIAN-INSPIRED WHEAT BERRY AND TUNA SALAD

⅔ cup wheat berries, preferably hard red wheat berries

1 celery stalk, minced

1 can (7 ounces) Italian-style tuna packed in olive oil

8 large pitted green olives

1 tablespoon capers, rinsed

Up to 1½ tablespoons fresh rosemary leaves

Up to 1½ tablespoons fresh oregano leaves

½ teaspoon red pepper flakes

1 garlic clove, quartered

1 jarred or tinned anchovy fillet

2 tablespoons olive oil

2 tablespoons balsamic vinegar

SERVES 2 (can be doubled or tripled)

Active time: 15 minutes
Total time: 1 hour 15 minutes, plus soaking the wheat berries for at least 8 hours

Make ahead: Store, covered, in the fridge for 1 or 2 days.

Save time: Use 2 cups cooked hard red wheat berries and omit soaking and cooking the raw grains.

GRAIN SWAPS

▨ Substitute ⅔ cup Kamut for the wheat berries. To compensate for the differences in flavors between the grains, also substitute thyme for the rosemary.

TESTERS' NOTES

▨ Whole-grain farro may seem a more standard choice for this Italian-inspired salad, but we found the firm texture of hard red wheat berries works better against the soft, silky tuna.

▨ Italian-style canned tuna is often yellowtail tuna and is usually packed in olive oil. It's prized for its moist texture and mild flavor.

▨ We love fresh herbs—and like lots of them in salads for a real brawl in the bowl. If you prefer a gentler taste, consider using 1 tablespoon each of rosemary and oregano—or even just 2 teaspoons of each.

1. Soak the wheat berries in a big bowl of cool water for at least 8 and up to 16 hours. Drain them in a fine-mesh sieve or small-holed colander set in the sink. Pour them into a large saucepan, cover with water by several inches, and bring to a boil over high heat. Reduce the heat to low and simmer until tender, about 1 hour. Drain again in that sieve or colander, then run under cool water until the wheat berries are at room temperature. Drain thoroughly.

2. Pour those cooked wheat berries into a large serving bowl. Stir in the celery. Drain the tuna and crumble it into the bowl as well.

3. Mince together the olives, capers, rosemary, oregano, red pepper flakes, garlic, and anchovy fillet on a cutting board by repeatedly rocking a large, heavy knife through the mixture, rotating the knife this way and that, scraping the mess together, and rocking the knife again and again until it's a grainy, coarse amalgam. Scrape this aromatic paste into a small bowl. Whisk in the olive oil and balsamic vinegar.

4. Pour the olive oil dressing into the bowl with the wheat berries. Toss gently to avoid breaking the tuna into shards but also thoroughly to make sure everything's well combined.

WHEAT BERRIES WITH FETA AND OLIVES

CHEF IT UP!

▪ Try goat feta, rather than the standard sheep's milk variety. It'll offer a bigger contrast to the olives.

GRAIN SWAPS

▪ Substitute 1 cup Kamut for the wheat berries.

TESTERS' NOTES

▪ A simple salad like this is all about the quality of the ingredients. Buy the best you can comfortably afford.

▪ The best sun-dried tomatoes are not necessarily packed in oil, which can obscure their summery taste. Rather, look for dried ones in the supermarket's produce section. They should be pliable and vibrantly colored. Remember: A good sun-dried tomato should smell like a fresh tomato.

▪ Pre-crumbled feta, while a convenience, isn't always up to snuff in its quality. Better to buy a small block packed in brine, or a high-quality block of feta shrink-wrapped for storage, then crumble it yourself.

▪ There's no additional salt because the olives and feta carry enough into the salad.

1 cup wheat berries, preferably hard red wheat berries

12 dry-pack sun-dried tomatoes, thinly sliced

½ cup pitted oil-cured black olives, chopped

1 tablespoon minced shallot

4 ounces feta

3 tablespoons olive oil

1 teaspoon finely grated lemon zest

2 tablespoons fresh lemon juice

1 teaspoon minced fresh dill fronds or ½ teaspoon dried dillweed

½ teaspoon ground black pepper

1. Soak the wheat berries in a big bowl of cool water for at least 8 and up to 16 hours. Drain them in a fine-mesh sieve or small-holed colander set in the sink. Pour them into a large saucepan, cover with water by several inches, and bring to a boil over high heat. Reduce the heat to low and simmer until tender, about 1 hour. Drain again in the sieve or colander, then run under cool water until the wheat berries are room temperature. Drain thoroughly.

2. Pour the cooked wheat berries into a large serving bowl. Stir in the sun-dried tomatoes, olives, and shallot. Crumble in the feta.

3. Whisk the olive oil, lemon zest, lemon juice, dill, and black pepper in a small bowl. Pour into the bowl with the wheat berries; stir and toss to coat.

Active time: 20 minutes

Total time: 1 hour 15 minutes, plus soaking the wheat berries for at least 8 hours

Make ahead: Store, covered, in the fridge for up to 5 days.

Save time: Use 2⅔ cups cooked soft white wheat berries and omit soaking and cooking the raw grains.

Make It Vegetarian: Use vegan-friendly Worcestershire sauce.

MAKE IT EASIER!

▥ Many high-end and specialty food markets have prepared food counters and salad bars with cooked wheat berries among the offerings. Take a carton home and you've got a jump on this salad—or many others in this section.

TESTERS' NOTES

▥ Just about any tomatoes will work here: globe, plum, or even cherry tomatoes. Just make sure they have that characteristic "tomato" smell before you buy them at the grocery store.

▥ There's no need to seed those tomatoes. If you do, you'll inadvertently juice them a bit—and you want to retain all that juice to make the dressing.

▥ This salad gets a little watery—on purpose. The vegetables break down and release their trapped liquids, thereby making a soupy dressing, a soup/salad hybrid. Serve it in bowls.

GAZPACHO-STYLE WHEAT BERRY SALAD

1 cup wheat berries, preferably soft white wheat berries

1 pound tomatoes, finely chopped

1 green bell pepper, finely chopped

1 cucumber, halved lengthwise, seeds scraped out, finely chopped

3 celery stalks, cut lengthwise into thirds and then finely chopped

½ small red onion, finely chopped

2 tablespoons olive oil

2 tablespoons fresh lemon juice

2 tablespoons red wine vinegar

2 teaspoons Worcestershire sauce

½ teaspoon salt (optional)

Several dashes hot red pepper sauce, such as Tabasco

1. Soak the wheat berries in a big bowl of cool water for at least 8 and up to 16 hours. Drain them in a fine-mesh sieve or small-holed colander set in the sink. Pour the wheat berries into a large saucepan, fill it about two-thirds of the way with water, and bring to a boil over high heat. Reduce the heat to medium and simmer until the grains are tender with some chew still left, about 1 hour. Drain again in that sieve or colander, then run under cool water to bring the wheat berries to room temperature. Drain thoroughly.

2. Place the cooked wheat berries in a large bowl and stir in the remaining ingredients: the tomatoes, bell pepper, cucumber, celery, onion, olive oil, lemon juice, vinegar, Worcestershire sauce, salt (if using), and hot sauce. Set aside to marinate at room temperature for 20 minutes before serving.

WHEAT BERRIES WITH OVEN-ROASTED TOMATOES AND FAVA BEANS

1 cup wheat berries, either soft white wheat berries or hard red wheat berries

2 pints cherry or grape tomatoes, halved

4 tablespoons olive oil, divided

3 medium shallots, chopped

1 pound peeled fava beans, either canned (drained and rinsed) or frozen (thawed)

2 tablespoons white wine vinegar

1 tablespoon minced fresh oregano leaves

1 tablespoon minced fresh marjoram leaves

½ teaspoon salt

½ teaspoon ground black pepper

1. Souse the wheat berries in a big bowl of cool water for at least 8 and up to 16 hours.

2. Preheat the oven to 200°F. Line a baking sheet with parchment paper or a nonstick liner. Arrange the tomatoes cut side up on the baking sheet and bake until slightly dehydrated and condensed, and a little brown just at the edges, about 3 hours.

3. As the tomatoes roast, drain the wheat berries in a fine-mesh sieve or a small-holed colander set in the sink. Pour the wheat berries into a big saucepan, cover with water by several inches, and bring to a boil over high heat. Reduce the heat to low and simmer until tender but still chewy, about 1 hour. Drain again in that sieve or colander, then run under cool water until the wheat berries are room temperature, stirring them around to get rid of any hot pockets. Drain thoroughly.

4. When the tomatoes and wheat berries are ready, heat a large skillet over medium heat and swirl in 1 tablespoon of the oil. Add the shallots, reduce the heat to medium-low, and cook, stirring often, until softened and sweet, about 5 minutes.

5. Scrape the contents of the skillet into a large bowl. Add the tomatoes, drained wheat berries, and fava beans. Stir in the remaining 3 tablespoons oil, the vinegar, oregano, marjoram, salt, and pepper.

SERVES 4

Active time: 20 minutes

Total time: 3 hours 20 minutes, plus soaking the wheat berries for at least 8 hours

Make ahead: Store, covered, in the fridge for up to 5 days.

Save time: Use 2⅔ cups cooked soft wheat berries or 2¾ cups cooked hard red winter wheat berries and omit steps 1 and 3.

CHEF IT UP!

▥ For a more intense flavor, do not chop—or even peel—the shallots. Instead, seal them in a foil packet and set the packet directly over an open, medium flame on a gas stove or a bit longer over direct heat on a grill grate. Cook for 10 minutes, then use long-handled tongs to turn the packet and continue cooking for 10 more minutes or up to 15 minutes on the grill. The packet must have no holes in it—the seal cannot break. Cool for about 20 minutes, then open the packet. The shallots will have taken on an almost smoky flavor because of the intense caramelization that goes on over the open flame. Peel them and chop them up. Use the full amount of olive oil in the dressing for the salad (rather than using 1 tablespoon to sauté the shallots).

GRAIN SWAPS

▥ Substitute 1 cup spelt berries for a more pronounced, slightly sour flavor.

Make ahead: Store, covered, in the fridge for no longer than 1 day.

CHEF IT UP!

▦ We believe the key to this dish is to keep the tuna medium-rare, if not rare, so that it offers a creamy luxuriance against the grainy farro. Buy sushi-quality tuna if you do intend to keep it rare. And always ask to smell the fish at the fish counter. It should smell like the ocean at high tide on a spring morning, never like the tidal flats in August.

GRAIN SWAPS

▦ Substitute 1 cup hard red wheat berries for the farro.

TESTERS' NOTES

▦ This salad is modeled on the Mediterranean classic, except this version is all tossed together, the better to be able to make it ahead and have it for lunch the next day.

▦ Since the tuna is cooked to medium-rare (or even rare), keep the salad refrigerated, below 40°F. And don't store it for more than a day in the fridge.

▦ Look for the smallest potatoes you can find so you can keep this salad from being a knife-and-fork affair.

▦ Niçoise olives are often sold pitted. If you find them with the pits intact, use 8 ounces and pit them yourself.

FARRO NIÇOISE

1 cup whole-grain farro

8 ounces small red-skinned potatoes, halved

8 ounces green beans, cut into 1-inch pieces

12-ounce tuna steak

4 tablespoons olive oil, divided

½ teaspoon salt

½ teaspoon ground black pepper

¼ cup chopped parsley leaves

6 ounces pitted Niçoise olives, halved

10 dry-pack sun-dried tomatoes, slivered

3 tablespoons red wine vinegar

1. Soak the farro in a big bowl of cool water for at least 8 and up to 16 hours. Drain in a fine-mesh sieve or small-holed colander set in the sink. Pour the farro into a large saucepan, cover with water by several inches, and bring to a boil over high heat. Reduce the heat to low and simmer for 50 minutes.

2. Add the potatoes to the pan and continue cooking until the spuds are tender when poked with a fork and the farro is tender but still has some chew left in its texture, about 10 minutes.

3. Place the green beans in a small-holed colander set in the sink, then pour the contents of the saucepan over the beans, blanching them as everything else gets drained. Leave all this to steam a bit while you cook the tuna.

4. Rub the tuna with 1 tablespoon of the oil; sprinkle the salt and pepper over both sides of the fish. Heat a large grill pan or non-stick skillet over medium heat. Slip the tuna into the pan or skillet. Cook for 6 minutes, turning once, until lightly browned on the outside but still pink within. Transfer to a cutting board, let the tuna rest for a couple of minutes, and then cut the steak into ½-inch cubes.

5. Dump the cubes into a large bowl and stir in the parsley, olives, sun-dried tomatoes, cooked farro, potatoes, and green beans. Add the vinegar and the remaining 3 tablespoons oil. Stir gently, just to make sure everything's mixed up and glistening.

FARRO WITH NECTARINES, BASIL, AND TOASTED PINE NUTS

1 cup whole-grain farro

6 tablespoons pine nuts

2 nectarines, chopped

4 ounces ricotta salata, finely crumbled

16 basil leaves, minced

2 tablespoons almond oil

1 tablespoon white balsamic vinegar

½ teaspoon salt

½ teaspoon ground black pepper

1. Soak the farro in a big bowl of cool water for at least 8 and up to 16 hours. Drain in a fine-mesh sieve or small-holed colander set in a sink. Pour the farro into a large saucepan, cover with water by several inches, and bring to a boil over high heat. Reduce the heat to low and simmer until tender, about 1 hour. Drain again in that sieve or colander, then run under cool water to stop the cooking. Drain thoroughly.

2. Scatter the pine nuts in a dry skillet and set it over medium heat. Cook, stirring often, until lightly toasted and fragrant, about 4 minutes.

3. Pour the pine nuts into a large serving bowl. Add the cooked farro. Stir in everything else: the nectarines, ricotta salata, basil, oil, vinegar, salt, and pepper.

SERVES 4

Active time: 15 minutes

Total time: 1 hour 15 minutes, plus soaking the farro for at least 8 hours

Make ahead: Store, covered, in the fridge for up to 4 days. For a fresher taste, omit the ricotta salata until ready to serve, and add small amounts of the grated cheese to individual servings.

Save time: Use 2⅓ cups cooked whole-grain farro and omit soaking and cooking the raw grains.

CHEF IT UP!

▥ Chiffonade the basil: Set half the leaves one on top of the other in a pile. Roll them up the long way like a tiny cigar. Starting at one end, slice crosswise into bits as thin as you can get them. Repeat with the other leaves, then spread these threads out before adding them to the salad.

TESTERS' NOTES

▥ This is a great place to start your discovery of whole-grain farro. We designed the dish to pit the nectarines and sweeter white balsamic vinegar against the more assertive taste of the whole grain (not against the sweeter taste of pearled or semi-pearled farro).

▥ Ricotta salata is a salted, pressed, and dried whey cheese, a variant of the more common, creamy ricotta. It's mild, almost floral, a bridge between the sweet nectarines and the earthy farro.

▥ Although we loved the slightly sweet taste of almond oil in this salad, you could also use olive oil for a slightly grassy, more summery flavor.

FARRO AND SMOKED CHICKEN SALAD WITH CARDAMOM AND CHUTNEY

1 cup whole-grain farro

¾ pound smoked skinless chicken breast, chopped

¾ cup pecan pieces, chopped

⅓ cup mayonnaise (regular or low-fat)

⅓ cup plain yogurt (whole-milk or low-fat)

¼ cup chutney

3 celery stalks, minced

4 small jarred pickled pearl onions, chopped

2 tablespoons fresh lemon juice

1 tablespoon minced fresh ginger

1 teaspoon ground cumin

1 teaspoon salt

Up to 1 teaspoon red pepper flakes

½ teaspoon ground cardamom

1. Soak the farro in a big bowl of cool water for at least 8 and up to 16 hours. Drain in a fine-mesh sieve or small-holed colander set in the sink. Pour the farro into a large saucepan. Swamp with plenty of water and bring to a boil over high heat. Reduce the heat and simmer until tender, about 1 hour. Drain again in that sieve or colander, then run under cool water to stop the cooking.

2. Dump the cooked farro into a large bowl and stir in everything else: the smoked chicken, pecans, mayonnaise, yogurt, chutney, celery, pickled onions, lemon juice, ginger, cumin, salt, red pepper flakes, and ground cardamom.

TESTERS' NOTES

▥ Looked for smoked chicken breasts in the deli case of your supermarket. Choose low-sodium offerings, whenever possible.

▥ Look for jars of pickled pearl onions in the condiment aisle of your supermarket. To keep the flavors of this salad from becoming too ridiculously baroque, look for a plain bottling, without the bells and whistles of added herbs and spices.

SERVES 6

Active time: 20 minutes
Total time: 1 hour 30 minutes, plus soaking the farro for at least 8 hours

Make ahead: Store, covered, in the fridge for up to 4 days.

Save time: Use 2⅓ cups cooked farro and omit soaking and cooking the raw grains.

MAKE IT EASIER!

▥ Jarred, minced ginger is a time-saver in the kitchen. However, read the label to make sure there's no added sugar. And make sure the ginger in your bottling is pale beige, not brown. The bits should be moist and retain their characteristic smell, not an acrid tang. Keep the sealed jar refrigerated to hold the freshness.

CHEF IT UP!

▥ You can vary this salad dramatically by choosing bottlings of chutney far beyond the mango standard—like a hot tomato chutney.

▥ Smoke your chicken breasts. Set up a grill for indirect, low-heat cooking with a smoker box or wood-chip pan near the heat source on a gas grill. Set 3 boneless, skinless chicken breast halves (6 ounces each) on the grate over the unheated portion of the grill. Add a handful of drained, presoaked wood chips to the coals or the smoker box, cover the grill, and cook at a low temperature, about 250°F, until an instant-read meat thermometer inserted into the thickest center of the breasts registers 160°F, about 4 hours. Maintain the heat by adjusting the burners or air vents; add more charcoal and more drained chips about every hour.

Active time: 15 minutes

Total time: 1 hour 45 minutes, plus soaking the farro for at least 8 hours

Make ahead: Store, covered, in the fridge for up to 4 days.

Save time: Use 2⅓ cups cooked farro and omit soaking and cooking the raw grains.

CHEF IT UP!

▪ Use a coarse-grained mustard instead of Dijon mustard.

▪ Add up to ½ cup minced onion with the celery.

▪ Add 1 tablespoon minced dill with the black pepper.

TESTERS' NOTES

▪ Whole-grain farro and potatoes are a match made in heaven: Both have a scented earthiness that harmonizes their opposing textures.

▪ If you want more protein, add some chopped rotisserie chicken breast meat.

CREAMY FARRO POTATO SALAD

1 cup whole-grain farro

1 pound very small red potatoes, halved

⅔ cup mayonnaise (regular, low-fat, light, or fat-free)

2 tablespoons Dijon mustard

1 tablespoon brine from the dill pickle jar

1 teaspoon ground black pepper

3 celery stalks, thinly sliced

3 scallions, thinly sliced

1 large dill pickle, diced

1. Soak the farro in a big bowl of cool water for at least 8 and up to 16 hours. Drain in a fine-mesh sieve or a small-holed colander set in the sink. Pour the grains into a large saucepan, fill two-thirds of the way with water, and bring to a boil over high heat. Reduce the heat somewhat and simmer under tender but with some chew, about 1 hour. Drain in that same sieve or colander. (Are you getting used to this process yet?) Run under cool water to stop the cooking. Drain thoroughly.

2. Set up a vegetable steamer in a large saucepan or on top of a pot. Bring a little water in the bottom to a boil over high heat, add the potatoes, cover, and steam until tender when pierced with a fork, about 15 minutes. Cool the potatoes by running tap water over the potatoes in the steamer basket. Drain thoroughly.

3. Whisk the mayonnaise, mustard, pickle brine, and pepper in a large serving bowl. Stir in the celery, scallions, and diced pickle. Add the cooked farro and potatoes. Toss well.

KAMUT SALAD WITH CAULIFLOWER, OLIVES, AND RAISINS

TESTERS' NOTES

▪ Light but still satisfying, hearty but not heavy, this salad will knock your socks off. It stopped our friends and testers cold on first taste. Pretty swift for a whole grain!

▪ Make sure the cauliflower florets are very small, no more than an inch or so across. Slice larger florets down to size. This should not be a knife-and-fork salad, but a spoon one.

1 cup Kamut

¼ cup almond oil

1 medium shallot, minced

1 tablespoon minced fresh ginger

2 garlic cloves, minced

6 cups small cauliflower florets

4 ounces pitted green olives, sliced (about 1 cup)

¾ cup golden raisins

½ teaspoon ground cinnamon

½ teaspoon salt

½ teaspoon ground black pepper

½ cup dry white wine or dry vermouth

1. Soak the Kamut in a big bowl of cool water for at least 8 and up to 16 hours. Drain in a fine-mesh sieve or a small-holed colander set in the sink. Pour the grains into a large saucepan, cover with water by several inches, and bring to a boil over high heat. Reduce the heat to low and simmer until tender, about 1 hour. Drain again in that sieve or colander, then run under cool water until the grains are at room temperature. Drain thoroughly.

2. Heat a large pot or a Dutch oven over medium heat. Add the oil, then the shallot, ginger, and garlic. Cook, stirring almost constantly, until the shallot softens, about 1 minute.

3. Dump in the cauliflower florets. Continue cooking, stirring frequently, until they begin to soften and even lightly brown at the edges, about 5 minutes.

4. Stir in the olives, raisins, cinnamon, salt, and pepper. Stir over the heat until very fragrant, a minute or so. Then pour in the wine or vermouth and bring to a full simmer. Bubble for 2 minutes to steam the vegetables a bit and to reduce the wine or vermouth until it's the consistency of a dressing. Scrape the entire contents of the pot into a large bowl. Stir in the cooked Kamut.

DECONSTRUCTED KAMUT CAESAR SALAD

1 cup Kamut

3 large eggs

4 to 6 jarred or tinned anchovy fillets

1 small garlic clove

⅓ cup dry-pack sun-dried tomatoes, thinly sliced

¼ cup olive oil

1½ tablespoons fresh lemon juice

1 tablespoon Worcestershire sauce

2 teaspoons minced fresh rosemary leaves

2 teaspoons minced fresh oregano leaves

1 teaspoon capers, rinsed and chopped

½ teaspoon ground black pepper

SERVES 4

Active time: 10 minutes

Total time: 1 hour 30 minutes, plus soaking the Kamut for at least 8 hours

Make ahead: Cool the salad completely and store, covered, in the fridge for up to 4 days.

Save time: Use 2¾ cups cooked Kamut and omit soaking and cooking the raw grains.

MAKE IT EASIER!

▩ Look for hard-boiled eggs on the salad bar at your supermarket—or sometimes in the dairy section of high-end markets.

TESTERS' NOTES

▩ We created this recipe after we had a rather perfunctory Caesar salad at a burger joint. We said, "You know, a grain would keep this sort of thing from being a cliché." Kamut to the rescue.

▩ If you've got fat, thick anchovy fillets (and you may need to bone them), or if you prefer a milder, brighter taste with more standard anchovies, use only 4 of them in this easy salad.

1. Soak the Kamut in a big bowl of cool water for at least 8 and up to 16 hours. Drain in a fine-mesh sieve or small-holed colander set in the sink. Pour the grains into a large saucepan, cover with water by several inches, and bring to a boil over high heat. Reduce the heat to low and simmer until tender, about 1 hour. Drain again in that sieve or colander, then run under cool water until the grains are room temperature. Drain thoroughly.

2. While the Kamut cooks, place the eggs in a saucepan large enough to hold them in one layer. Fill the pan with cool water so that it comes 1 inch over the eggs. Cover, place over high heat, and bring the water to a full boil. Boil for 1 minute. Remove the pan from the heat, cover, and set aside for 5 minutes. Pour off most of the water in the pan, add a few ice cubes, and run cold water into the pan to cool the eggs quickly to room temperature. Tap the shells against a counter to crack them in several places, then roll them gently between your palms. Peel off the shells, starting at the large ends. Chop the hard-boiled eggs and place them in a large serving bowl. (If the Kamut is not ready yet, set the bowl in the fridge to keep the eggs safe.)

3. Stir the cooked Kamut into the bowl. Put the anchovy fillets and garlic clove through a garlic press, letting the mushed bits drip into the serving bowl. Stir in everything else: the sun-dried tomatoes, olive oil, lemon juice, Worcestershire sauce, rosemary, oregano, capers, and pepper.

Active time: 10 minutes

Total time: 1 hour 15 minutes, plus soaking the spelt berries for at least 8 hours

Make ahead: Cover and refrigerate for up to 4 days.

Save time: Use 2⅔ cups cooked spelt berries and omit soaking and cooking the raw grains.

TESTERS' NOTES

■ Here, you'll see that spelt berries offer a big flavor, a sour/sweet/savory mélange, best balanced by other big-flavored items (enter the ham).

■ Because spelt berries are chewy, pair this salad with a dollop of hummus on the plate. Both take well to baked pita chips or crunchy bread.

SPELT BERRY SALAD WITH WHITE BEANS, SAGE, AND HAM

1 cup spelt berries

1 can (15 ounces) white beans, drained and rinsed

6 ounces chopped deli smoked ham

8 radishes, grated through the large holes of a box grater

3 tablespoons olive oil

3 tablespoons sherry vinegar

½ teaspoon salt

½ teaspoon ground black pepper

1. Soak the spelt berries in a big bowl of cool water for at least 8 and up to 16 hours. Drain them in a fine-mesh sieve or small-holed colander set in the sink. Pour them into a large saucepan, cover with water by several inches, and bring to a boil over high heat. Reduce the heat a bit and simmer until tender, about 1 hour. Drain again in that sieve or colander, then run under cool water to bring the grains to room temperature. Drain thoroughly.

2. Dump the cooked spelt berries into a big serving bowl. Stir in the beans, ham, radishes, oil, vinegar, salt, and pepper.

SPELT BERRY SALAD WITH CHERRY TOMATOES, PECANS, AND BASIL

1 cup spelt berries

2 cups cherry or grape tomatoes, halved

1 cup packed basil leaves, minced

¾ cup pecan pieces

2½ ounces Parmigiano-Reggiano, finely grated

3 tablespoons white balsamic vinegar

1 garlic clove, minced

½ teaspoon salt

½ teaspoon ground black pepper

⅓ cup olive oil

1. Soak the spelt berries in a big bowl of cool water for at least 8 and up to 16 hours. Drain them in a fine-mesh sieve or a small-holed colander set in the sink. Pour them into a large saucepan, cover with water by several inches, and bring it all to a boil over high heat. Reduce the heat to low and simmer until tender, about 1 hour. Drain in that sieve or colander and run under cool water until room temperature. Drain thoroughly.

2. Pour the cooked spelt berries into a large bowl. Stir in the tomatoes, basil, pecans, and Parmigiano-Reggiano.

3. Whisk the vinegar, garlic, salt, and pepper in a small bowl to combine. Whisk in the olive oil in dribs and drabs to make a creamy, smooth dressing. Pour this over the spelt mixture and toss to coat.

SERVES 4

Active time: 15 minutes

Total time: 1 hour 20 minutes, plus soaking the spelt berries for at least 8 hours

Make ahead: Store, covered, in the fridge for up to 4 days.

Save time: Use 2⅔ cups cooked spelt berries and omit soaking and cooking the raw grains.

CHEF IT UP!

■ For more flavor, toast the pecan pieces in a dry skillet over medium-low heat until lightly browned and fragrant, about 5 minutes, stirring often.

■ Don't grate the Parmigiano-Reggiano. Shave it into paper-thin pieces with a cheese plane.

TESTERS' NOTES

▦ Try this salad in early summer, whenever the basil and cherry tomatoes first appear in your area.

▦ White balsamic vinegar is made from white Trebbiano grape pressings, the same fruit used to make the syrupy, black, aged balsamic. However, the pressings (or "must") are not first cooked to a dark glaze but rather mixed raw with white wine vinegar and cooked very lightly. Some bottlings are aged in barrels; others, in stainless steel. The result is a light, sweet, summery vinegar.

▦ Why are some dressings whisked (as here) and others just dumped into the bowl? It's all based on the desired texture. Whisking a dressing allows the oil to emulsify a bit; it then becomes both creamier and (intriguingly) lighter on the tongue.

RICE AND WILD RICE SALADS

Although these rice and wild rice salads are among the tastiest and easiest whole-grain salads you can make, there's no doubt about it: Growing rice is hard on the land. This aquatic grass requires that the fields be flooded at least once a year, sometimes twice, depending on what the climate will allow—all of which then causes the fields to silt up with unusable muck, a sort of thick clay. Eventually, rice paddies turn into disasters.

Actually, post-apocalyptic landscapes. The traditional way around the flooding problems is to burn the harvested fields. For one thing, doing so incinerates the chaff and the accompanying weeds, getting rid of the unwanted leftovers. It also reduces the acidity of the silted soil and rebalances the nitrogen content. Unfortunately, it puts plumes of smoke into the air, a respiratory irritant and source of global pollution. The enormous rice fields in the central valley of California can sometimes look like the final scene of some Hollywood-produced alien-invasion blockbuster.

Wild rice hasn't escaped these problems. Modern production favors hybrids that suffer the same problems as more standard rice. No, wild rice is not rice. (See page 32 for more information.) But agricultural practices have bound them in a common harvest.

Still, there are ways around these problems. With wild rice, you can opt out of this eco-nightmare by finding producers who still gather the grains by hand, a laborious process. A quick Internet search will lead you to many producers in the upper Midwest as well as across the Canadian border, particularly on Native American lands.

But there are other ways to be sustainable. Big farming doesn't necessarily mean bad farming. Some producers are doing all they can to mitigate the problem of growing rice to feed our ever-expanding population. Take, for example, the Lundbergs in California's Central Valley, a family-run company of organic rice farmers. At harvest, their threshing machines strip the stalks of their seeds, leaving the chaff behind, just as all rice farmers do. But while organic farming does not require farmers to use that chaff, the Lundbergs see it as next year's fertilizer, natural decay that strengthens the soil and keeps the top layer of clay from turning into cement under the California sun.

However, the chaff is also full of weeds. Leave it on the ground and those weeds reseed. Then all the seeds, edible or not, pass through the threshing machine and end up in the bags. No one wants bitter bull rush seeds in their cooked rice. Thus, many farmers burn it all, no matter the cost to the air.

The Lundbergs practice a dangerous game of letting water, not fire, do the work. After planting, their fields are flooded for about 3 weeks so the broadleaf dies off. But the more conventional rice plants will die if submerged for over 35 days. In other words, drain the water too soon and the broadleaf doesn't die; drain it too late and the rice dies. If everything works out right, the broadleaf drowns, then the aquatic weeds wither in the dry fields before harvest. Farmers like these end up with a more natural cycle of growth and decay that puts essential nutrients back into the soil.

Make your discovery of rice and wild rice twofold: of the grains themselves in cold salads for meals in the days ahead, of course; but also of hand-gatherers practicing old methods of wild-rice production or modern farmers who grow rice responsibly, conserving the land for future generations. In this way, you can spend your hard-earned dollars authentically and ethically.

Look, despite all the hoopla about farm-to-table eating, we live—no, we thrive—in a system of national distribution. So choose to support large *and* small farmers who care for the land. In this way, you can find whole grains that not only contribute to *your* health, but to the planet's, too. And by doing so, you'll get even more satisfaction out of every bite. We know whole grains are good for the body. We hope you're seeing they're good for the foodie palate, too. But who knew they could be good for the soul as well?

RICE AND WILD RICE SALADS

Active time: 20 minutes
Total time: 1 hour 20 minutes

Make ahead: Immediately after preparing, cover and store in the fridge for up to 4 days.

Save time: Use 3⅓ cups cooked long-grain brown rice and omit soaking and cooking the raw grains.

Make It Vegan: Omit the chicken and substitute 12 ounces smoked, dried tofu, sliced into match-sticks; also use *nama shoyu* or *tamari* soy sauce to give the dish a little more heft.

MAKE IT EASIER!

- For this or any brown rice salad, stop by a Chinese restaurant and pick up a couple of containers of cooked brown rice.

SPICY BROWN RICE SALAD WITH CHICKEN AND PEANUTS

2¼ cups water

1 cup long-grain brown rice, such as brown basmati or brown jasmine

12 dried Chinese black mushrooms

1 tablespoon toasted sesame oil

1 teaspoon five-spice powder

2 boneless, skinless chicken breast halves (6 ounces each)

1 can (11 ounces) water-packed mandarin oranges, drained

1 red bell pepper, seeded and chopped

2 celery stalks, halved lengthwise and thinly sliced

½ cup unsalted roasted peanuts, chopped

2 tablespoons soy sauce (regular or reduced-sodium)

2 tablespoons rice vinegar (page 97)

2 teaspoons honey

Up to 1 teaspoon red pepper flakes

1. Combine the water and rice in a medium saucepan and bring to a boil over high heat. Cover, reduce the heat to low, and simmer until the rice is tender and the water has been absorbed, about 40 minutes. Set aside, covered, to steam for 10 minutes.

2. Meanwhile, put the mushrooms in a small heatproof bowl. Bring a kettle of water to a boil and pour over the mushrooms. Soak for 20 minutes.

3. And while those first two steps are going on, heat a large nonstick skillet or grill pan over medium heat. Rub the sesame oil and five-spice powder into the chicken breasts. Slip them into the skillet or pan and cook, turning once, until well browned and an instant-read meat thermometer inserted into the thickest part of a breast registers 160°F, about 10 minutes. Transfer to a cutting board to cool for 5 minutes.

(continued)

4. Dump the cooked rice into a large serving bowl. Drain the mushrooms in a colander, remove the stems and discard them, then slice the caps into thin strips and add them to the bowl. Finally, chop the chicken into ½-inch bits and toss these into the bowl as well.

5. Stir in everything else: the orange segments, bell pepper, celery, peanuts, soy sauce, vinegar, honey, and red pepper flakes.

TESTERS' NOTES

■ The flavors of this salad are modeled on kung pao, the popular dish in North American Chinese restaurants. If you want it even more fiery, up the red pepper flakes to 2 teaspoons.

■ Cooked rice is prone to a type of food poisoning from bacteria found dormant on the grains. Some rice salads are safe because the added vinegar keeps the bad bugs from coming to life and interfering with your fun. But always err on the safe side: Refrigerate cooked rice salads quickly after making.

■ Bags of dried Chinese black mushrooms have shown up in even run-of-the-mill supermarkets these days—although they're available in copious supply at Asian specialty markets and from online suppliers. They make an excellent pantry staple; a quick mushroom stock is no more than 20 minutes away after soaking them. However, they can be sandy or gritty; you may need to strain that stock through cheesecloth. And the mushrooms themselves can fall victim to rot after long storage. Always inspect them before you use them.

■ If you can't find the more esoteric dried Chinese black mushrooms, substitute dried shiitake mushrooms (stems removed after soaking).

BROWN RICE SALAD WITH RED PEPPERS AND DRIED APRICOTS

2¼ cups water

1 cup long-grain brown rice, such as brown basmati

1 can (15 ounces) pinto beans, drained and rinsed

¾ cup walnut pieces, chopped

3 large jarred roasted red peppers or pimientos, chopped, plus 2 tablespoons liquid from the jar

4 scallions, thinly sliced

16 dried apricots, thinly sliced

2 tablespoons fresh lime juice

2 tablespoons toasted walnut oil

1 tablespoon minced fresh oregano leaves or 2 teaspoons dried oregano

1 teaspoon ground cumin

1 teaspoon ground pure chile powder, preferably chipotle chile powder

½ teaspoon ground cinnamon

SERVES 6

Active time: 15 minutes
Total time: 55 minutes

Make ahead: Immediately after preparing, cover and store in the fridge for up to 4 days.

Save time: Use 3⅓ cups cooked long-grain brown rice and omit soaking and cooking the raw grains.

CHEF IT UP!

▪ Roast 3 red bell peppers over an open flame; seal them in a large bowl covered with plastic wrap for 10 minutes before peeling off the blackened bits. Then seed and stem the peppers and chop them up. No reason just to use red bell peppers! Try poblanos for lots more kick. In any event, you'll need to add 2 tablespoons canned broth to the salad to moisten it (since you won't be using the liquid from the jarred peppers). Also, check the salad for salt when done since we've used the liquid from the jarred peppers to carry salt into the salad.

1. Combine the water and rice in a medium saucepan and bring to a boil over medium-high heat. Cover, reduce the heat to low, and cook until the rice is tender and the water has been absorbed, about 40 minutes. Set aside, covered, to steam for 10 minutes.

2. Transfer the cooked rice to a large bowl and toss in all the other ingredients: the beans, walnuts, roasted peppers (and the liquid from the jar), scallions, dried apricots, lime juice, walnut oil, oregano, cumin, chile powder, and cinnamon. Stir well.

TESTERS' NOTES

▪ A fairly straightforward salad, you want the most present flavors from each of the ingredients. Toasted walnut oil adds a pop of nuttiness to the salad, an excellent pairing with the brown rice. Once you've opened the can or jar, store the oil in your fridge for up to 3 months.

▪ Long-grain brown rice is the best choice for salads. While medium-grain and short-grain brown rices are lovely in hot dishes, they can gum up a salad, especially after storage in the fridge.

▪ That said, long-grain rice does have an Achilles heel: It sucks up any available moisture. Thus, a rice salad can dry out after a couple of days. Keep yours well covered in the fridge to prevent inadvertent evaporation that can worsen the problem. And add a little more oil or some canned broth to loosen up a salad that's become too dry.

SERVES 6

Active time: 15 minutes
Total time: 55 minutes

Make ahead: Immediately after preparing, cover and store in the fridge for up to 4 days.

Save time: Use 2½ cups cooked long-grain brown rice and omit soaking and cooking the raw grains.

CHEF IT UP!

▪ Substitute ground sumac for the paprika; also substitute ground Aleppo pepper for the black pepper.

▪ For more flavor, toast the sesame seeds in a small dry skillet over medium-low heat until lightly browned and fragrant.

TESTERS' NOTES

▪ We morphed the flavors of a light, fresh, summer soup of chickpeas and grapes, sometimes called "Lebanese gazpacho," into this brown rice salad.

▪ If tomatoes are beyond their prime or out of season, substitute 8 ounces chopped cherry or grape tomatoes.

LEBANESE-INSPIRED BROWN RICE SALAD WITH CHICKPEAS AND GRAPES

1¾ cups plus 2 tablespoons water

¾ cup long-grain brown rice, preferably brown jasmine rice

1 can (15 ounces) chickpeas, drained and rinsed

¾ cup red grapes, halved and seeded

1 tomato, chopped

1 small garlic clove, put through a garlic press or finely minced

3 tablespoons olive oil

1 tablespoon fresh lime juice

2 teaspoons minced fresh marjoram leaves or 1 teaspoon dried marjoram

2 teaspoons fresh thyme leaves or 1 teaspoon dried thyme

1 teaspoon sesame seeds

1 teaspoon mild paprika

1 teaspoon salt

½ teaspoon ground black pepper

1. Mix the water and rice in a medium saucepan and crank it up to a boil over high heat. Cover, reduce the heat to low, and simmer until the water has been absorbed and the grains are tender, about 40 minutes. Set aside, covered, for 10 minutes to steam.

2. Dump the cooked rice into a large serving bowl. Stir in everything else: the chickpeas, grapes, tomato, garlic, oil, lime juice, marjoram, thyme, sesame seeds, paprika, salt, and pepper. Toss it all before serving.

RED RICE ROMESCO SALAD

1½ cups water

1 cup long-grain red rice, preferably red Himalayan or red Cargo rice

⅓ cup hazelnuts

2 tomatoes

1 large fennel bulb

3 tablespoons olive oil, divided

2 jarred roasted red peppers or pimientos, chopped

2 tablespoons sherry vinegar

½ teaspoon salt

½ teaspoon ground black pepper

SERVES 4

Active time: 30 minutes
Total time: 1 hour

Make ahead: Immediately after preparing, cover and store in the fridge for up to 3 days.

Save time: Use 3½ cups cooked red rice and omit soaking and cooking the raw grains.

1. Combine the water and rice in a medium saucepan and bring to a boil over high heat. Cover, reduce the heat to low, and cook until the rice is tender and the water has been absorbed, 30 to 40 minutes, depending on the residual moisture in the grains after storage. Set aside, covered, to steam for 10 minutes.

2. Meanwhile, preheat the oven to 400°F. Spread the hazelnuts on a large rimmed baking sheet and roast them until lightly browned and fragrant, stirring occasionally, about 7 minutes. Pour the nuts into a clean kitchen towel and wrap it around them. Set aside for 5 minutes or until cool enough to handle, then rub the hazelnuts together in the towel to remove most of their papery skins by grating them against each other and the towel. Pick the hazelnuts out of the towel, then coarsely chop the nuts.

3. Also while the rice cooks, halve the tomatoes through their stem ends. Remove the stalks and fronds from the fennel bulb, as well as any tough bottom and/or browned, squishy bits. Slice the bulb lengthwise into ½-inch slabs. Rub the cut side of the tomatoes and fennel with 1 tablespoon of the oil.

4. Heat a grill pan over medium-high heat or prepare a grill for high-heat cooking. Place the tomatoes, cut side down, and the fennel slices on the pan or grill grate. Grill for 6 minutes. Turn everything and continue grilling until soft and marked, about 6 more minutes. Transfer the vegetables to a cutting board.

5. Chop the grilled tomatoes and fennel and place in a large bowl. Add the hazelnuts, roasted peppers, vinegar, salt, pepper, and remaining 2 tablespoons oil. Fluff the rice with a fork and stir it in.

MAKE IT EASIER!

▨ Skip step 3 by looking for roasted, skinned hazelnuts among the dried fruit and other nuts at your supermarket. Chop these into small bits before adding them to the salad.

▨ You needn't buy a jar of roasted red peppers. They're available at the salad bar, olive bar, or antipasto bar of many supermarkets.

TESTERS' NOTE

▨ The flavors here are not strictly romesco, a Catalan concoction. Traditionally, romesco uses fennel fronds; but we deconstructed the sauce to create a salad—and used the fennel bulb for crunch and zip against the sweet rice.

CHEF IT UP!

- Substitute golden raisins for the black raisins.

- Substitute avocado oil for the olive oil.

- Consider using Aleppo pepper, rather than the more standard black peppercorns.

TESTERS' NOTES

- We found the combination of long-grain red rice and lentils to be almost irresistible because of the contrast of textures: dry and chewy paired with soft and luxurious.

- Don't cook the lentils until they're falling apart, just tender to the bite. The only way to tell if they're perfect is to scoop a few out of the pot as they boil, cool them by blowing on them, then taste them.

RED RICE AND LENTILS

2 cups water

1 cup long-grain red rice, preferably red Himalayan or red cargo rice

¾ cup green lentils du Puy

½ cup pine nuts

8 celery stalks, cut lengthwise into thin spears and then minced

2 small shallots, minced

1 cup raisins, chopped

5 tablespoons olive oil

¼ cup white balsamic vinegar

1 teaspoon salt

1 teaspoon ground black pepper

1. Combine the 2 cups water and the rice in a medium saucepan and bring to a boil over high heat. Cover, reduce the heat to low, and cook until the rice is tender and the water has been absorbed, 30 to 40 minutes. Set aside, covered, to steam for 10 minutes.

2. Meanwhile, bring a large saucepan of water to a boil over high heat. Add the lentils, reduce the heat to medium or so, and boil until the lentils are tender, about 15 minutes. Drain in a colander set in the sink, then run cool water over them to stop the cooking and bring them back to room temperature.

3. As those cook, scatter the pine nuts into a large dry skillet and set it over medium-low heat. Toast gently, just until golden, stirring occasionally, about 4 minutes.

4. Pour the pine nuts into a serving bowl. Add the lentils. Fluff the rice with a fork and add it, too. Then add all the remaining ingredients: the celery, shallots, raisins, oil, vinegar, salt, and pepper. Toss well to serve.

WILD RICE SALAD WITH ORANGE SUPREMES, SHAVED FENNEL, AND PISTACHIOS

1½ cups wild rice

4 navel oranges

1 large fennel bulb, trimmed of its fronds and stalks

1 cup chopped pistachios

¼ cup olive oil

2 tablespoons sherry vinegar

½ teaspoon salt

1. Pour the wild rice into a large saucepan, cover with a generous amount of water, and bring to a boil over high heat. Reduce the heat a bit and simmer steadily until tender, between 30 and 55 minutes, depending on the varietal and the grains' residual moisture content. Check the package for more information.

2. Make orange supremes from those oranges: Cut a small slice off each fruit's top and bottom so the round fruit can stand steadily on a cutting board. Use a sharp paring knife to cut the rind off the flesh in long arcs, starting at the top and following down along the natural curve of the fruit. Cut far enough into the flesh to remove the white pith and membranes but not so far as to damage the pulp. Once peeled, hold the fruit in one hand over a serving bowl, then use that paring knife to cut between the flesh and the white membranes separating the individual segments, allowing the segments to fall into the bowl along with any juice. Discard the membranes and peel.

3. Shave the fennel into thin strips: You can either do this over the shaving blade on a box grater or with a mandoline, provided you have the hand-guard in place to hold the bulb as you run it over the blade. You want very thin, limp pieces, almost translucent. Cut them into bite-sized bits and add them to the bowl with the oranges.

4. Drain the wild rice in a fine-mesh sieve or a lined colander set in the sink. Run cool water over the grains to return them to room temperature. Drain thoroughly, shaking the sieve to get rid of excess moisture.

5. Scrape the wild rice into the bowl. Add the pistachios, oil, vinegar, and salt. Toss well.

SERVES 6

Active time: 40 minutes
Total time: 1 hour 20 minutes

Make ahead: Store, covered, in the fridge for up to 4 days.

Save time: Use 5¼ cups cooked wild rice and omit steps 1 and 4.

MAKE IT EASIER!

▥ Substitute canned mandarin orange segments, drained, for the orange supremes. Use only those packed in water or juice, not heavy syrup. You may need a little of the liquid in the can to moisten the salad when you're done.

CHEF IT UP!

▥ Substitute avocado oil for the olive oil.

TESTERS' NOTE

▥ As we've noted, there are many varietals of wild rice, from the heritage rices gathered by hand in Minnesota to the industrially harvested strains grown in central California. Both will work here, although we tested the recipe with hand-picked grains. We balanced the vinegar, in particular, against their nuttier flavor. If you have the black, industrially harvested wild rice, taste the salad before serving, adding a little more vinegar if you find it leaning too sweet.

WILD RICE SALAD WITH APPLES AND BACON

1 cup wild rice

6 ounces bacon slices

1 cup pecan pieces

2 large tart apples, peeled and chopped

3 scallions, thinly sliced

¼ cup cider vinegar

2 tablespoons toasted nut oil, preferably pecan

1 tablespoon fresh thyme leaves or 2 teaspoons dried thyme

½ teaspoon ground black pepper

1. Pour the wild rice into a large saucepan, cover with water by several inches, and bring it all to a boil over high heat. Reduce the heat a bit and simmer steadily until tender, between 30 and 55 minutes, depending on the varietal and the grains' residual moisture content. Check the package for more information. Drain in a fine-mesh sieve or a lined colander set in the sink, then rinse under cool water to stop the cooking. Drain thoroughly.

2. Fry the bacon in a dry skillet set over medium heat, turning occasionally, until crisp and dark brown, about 5 minutes. Transfer the slices to a cutting board.

3. Maintain the heat under that skillet of bacon grease. Dump the pecan pieces in it. Toast lightly until browned and irresistible. Scoop up the pecan pieces with a slotted spoon and drain on paper towels.

4. Chop the bacon into small bits; chop those pecan pieces, too, until they're about the size of the grains of wild rice. Put both in a serving bowl. Stir in the wild rice, apples, scallions, vinegar, nut oil, thyme, and pepper.

SERVES 6

Active time: 15 minutes
Total time: 1 hour 10 minutes

Make ahead: Store, covered, in the fridge for up to 3 days.

Save time: Use 3½ cups cooked wild rice and omit soaking and cooking the raw grains.

TESTERS' NOTES

■ Very hearty, this salad is best for a late fall day when the apples are at their crispest.

■ Look for firm, tart apples like Cortland, Empire, Northern Spy, or Granny Smith. They'll balance the rice, bacon, and nut oil to create a more satisfying salad than a soft, sweet apple like a Fuji or a Mutsu.

■ For even more flavor, use pepper bacon—but if you do, omit the pepper in the recipe.

■ Frying pecan pieces in bacon fat to add to a salad—does it get any better than that?

MORE WHOLE-GRAIN SALADS

We're both lapsed vegetarians. Bruce's stint into the meatless world came about because he watched an instructor in chef school break down a whole duck. Given that he now routinely breaks down various birds in our kitchen, not to mention whole goats, he's probably over his initial horror.

Mark's foray was all about politics after grad school in Madison, Wisconsin, in the mid-'80s. Although it was a decade and a half after the free-love fest of the '60s, the town still had a hippie vibe. The amazing farmers' market sported an amazing amount of tie-dye.

We both have something else in common, a secret from our vegetarian days: Neither of us cared for the iconic meal of our former tribe—tabbouleh. Too often it's just a big bowl of too many raw onions, too much parsley, too much oil—and way too little grain. Sure, tabbouleh is actually a parsley salad, but we both dug for the grain when presented with a plate of the stuff. And otherwise tried to smile.

Things changed long after we'd given up our vegetarian ways—when we found whole-grain bulgur, in fact. We now look forward to a big bowl of tabbouleh for lunch, mostly because the more savory, slightly bitter, and certainly more sophisticated taste of the whole grain. In copious supplies, it keeps the salad from becoming quite so insipid.

We've discovered many more whole grains in the years since, some grains that would surprise even tie-dyed-in-the-wool tabbouleh lovers still among our friends: sour/sweet rye berries, best in salads with big flavors; the earthy nose of triticale that can stand up to even smoked trout; or Job's tears, probably the surprise here, maybe a grain you've never heard of, but one popular in Asia and one that offers a fine, dry, less-sweet-than-black-eyed-peas flare to a salad.

In other words, we had to eat more things to find more things to eat. But it's ever thus—and one of the reasons we all should keep expanding our culinary repertoire. Our palates learn. As we've said, they're directly linked to the memory centers of our brains. And they can keep on learning. In fact, boredom is one of the primary reasons we overeat, whether vegetarians or committed carnivores. We get locked into a limited range, decide we'd rather not eat this or that, limit our choices further, and soon eat without much thought at all. Eat *too much* without much thought at all, in fact.

Whole grains can change that. There's an amazing range in this section, much of it undiscovered by many of us. And the research is pretty solid: To eat less, eat more things. Expand your tastes, your likes. Reach beyond the horizon with something as simple as these cold salads, made from triticale berries, oat groats, millet, rye berries, and Job's tears. There are even twists on the standard tabbouleh in this mix!

Soon enough, you'll find yourself no longer locked into choices you made years ago for no apparent reason. You'll find more satisfaction in every bite. All from whole grains. Not too shabby, eh?

MORE WHOLE-GRAIN SALADS

Active time: 20 minutes
Total time: 1 hour 10 minutes

Make ahead: Store, covered, in the fridge for up to 3 days. If the bulgur clumps, stir in a little more oil or reduced-sodium chicken broth to loosen it up.

MAKE IT EASIER!

▥ Look for peeled and cored pineapple cubes in the refrigerator case of your supermarket's produce section. Dice these into smaller, more manageable bits so the salad can be eaten at the table or your desk with a spoon or a fork, no knife in sight.

GRAIN SWAPS

▥ Substitute 2½ cups *cooked* quinoa for the bulgur and omit soaking and cooking the raw grains.

TESTERS' NOTES

▥ We almost called this a "Polynesian Salad," because, well, you can take the boys out of the '70s but you can't take the '70s out of the boys. Still, it's a nice way to gussy up a standard tabbouleh with the flavors of the old Trader Vic's.

▥ Rice vinegar comes in two forms: seasoned and unseasoned. Basically, seasoned means sweetened and salted. Check the labeling on your bottle to see which you have. A perfect pantry has both; a good pantry, just unseasoned. You can always add ¼ teaspoon sugar per tablespoon of vinegar to bring some sweetness to a dish that calls for "seasoned rice vinegar."

TABBOULEH WITH CHICKEN AND PINEAPPLE

1 cup quick-cooking whole-grain bulgur

1 cup boiling water

½ pound boneless, skinless chicken breasts

1 tablespoon almond oil

8 ounces diced fresh pineapple

5 scallions, white and pale green parts only, thinly sliced

2 tablespoons fresh lime juice

2 tablespoons seasoned rice vinegar

2 tablespoons soy sauce (regular or reduced-sodium)

1. Dump the bulgur into a large heatproof bowl; pour the boiling water over the wheat. Stir, cover with a plate, and set aside for 1 hour.

2. Meanwhile, heat a large grill pan over medium heat or prepare the grill for direct, high-heat cooking. Rub the chicken breasts with the oil. Grill them on the pan or over direct heat on the grill until an instant-read meat thermometer inserted into the middle of a breast registers 160°F, about 8 minutes, turning once after 4 minutes.

3. Transfer the chicken to a cutting board, wait a couple minutes to let the juices slip back among the muscle fibers, and slice the breasts lengthwise into long, thin strips. Place them in a serving bowl.

4. Fluff the bulgur with a fork, then dump the grains into the bowl. Add the remaining ingredients: the pineapple, scallions, lime juice, vinegar, and soy sauce. Toss well.

CURRIED CARROT AND BULGUR SALAD

1 cup quick-cooking whole-grain bulgur

1 cup boiling water

3 tablespoons toasted walnut oil

1 small leek, white and pale green parts only, halved lengthwise, well washed, and thinly sliced crosswise

2 large carrots, shredded through the large holes of a box grater

2 teaspoons curry powder

¼ cup dry white wine or dry vermouth

2 tablespoons white wine vinegar

2 teaspoons Worcestershire sauce

1. Dump the bulgur into a large heatproof bowl. Pour the boiling water over the wheat, stir, cover with a plate, and set aside for 1 hour.

2. After the bulgur has softened, heat a large skillet over medium heat. Swirl in the oil, then add the leek. Cook, stirring often, until softened, about 2 minutes. Stir in the carrots and cook for 1 minute.

3. Add the curry powder and stir over the heat for 30 seconds. Pour in the wine or vermouth. Bring to a full simmer, scraping up any dried bits in the skillet. Continue simmering until the wine has reduced to a thick glaze, about 2 minutes.

4. Stir in the vinegar and Worcestershire sauce. Toss well, then pour and scrape the contents of the skillet into the bowl with the bulgur. Stir well, breaking up the grains to coat them in the dressing.

SERVES 4

Active time: 10 minutes
Total time: 1 hour 15 minutes

Make ahead: Store, covered, in the fridge for up to 3 days. If the bulgur gets hard or dry, moisten it with a little extra oil or reduced-sodium vegetable broth.

Make It Vegetarian: Use vegan-friendly Worcestershire sauce.

CHEF IT UP!

▪ Curry is not one thing but a multitude. Search out blends that are more aromatic than the standard yellow powder, particularly those found at East Indian grocery stores or online spice outlets. Or make your own: Mix 4 teaspoons ground coriander, 2 teaspoons ground celery seeds, 2 teaspoons ground dried orange peel, 1 teaspoon ground fenugreek, 1 teaspoon ground cinnamon, 1 teaspoon ground ginger, 1 teaspoon salt, ½ teaspoon ground mace. Pour into a small bottle and store in a cool, dark place for up to 3 months.

GRAIN SWAPS

▪ Substitute 2½ cups *cooked* quinoa for the bulgur and omit soaking and cooking the raw grains.

TESTERS' NOTES

▪ Walnut oil offers the perfect contrast to the bulgur, a balance of soft, earthy flavors. Store all opened containers in the fridge.

▪ Leeks are very sandy, particularly in the inner layers. Make sure you get rid of all of the grit by opening the layers under running water.

▪ Why all this insistence on "reduced-sodium" broths? Because 1) the watery taste of poor-quality broth should not be covered up with salt and 2) no one else should control the sodium content of your food.

▪ Because the flavors of curry can be intense, the portion size is a little smaller for this salad. If you're concerned about having enough on hand, this recipe is easily doubled.

Active time: 10 minutes
Total time: 30 minutes

Make ahead: Store, covered, in the fridge for up to 3 days.

Save time: Use 3½ cups cooked quinoa and omit cooking the raw grains.

CHEF IT UP!

▥ For a deeper flavor, toast the quinoa in a dry skillet over medium heat for a couple of minutes before boiling it.

▥ Substitute skinned smoked duck for the Canadian bacon. You could even call in an order of smoked tea duck from a Chinese restaurant, skin the meat, take it off the bones, and dice the meat into small bits for this salad.

ASIAN-INSPIRED QUINOA WITH CANADIAN BACON

1 cup quinoa, preferably white quinoa

2 tablespoons toasted sesame oil

8 ounces sliced cremini mushrooms

8 ounces Canadian bacon, diced

3 to 4 scallions, minced

2 tablespoons oyster sauce

2 tablespoons rice vinegar (see page 97)

Up to 1 tablespoon Asian black bean chili paste

2 teaspoons minced fresh ginger

1. Fill a large saucepan about two-thirds full with water and bring it to a boil over high heat. Stir in the quinoa, reduce the heat to low, and cook until the grains have developed their halos and are tender, about 12 minutes. Drain in a fine-mesh sieve or a lined colander set in the sink.

2. Heat a large skillet or wok over medium-high heat. Pour in the oil, then add the mushroom slices. Cook, stirring often, until the mushrooms give off their liquid and most of it evaporates, about 6 minutes.

3. Stir in the drained quinoa and the Canadian bacon. Cook for a couple of minutes, stirring constantly, to heat through. Pour into a large bowl. Toss in the scallions, oyster sauce, rice vinegar, chili paste, and ginger. The salad tastes best if you chill it in the fridge for a couple of hours before serving.

TESTERS' NOTES

▥ This easy quinoa salad is great alongside a creamy dip like baba ghanoush.

▥ Sesame oil is available in dark, toasted bottlings as well as pale, untoasted ones. The recipes in this book only call for the former, a better match to whole grains.

▥ There's a range of scallions here because tastes vary. Add all 4 for balance if you use the full amount of the black bean chili paste.

▥ The sheer number of bottlings of chili pastes and sauces in an Asian grocery store can be boggling.

Even neighborhood supermarkets can have a full offering. For this recipe, use a chili sauce that includes preserved black beans. You may need to stir it up if there's a layer of chile oil floating on top. The mix of preserved black beans and chiles is a salty/spicy combo that can balance the scallions, sesame oil, and pork in the salad.

▥ Canadian bacon, as sold in the United States, is actually smoked pork loin, not the peameal bacon sold in Canada. Our "Canadian" bacon is lighter and brighter than both Canada's peameal bacon and the standard American "streaky" bacon.

Active time: 15 minutes
Total time: 30 minutes

Make ahead: Store, covered, in the fridge for up to 4 days.

Save time: Use 3½ cups cooked quinoa and omit soaking and cooking the raw grains.

MAKE IT EASIER!

▪ You can forgo most of the cooking: Skip the asparagus and shiitake caps, and use ½ pound frozen mixed Asian vegetables. No need to cook them; just thaw and toss.

TESTERS' NOTES

▪ Quinoa takes a little time to absorb more complex flavors— which is why quinoa salads like this one are better the day after.

▪ We went back and forth on adding some heat to this salad. If you want to spice it up, mince a couple of pickled jalapeño rings and add them to the mix.

QUINOA WITH ASPARAGUS AND SHIITAKES

1 cup white or red quinoa

1 pound thin asparagus spears

1 tablespoon olive oil

½ pound shiitake mushrooms, stems discarded

1½ tablespoons soy sauce (regular or reduced-sodium)

1½ tablespoons rice vinegar (see page 97)

1 tablespoon mirin (see page 156)

1 teaspoon finely grated orange zest

1 tablespoon orange juice

1. Fill a large saucepan about two-thirds full with water and bring it to a boil over high heat. Stir in the quinoa, reduce the heat to low, and cook until the grains have developed their halos and are tender, about 12 minutes. Drain in a fine-mesh sieve or a lined colander set in the sink.

2. Heat a grill pan over medium heat or fire up the grill for direct, high-heat cooking. Coat the asparagus spears with the oil, then grill until browned, marked, and tender, about 8 minutes, turning occasionally. Maintain the heat under the pan or on the grill. Transfer the spears to a cutting board and slice them into 1-inch segments.

3. Set the shiitake mushroom caps in the pan or on the grill grate over direct heat. Set a heavy flameproof lid—like the lid to a cast iron Dutch oven or even a panini or sandwich press—on top of them to weight them down. Cook for 1 minute. Transfer to the cutting board and slice into thin strips.

4. Pour the asparagus bits and mushroom slices into a serving bowl. Fluff the quinoa and dump it in as well. Stir in the remaining ingredients: the soy sauce, vinegar, mirin, orange zest, and orange juice.

QUINOA WITH GRILLED SHRIMP AND PEPPERS

1 cup quinoa, preferably white quinoa

1 green bell pepper

1 red bell pepper

1 yellow bell pepper

½ pound peeled and deveined medium (about 30 per pound) shrimp

3 tablespoons olive oil, divided

2 tablespoons fresh lemon juice

1½ teaspoons minced fresh rosemary or 1 teaspoon crumbled dried rosemary

1 small garlic clove, minced or put through a garlic press

½ teaspoon salt

½ teaspoon ground black pepper

1. Fill a large saucepan about two-thirds full with water and bring it to a boil over high heat. Stir in the quinoa, reduce the heat to low, and cook until the grains have developed their halos and are tender, about 12 minutes. Drain in a fine-mesh sieve or a lined colander set in the sink.

2. Meanwhile, fire up the grill for direct, high-heat cooking. Set the peppers on the grate, cover the grill, and cook until sizzling and blackened, about 10 minutes, turning often with tongs. (You can also get the job done by setting the peppers on a large lipped baking sheet and broiling them 4 to 6 inches from the preheated element, turning them several times.) Transfer the peppers to a bowl and cover the bowl with plastic wrap. Set aside for 15 minutes while you grill the shrimp.

3. Toss the shrimp in a bowl with 1 tablespoon of the oil. Set them on the grill grate or in a preheated grill pan set over medium–high heat and cook until pink and firm, about 6 minutes, turning once. Transfer to a cutting board, chop them into bite-size bits, and scrape into a serving bowl.

4. Peel the blackened bits off the peppers. Stem and core them and chop the flesh into small bits, about the size of the shrimp pieces. Scrape these into the serving bowl as well.

5. Dump in the cooked quinoa, the remaining 2 tablespoons olive oil, and everything else: the lemon juice, rosemary, garlic, salt, and pepper. Toss well to serve.

SERVES 6

Active time: 35 minutes
Total time: 45 minutes

Make ahead: Store, covered, in the fridge for up to 3 days.

Save time: Use 3½ cups cooked quinoa and omit soaking and cooking the raw grains.

MAKE IT EASIER!

▥ Substitute ½ pound packaged lump crabmeat, picked over to remove bits of shell and cartilage, for the shrimp. No need to grill it! Just toss the crabmeat into the bowl with the quinoa (but stir gently so as not to break it up too much). If you really want to go easy, also substitute 3 jarred roasted red peppers, chopped up.

TESTERS' NOTES

▥ Can you use other sorts of quinoa here? Of course, but just remember that the flavor of black quinoa is more insistent; the texture, often drier.

▥ Use a high-quality, deeply flavored olive oil. No, you don't need a wallet-emptying bottle for this salad; but you do need a flavorful, aromatic oil, made from the first cold press of ripe olives. If you want to be economical, use a sturdier, less expensive olive oil to coat the shrimp and then a high-end one in the salad at the end.

MILLET SALAD WITH CORN AND PEANUTS

SERVES 6

Active time: 15 minutes
Total time: 30 minutes

Make ahead: Store, covered, in the fridge for up to 4 days.

CHEF IT UP!

▪ You can use fresh corn kernels, cut right off the cob—or you can grill ears of corn over a high-heat fire for a few minutes, then slice the kernels off. In fact, you can even do this several days in advance, storing the grilled kernels until you're ready to make this salad.

TESTERS' NOTES

▪ We've used the sweeter, more familiar taste of corn to balance the crunchy millet. The resulting combo yields a sweet/savory perfection.

▪ If the millet gets dry or crunchy, moisten the salad with extra peanut oil or some reduced-sodium vegetable broth.

1 cup millet

8 ounces frozen corn kernels, thawed

1 large tomato, chopped

½ cup chopped fresh parsley leaves

½ cup unsalted roasted peanuts, chopped

½ teaspoon salt

3 tablespoons peanut oil

1 large yellow onion, chopped

2 garlic cloves, minced

1 tablespoon minced fresh ginger

1 teaspoon packed dark brown sugar

1 teaspoon mild paprika

½ teaspoon ground allspice

¼ teaspoon cayenne pepper

3 tablespoons fresh lemon juice

1. Place the millet in a large saucepan and fill it about halfway with water. Bring to a boil over high heat, then reduce the heat and cook until the grains are tender but still a little chewy, even with a slight crunch at their centers, about 12 minutes. Drain in a fine-mesh sieve or a colander lined with a coffee filter, paper towels, or cheesecloth.

2. Scrape the cooked millet into a large bowl. Stir in the corn, tomato, parsley, peanuts, and salt.

3. Heat a large skillet over medium heat. Swirl in the oil, then add the onion. Cook, stirring often, until softened, about 3 minutes. Add the garlic and ginger; stir over the heat for about 30 seconds.

4. Mix in the brown sugar, paprika, allspice, and cayenne. Heat them through for a few seconds, then pour in the lemon juice. Scrape up any browned bits in the skillet, then scrape the contents of the skillet into the bowl with the millet mélange. Toss well.

REUBEN SALAD

1 cup rye berries

1 large head green cabbage
(about 2 pounds)

2 tablespoons salt

½ pound thick-cut deli pastrami,
cut into ¼-inch dice

½ pound thick-cut Swiss cheese,
diced to match the pastrami

6 tablespoons mayonnaise
(regular, low-fat, light, or
fat-free)

2 tablespoons pickle relish

1 tablespoon ketchup

3 tablespoons cider vinegar

1. Soak the rye berries in a big bowl of cool water for at least 8 and up to 16 hours. Drain the rye berries in a fine-mesh sieve or small-holed colander set in the sink. Pour the rye berries into a large saucepan, cover with water by several inches, and bring to a boil over high heat. Reduce the heat to low and simmer until tender, about 1 hour 15 minutes. Drain again in that sieve or colander, then run under cool water to stop the cooking. Drain thoroughly.

2. Slice the cabbage head in half. Cut out the thick, pyramidal core at the base of each half. Set the halves cut side down on the cutting board; make thin slices parallel to the core's former point up in the heart of the cabbage. Separate the shreds from each other and toss them in a large bowl with the salt. Set aside at room temperature for 30 minutes.

3. Rinse the cabbage to get rid of the excess salt, then squeeze it by handfuls to remove any excess water. Dump these handfuls into a large serving bowl as you go. Pour in the cooked rye berries, diced pastrami, and cheese. Toss well.

4. Whisk the mayonnaise, pickle relish, and ketchup in a small bowl; whisk in the vinegar. Pour this dressing onto the salad and toss it up.

SERVES 8

Active time: 15 minutes
Total time: 2 hours, plus soaking the rye berries for at least 8 hours

Make ahead: Store, covered, in the fridge for up to 3 days.

Save time: Use 2⅔ cups cooked rye berries and omit soaking and cooking the raw grains.

CHEF IT UP!

■ Run the cut cabbage halves down a mandoline with a ⅛-inch blade to make perfectly thin strips. Use the safety guard to protect your fingers.

TESTERS' NOTES

■ Consider this the classic Reuben sandwich in a bowl—or a cross between that sandwich and coleslaw.

■ For the best results, buy the meat and cheese in single, thick slabs from the deli counter, then dice them at home, rather than trying to work with flimsy, paper-thin slices.

RYE BERRIES AND GOAT CHEESE IN A DIJON VINAIGRETTE

1 cup rye berries

6 tablespoons olive oil

1 large shallot, minced

3 carrots, finely diced

3 celery stalks, minced

3 tablespoons cider vinegar

1 tablespoon Worcestershire sauce

1 tablespoon Dijon mustard

1 teaspoon fresh thyme leaves or ½ teaspoon dried thyme

½ teaspoon salt

½ teaspoon ground black pepper

4 ounces fresh chèvre or soft goat cheese

SERVES 4

Active time: 15 minutes
Total time: 1 hour 45 minutes, plus soaking the rye berries for at least 8 hours

Make ahead: Store, covered, in the fridge for up to 4 days.

Save time: Use 2⅔ cups cooked rye berries and omit soaking and cooking the raw grains.

Make It Vegetarian: Use a vegan-friendly Worcestershire sauce.

1. Soak the rye berries in a big bowl of cool water for at least 8 hours or up to 16 hours. Drain in a fine-mesh sieve or small-holed colander set in the sink. Pour the grains into a large saucepan, cover with water by several inches, and bring to a boil over high heat. Reduce the heat to low and simmer until tender, about 1 hour 15 minutes. Drain again in that sieve or colander and run under cool water to stop the cooking. Drain thoroughly while you prepare the rest of the recipe.

2. Heat a large skillet over medium heat. Pour in the oil, then add the shallot, carrots, and celery. Stir until softened, about 4 minutes. Stir in the vinegar, Worcestershire sauce, mustard, thyme, salt, and pepper. Stir over the heat about 30 seconds; set aside for a couple of minutes to cool down.

3. Pour the rye berries into a large bowl, scrape the contents of the skillet into the bowl, and toss to coat and combine. Set aside for 15 minutes to blend the flavors.

4. Crumble the goat cheese into the bowl and stir gently to break it up throughout the salad without mushing it.

CHEF IT UP!

▪ Fry eggs in olive oil and lay them on top of servings of the salad.

GRAIN SWAPS

▪ Substitute 1 cup hull-less barley or 1 cup spelt berries for the rye berries. These substituted grains will take 45 minutes to 1 hour to get tender in the simmering water.

TESTERS' NOTE

▪ The true success of this simple recipe lies with how you mince the shallot, carrots, and celery: Get them into tiny pieces about the same size as the rye berries. That way, the salad becomes a gorgeous mosaic of colors and textures in every spoonful.

Active time: 15 minutes

Total time: 1 hour, plus soaking the triticale for at least 8 hours

Make ahead: Store, covered, in the fridge for up to 2 days.

Save time: Use 2⅔ cups cooked triticale berries and omit soaking and cooking the raw grains.

CHEF IT UP!

▦ Rather than using frozen artichoke hearts, poach well-trimmed, very tiny baby artichokes in a white wine and broth mixture until tender, then slice them into quarters.

GRAIN SWAPS

▦ Substitute 1 cup rye berries for the triticale berries. They'll need to simmer about 1 hour 15 minutes to get tender.

TESTERS' NOTE

▦ Triticale berries have a somewhat pungent, forceful taste—and thus the smoked trout is here as a good balance. Look for it near the smoked salmon in most well-stocked markets. Of course, you could flake smoked salmon into the salad as well, although its texture will be a little softer, not quite as good a contrast to the artichoke hearts.

TRITICALE WITH SMOKED TROUT AND ARTICHOKES IN A LEMON TAHINI DRESSING

1 cup triticale berries

2 tablespoons fresh lemon juice

1½ tablespoons tahini

1 tablespoon white balsamic vinegar

1 tablespoon Dijon mustard

½ teaspoon salt

½ teaspoon ground black pepper

½ cup olive oil

1 package (9 ounces) frozen artichoke heart quarters, thawed, squeezed gently by the handfuls to remove excess moisture, and chopped

8 ounces smoked trout, skinned and chopped

1. Soak the triticale berries in a big bowl of cool water for at least 8 and up to 16 hours. Drain the berries in a fine-mesh sieve or small-holed colander set in the sink, then pour them into a large saucepan. Cover with more water, until they're submerged by several inches. Bring to a boil over high heat. Reduce the heat to low and simmer until tender, about 45 minutes. Drain once again in that sieve or colander; rinse with cool tap water until the grains are at room temperature. Shake the colander to drain the berries.

2. Place the lemon juice, tahini, vinegar, mustard, salt, and pepper in a mini food processor or blender. Turn it on, then drizzle in the oil in dribs and drabs to make a rich dressing. You can also make this dressing in a small bowl with a whisk, but you'll need to give your forearm a workout. Whisk the first ingredients together, then whisk in the oil in a very small, steady stream.

3. Pour the cooked triticale into a large bowl. Pour and scrape the salad dressing into the bowl as well. Add the artichoke hearts and smoked trout. Stir gently to avoid breaking the trout into minuscule threads but nonetheless make sure everything's well combined.

OAT GROAT AND BLACK-EYED PEA SALAD

1 cup oat groats

1 cup dried black-eyed peas

½ cup finely chopped pitted green olives (about 4 ounces)

½ cup finely chopped dry-pack sun-dried tomatoes

1 garlic clove, minced

3 tablespoons olive oil

2 tablespoons white wine vinegar

1 tablespoon minced fresh oregano leaves

2 teaspoons pomegranate molasses

½ teaspoon red pepper flakes

½ teaspoon grated nutmeg

1. Soak the oat groats in a big bowl of cool water for at least 8 and up to 16 hours. Do the same thing with the black-eyed peas.

2. Pour the oat groats into a large saucepan, cover with water by several inches, and bring to a boil over high heat. Reduce the heat to low and simmer until tender if still with a little tooth, about 45 minutes. Drain again in that sieve or colander, then run under cool water to stop the cooking. Drain thoroughly.

3. As the groats cook, drain the black-eyed peas in a colander and pour them into a second saucepan and cover with a good amount of water. Bring to a boil over high heat, then reduce the heat to low and simmer until tender, about 45 minutes. Drain these as well in a colander in the sink, cooling them off with tap water, too.

4. Pour the groats and the black-eyed peas into a big bowl. Add everything else: the olives, sun-dried tomatoes, garlic, oil, vinegar, oregano, pomegranate molasses, red pepper flakes, and nutmeg. Toss to serve.

SERVES 4

Active time: 15 minutes

Total time: 1 hour, plus soaking the groats and peas for at least 8 hours

Make ahead: Store, covered, in the fridge for up to 4 days.

Save time: Substitute 2 cups cooked oat groats.

MAKE IT EASIER!

▥ Use a 15-ounce can of black-eyed peas. Drain and rinse the peas before tossing them into the salad.

TESTERS' NOTES

▥ Oat groats have a sweet yet savory flavor that goes well with the more earthy black-eyed peas. Since the flavors here have to be pretty present, even pumped up, avoid dried oregano and go for the fresh.

▥ Pomegranate molasses is a Middle Eastern condiment, a thick concentrate of pomegranate juice with a sweet/sour flavor. If you can't lay your hands on a bottle, substitute aged, thick balsamic vinegar for a spikier, more aggressive taste.

▥ There's no added salt here because of the olives. If you'd like a saltier salad, add ½ teaspoon with the nutmeg—or pass salt on the side for sprinkling on individual servings.

SERVES 4

Active time: 10 minutes
Total time: 1 hour 25 minutes

JOB'S TEARS AND EDAMAME IN A CARROT DRESSING

GRAIN SWAPS

▦ Substitute ⅔ cup hull-less barley for the Job's tears; soak the barley for at least 8 and up to 16 hours before cooking with the East Indian method (see page 11).

TESTERS' NOTES

▦ Job's tears easily lend themselves to Asian palettes, a little bit of whole grain goodness among the ginger and flavorings.

▦ Tamari is an ultra-smooth, Japanese-style soy sauce, often available in wheat-free bottlings.

⅔ cup Job's tears (*hato mugi*), preferably dark (*yuuki hato mugi*)

1 cup frozen shelled edamame, thawed

8 ounces firm tofu, diced

1 large carrot, grated through the large holes of a box grater

2 tablespoons minced fresh ginger

2 tablespoons white miso paste

1 tablespoon tamari sauce

1 tablespoon rice vinegar

1 teaspoon toasted sesame oil

1. Pour the Job's tears into a large saucepan, cover them with cool water by several inches, and bring to a boil over high heat. Reduce the heat to low and simmer until soft but starchy, sort of like al dente soba noodles, between 1 hour and 1 hour 15 minutes, depending on the grains' residual moisture content from long storage. Drain in a fine-mesh sieve or small-holed colander set in the sink. Run under cool water to stop the cooking. Drain thoroughly.

2. Scrape the grains into a large bowl. Stir in the edamame. Lay the diced tofu on top without stirring it in.

3. Puree the carrot, ginger, miso, tamari, rice vinegar, and sesame oil in a food processor or even a mini food processor. Add water—up to ¼ cup—until the mixture processes into a thick, coarse dressing. Pour this over the salad, then toss gently, keeping the tofu pieces whole as you stir them through the grains.

ASIAN PICADILLO WITH JOB'S TEARS

1 cup Job's tears *(hato mugi)*, preferably dark *(yuuki hato mugi)*

3 tablespoons sesame seeds

1 tablespoon toasted sesame oil

6 scallions, green and white parts kept separate, each thinly sliced

3 garlic cloves, minced

1 to 2 tablespoons minced fresh ginger

3 tablespoons tahini

3 tablespoons fresh lime juice

3 tablespoons Asian fish sauce

1 tablespoon packed dark brown sugar

1 teaspoon ground black pepper

Up to 1 teaspoon Asian chili paste or sauce, or sambal olek

4 radishes, diced

⅓ cup fresh cilantro leaves, minced

About 16 leaves of red leaf, green leaf, or Romaine lettuce for wrapping

SERVES 4

Active time: 20 minutes
Total time: 1 hour 40 minutes

Make ahead: Job's tears do not store well; covered, this salad can last in the fridge about 1 day.

GRAIN SWAPS

- Substitute 1 cup oat groats for the Job's tears. Soak the groats in a big bowl of cool water for at least 8 and up to 16 hours before cooking them. They'll take about 45 minutes at a simmer to get tender with lots of water in a large saucepan.

1. Pour the Job's tears into a large saucepan, cover them with cool water by several inches, and bring to a boil over high heat. Reduce the heat to low and simmer until soft but starchy, sort of like al dente soba noodles, between 1 hour and 1 hour 15 minutes, depending on the grains' residual moisture content from long storage. Drain in a fine-mesh sieve or small-holed colander set in the sink. Run under cool water to stop the cooking. Drain thoroughly.

2. Heat a large skillet over medium heat. Pour in the sesame seeds and toast for a minute or two, just until aromatic. Scrape the seeds into a small bowl and set aside.

3. Return the skillet to the heat and swirl in the sesame oil. Add the scallion whites and stir over the heat until somewhat wilted, about 2 minutes. Stir in the garlic and ginger; cook for just a few seconds.

4. Add the tahini, lime juice, fish sauce, brown sugar, pepper, and chili paste. Stir over the heat just to scrape up any browned bits in the skillet.

5. When the mixture is bubbling, stir in the Job's tears, the toasted sesame seeds, scallion greens, radishes, and cilantro. Stir over the heat just until combined. Then set aside off the heat for at least 10 minutes before serving. To serve, place dollops in lettuce leaves and roll them up, sort of like an egg roll—or fold them closed, sort of like a burrito.

TESTERS' NOTES

▪ Okay, we'll admit it: This is a long way from a true picadillo of ground beef, spices, and veggies—a dish common in Cuban cooking that is often served over rice and beans. This one's been tweaked to Southeast Asia with the Job's tears standing in for the beef. You might also consider serving it over long-grain brown rice and warmed black beans.

▪ Bottled Asian chili sauces can range from very hot to insane. Basically, you're looking for ground chiles thinned with vinegar and seasoned with salt. In sambal olek, an Indonesian condiment, there are lots of seeds in the mix. In a pinch, you could substitute Sriracha, sometimes called "rooster sauce," a pureed red hot sauce from Thailand.

▪ One warning: Sesame seeds are notorious for picking up static and clinging to everything in sight. You may only be able to get them out of the skillet by scraping it repeatedly with a heat-safe (silicone) spatula.

▪ The amount of ginger called for is a fairly large range, so you can design the dish to your taste.

SERVES 6

Active time: 15 minutes

Total time: 1 hour 30 minutes, plus soaking the black barley for at least 8 hours

Make ahead: Store, covered, in the fridge for up to 4 days.

CHEF IT UP!

▪ Smoked paprika comes in many levels of heat, from incinerating to quite sweet. Choose the one that's right for you by reading labels while you're at the supermarket or when you're ordering online. Bittersweet smoked paprika has a slightly more complex finish, a nice contrast to the dates in this salad.

▪ Substitute tamari almonds for the whole almonds here. Omit toasting them; simply chop them up. Omit the salt in the salad as well.

TESTERS' NOTES

▪ This is our one recipe that specifically calls for black barley, sometimes called "hull-less purple barley." It's indigenous to Ethiopia but hasn't been grown there in centuries because of its low-yield production. Today, most of the black barley comes from Montana. It's a decided treat, a great balance between nutty and sweet—with its characteristic, gorgeous, purple color.

▪ You can also stir in some extra protein—for example, the chopped, skinned breast meat from a rotisserie chicken. But go easy on the meat. Use it more as a flavoring, rather than the central ingredient.

SPANISH-INSPIRED BLACK BARLEY SALAD WITH CHICKPEAS, DATES, AND TOASTED ALMONDS

1 cup black barley

⅔ cup whole almonds

3½ cups canned chickpeas, drained and rinsed

3 jarred roasted red peppers, chopped

6 large Medjool dates, pitted and chopped

1 small garlic clove, put through a garlic press or finely minced

⅓ cup olive oil

3 tablespoons red wine vinegar

1 teaspoon dried oregano

1 teaspoon sweet or bittersweet smoked paprika

1 teaspoon salt

½ teaspoon ground black pepper

1. Soak the black barley in a big bowl of cool water for at least 8 and up to 16 hours. Drain through a fine-mesh sieve or small-holed colander set in the sink, then dump the black barley into a large saucepan, cover with water by several inches, and bring to a boil over high heat. Reduce the heat to low and simmer until tender, about 1 hour 15 minutes. Drain again in that sieve or colander, then run under cool water until the grains are room temperature. Drain completely while you make the rest of the recipe.

2. Toast the almonds in a dry skillet over medium-low heat, stirring occasionally, until lightly browned and very fragrant, about 4 minutes. Pour them onto a cutting board, wait a few minutes, then chop them into bite-size pieces.

3. Pour the cooked black barley into a large bowl; stir in the chopped toasted almonds as well as the chickpeas, roasted peppers, dates, and garlic.

4. Whisk the remaining ingredients in a small bowl: the oil, vinegar, oregano, smoked paprika, salt, and pepper. Pour this dressing over the salad and toss to coat.

NOT SALADS AT ALL

Passengers on cruise ships can go a little nuts for whole grains. At least, that's what we've learned after doing cooking demonstrations on Holland America for years. People rush the stage. You have to be careful.

Maybe it's because whole grains are in such short supply on a ship. Yes, they can be stored for years, but moisture is their foe. Ancient grain warehouses were common in dry-as-sand Egypt, not so much in half-submerged Amazonia. You can eat fresh soft wheat berries right out of the field, a little crunchy, about like sunflower seeds. Dried, they become the tooth-crackers that can last for years—or rot in the damp environment of a ship's hold. Which is why you want to store whole grains at home in a cool, dry place, away from 1) moisture (including humidity), 2) light, and 3) heat (which can exacerbate the work of ambient moisture).

Last year, we were on the voyage-of-a-life-time from South America to Tahiti. We were several days out from Lima, Peru, but had stocked up on some whole grains for a demo of make-ahead summer deck food: things you can throw together days in advance to serve when the weather heats up. Truth be told, we were crowd-testing the very recipes in this section: stuffed tomatoes, summer rolls with quinoa, and a corn ceviche, as bright as Peru. It's always

good to find guinea pigs. Particularly on a cruise ship. Those people will tell you just what they think.

We finished the demo and lined the dishes across the counter to take questions. There were none. The crush was on.

One woman approached with her mouth full. "I've been dying for something like this," she said. "How'd you come up with it?"

We said something about the challenge of inspiration.

"No, I mean whose cookbook did you find this in?"

Yes, it's hard to imagine what food writers actually do. And it's boggling to think that the two of us have concepted, developed, and tested over 10,000 recipes in the last 12 years. But plagiarism?

"We don't steal," one of us stammered.

"Of course not," she assured us, chewing hell bent for leather. "But I mean, aren't there just two or three recipes? Everybody else just passes them around?"

Both to give her her due *and* to prove her wrong, here are four whimsical cold dishes—all departures *from* the standards, not a salad in the mix, most flights of fancy, based on established recipe concepts but all delightfully original with whole grains. From our own kitchen.

NOT SALADS AT ALL

TOMATOES STUFFED WITH BLACK RICE AND SHRIMP

1⅓ cups water

¾ cup Italian black rice such as venere rice (do not use Forbidden rice or Thai sweet sticky black rice)

¾ pound peeled and deveined small shrimp

4 tablespoons olive oil, divided

2 garlic cloves, minced

½ teaspoon red pepper flakes

1 teaspoon finely grated lemon zest

1 tablespoon fresh lemon juice

1 teaspoon ground black pepper

6 large globe tomatoes (6 ounces each)

¼ cup finely grated Parmigiano-Reggiano

1. Combine the water and rice in a small saucepan and bring to a boil over high heat. Cover, reduce the heat to low, and simmer slowly until the rice is tender and the water has been absorbed, about 40 minutes. Set aside, covered, to steam for 10 minutes.

2. Meanwhile, mix the shrimp, 2 tablespoons of the oil, the garlic, and red pepper flakes in a bowl. Set them aside at room temperature while you heat up a grill pan over medium heat until smoking or prepare the grill for direct high-heat cooking. Set the shrimp in the pan or on the grill grate over direct heat and cook until pink and firm, about 5 minutes, turning once or twice. Transfer to a cutting board and chop into tiny bits.

3. Place the chopped shrimp in a bowl. Fluff the rice with a fork and add it to the bowl. Stir in the remaining 2 tablespoons oil, the lemon zest, lemon juice, and black pepper.

4. Cut the tops off the tomatoes. Scoop out the flesh and seeds with a small spoon, preferably a serrated grapefruit spoon. Place ⅓ cup of the shrimp salad in each tomato. Top with some of the grated Parmigiano-Reggiano.

SERVES 6

Active time: 15 minutes
Total time: 55 minutes

Make ahead: Store the hollowed-out tomatoes and salad separately, for up to 2 days. Fill the tomatoes just before serving.

CHEF IT UP!

■ Shave the cheese, rather than grating it; lay paper-thin strips on the stuffed tomatoes.

TESTERS' NOTES

▦ Whole-grain, Italian, black rice is the sweetest of all the rices. For the best contrast, search out ripe but still firm tomatoes that will have just a hint of sour pop behind their summery freshness.

▦ We developed this recipe with very small shrimp, ones that take about 50 to make a pound. You can also use so-called "salad shrimp," sometimes called "baby shrimp" (although they are in fact fully adult shrimp caught in frigid, northern waters). Since these are sold precooked, skip step 2, adding the garlic and red pepper flakes directly to the salad. If you don't want the taste of raw garlic in the salad, cook the minced garlic and red pepper flakes in the oil for about half a minute in a small skillet set over medium heat. Or look to the salad bar of your supermarket for roasted garlic cloves, a really easy solution.

▦ There's no added salt in the recipe because the shrimp and cheese are both quite salty. If you'd like a little more salt, sprinkle a few grains over the stuffed tomato halves just before serving.

Active time: 15 minutes

Total time: 1 hour 15 minutes, plus soaking the wheat berries for at least 8 hours

Make ahead: Scrape the wheat berry puree into a small bowl, cover with plastic wrap, and store in the fridge for up to 5 days.

Save time: Use 1 cup plus 6 table-spoons cooked wheat berries and omit soaking and cooking the raw grains.

CHEF IT UP!

■ Substitute smoked olive oil for the regular olive oil.

■ Cook dried black-eyed peas for even more flavor. Follow the instructions on page 108 for cooking 1 cup dried black-eyed peas.

TESTERS' NOTES

■ Is this a "grain main"? Maybe we cheated a little, but we do so love this wheat berry and black-eyed pea hummus that lines the wrap. In fact, the spread itself is great to make even if you don't intend to make the wraps! It's a smooth, creamy addition to any plate with another chewier grain salad on it.

SANDWICH WRAP WITH A WHEAT BERRY SPREAD

½ cup wheat berries, preferably hard red wheat berries

1 can (15 ounces) black-eyed peas, drained and rinsed

6 tablespoons fresh lemon juice

2 tablespoons tahini

2 tablespoons olive oil

1 teaspoon ground cumin

1 garlic clove, minced or put through a garlic press

½ teaspoon salt

½ teaspoon ground black pepper

4 large thin flatbreads, lefse, whole wheat tortillas, or other breadish vehicles suitable for a wrap sandwich

About 1½ cups shredded iceberg lettuce

1 large tomato, very thinly sliced

1 Hass avocado, thinly sliced

Up to 8 pickled jalapeño rings (optional)

Up to 1 cup radish, sunflower, or other sprouts (optional)

1. Soak the wheat berries in a big bowl of cool water for at least 8 and up to 16 hours. Drain the wheat berries in a fine-mesh sieve or small-holed colander set in the sink. Pour the grains into a large saucepan, cover with water by several inches, and bring to a boil over high heat. Reduce the heat to low and simmer until tender but with a little chew, about 1 hour. Drain thoroughly in that sieve or colander, shaking the sieve or colander to get rid of excess moisture.

2. Place the cooked wheat berries in a large food processor. Add the black-eyed peas, lemon juice, tahini, oil, cumin, garlic, salt, and pepper. Process until fairly pasty, scraping down the inside of the bowl once or twice to make sure all the wheat berries take a death spiral. The mixture won't get as smooth as hummus, but close.

3. To make a wrap, lay a flatbread or tortilla on your work surface, then spread it with a rounded ½ cup of the wheat berry puree. Top with some lettuce, tomatoes, and avocado, as well as jalapeño rings and sprouts (if using). Roll it up and dig in!

ITALIAN-STYLE BLACK QUINOA AND SPINACH SUMMER ROLLS

½ cup black quinoa

1 package (10 ounces) frozen chopped spinach, thawed and squeezed dry

2 tablespoons raisins, chopped

2 tablespoons unseasoned dried whole wheat bread crumbs

2 tablespoons finely grated Parmigiano-Reggiano

2 tablespoons dry white wine, dry vermouth, or unsweetened apple juice

½ teaspoon dried dillweed

½ teaspoon fennel seeds, crushed under a heavy pot or rolling pin

½ teaspoon salt

½ teaspoon ground black pepper

8 dried rice paper rounds (for summer rolls)

1. Cover the black quinoa in large saucepan with cool water by a couple of inches. Bring to a boil over high heat. Reduce the heat to medium-low and cook until the quinoa is tender and the grains have bloomed their little halos, about 12 minutes. Drain in a fine-mesh sieve or small-holed colander set in the sink. Run under cool water to bring the quinoa back to room temperature and stop the cooking. Drain thoroughly.

2. Place the quinoa in a large bowl. Mix in everything but the rice paper rounds: the spinach, raisins, bread crumbs, cheese, wine or juice, dill, fennel seeds, salt, and pepper.

3. Fill a shallow bowl (such as a soup bowl from a standard place setting) or a small baking dish with hot tap water. Set one of the rice paper rounds in the water; soak for 10 seconds (about the time it takes to sing a standard-tempo chorus of "Happy Birthday"). Set the softened round on your work surface and place about ¼ cup of the filling in the center. Fold two "sides" of the circle over the filling, then roll it up. Place on a large baking sheet and continue making more summer rolls.

SERVES 4

Active time: 20 minutes
Total time: 35 minutes

Make ahead: Lay the rolls in a single layer on a baking sheet and cover with plastic wrap; store in the fridge for up to 2 days.

TESTERS' NOTES

▥ Summer rolls are like egg rolls—except they're not fried and they're made in rice paper wrappers. As such, they have a fresh, bright taste, usually paired with minimally cooked ingredients inside.

▥ Black quinoa has a more assertive, nutty flavor than white or even red.

▥ Look for rice paper summer roll wrappers in the Asian aisle of well-stocked supermarkets, at any Chinese grocery store, and from online suppliers.

▥ We debated the flavor profile here and decided that Asian spices didn't pair as well with more intense, drier, black quinoa; so we finally went Italian and added spinach for a slightly sour yet still savory counterpoint. The bread crumbs provide body but also soak up the excess moisture from the spinach, thereby preventing the rolls from getting soggy.

ROASTED CORN AND SHRIMP "CEVICHE"

4 ears of corn, husked

½ pound peeled and deveined
    medium shrimp

2 tablespoons olive oil, divided

¼ cup minced red onion

¼ cup minced fresh cilantro

3 radishes, minced

1 jalapeño chile, seeded and
    minced

¼ cup fresh lime juice

¼ teaspoon salt

¼ teaspoon ground black pepper

1. Position the rack 4 to 6 inches from the broiler heat source and preheat the broiler.

2. Lay the corn on a large rimmed baking sheet. Toss the shrimp with 1 tablespoon of the oil in a bowl, then spread them on the baking sheet, too. Broil, turning both the corn and shrimp, until the corn is lightly browned on all sides and the shrimp are pink and firm, about 5 minutes.

3. Cool the corn and shrimp a few minutes, then slice the kernels off the cobs. Dice the shrimp. Add both to a large nonreactive bowl. Stir in everything else: the onion, cilantro, radishes, jalapeño, lime juice, salt, pepper, and the remaining 1 tablespoon oil. Set aside at room temperature to marinate for 10 minutes before serving.

MAKE IT EASIER!

▥ Buy precooked peeled and deveined shrimp from the fish counter at your supermarket, chop them up, and add them with the corn.

CHEF IT UP!

▥ You can go all out and substitute an equivalent amount of fresh, raw, white-fleshed fish like bass or snapper for the shrimp, thereby making "real" ceviche in which the acid (a.k.a. lime juice) "cooks" the fish. Dice the fish into very small cubes. And use only the freshest fish, preferably sushi-quality fish. Tell the fishmonger at your market that you're making ceviche and need recommendations for the best fish on hand.

▥ Slice the jalapeño into paper-thin, almost see-through rings with the sharpest knife imaginable.

TESTERS' NOTES

▥ Ceviche is made from chopped raw fish that "cooks" in an acidic brine until somewhat firm—although technically still raw. This recipe is not a true ceviche (since you're using cooked shrimp); it's a dish in the spirit of ceviche, with its very bright flavors. Thus, we've put quotes around the word "ceviche" in the title.

▥ Sugar is often added to ceviches, but there's none here because the corn is so sweet. That said, you can always add a pinch if you find the lime juice overpowering.

▥ Serve this "ceviche" in lettuce leaf cups—or simply "up" in a martini glass.

3

WARM

This chapter may well be the heart of our project of moving grains to the center of our plates. These are dinner dishes, hot off the stove or out of the oven. There's even some dinner-party fare. You see, whole grains are not only the gourmet ingredients hiding in plain sight; they're gorgeously elegant, too.

Not everyone has seen it that way. Like all foods, whole grains have been subject to the whims of "what's in" and "what's out," the dictates of culinary fashion. And they have too often gotten the short end of the stick. To tell the story of why whole grains are not the first choice—this despite their long history with humans—we need to explore the rather loose, somewhat ineffable concept of "elegance."

At its baldest, elegance is a studied, conscious *subtraction* in the face of increasing abundance. Brooke Astor did not go out dripping in jewels, despite having hundreds in her collection. When we say "she wore it well," we mean "she didn't wear too much."

So it goes with food, too. Dainty portions are a hallmark of fine dining: a single scallop, sliced into thin coins, lined up on a plate, each covering a drop of a different sauce. The elaborate preparations that go on in high-end kitchens—the battalions of sous-chefs and prep cooks—all come down to a plate that belies their all-day work: a dribble of sauce, a perfectly turned potato, a sprinkling of stemmed thyme leaves. Against such elegance, whole grains appear like the bruisers at the ball.

So how did we get here? How'd we get to the point that you show your wealth by showing only the tip of it? We need to go back to the 1600s when the French invented dinner. Before then, the main meal was a midday affair, served as late as 2:00 p.m., thanks largely to the dictates of the fashionable Spanish court. Trouble was, the Iberian royalty and nobility had just come out from under Moorish rule; they celebrated their newfound power by breeding like rabbits with the British nobility. So, what with the dilution of the court among hundreds of intermarriages, plus a burgeoning love affair with British culture and most specifically its food, the Spanish court was quickly losing dominance across the

Continent, fast becoming an unfit taskmaster for fine dining.

At the time, France wasn't fit to pick up the slack. It was no more than a loose collection of fiefdoms, duchies, and landed estates, all of which swore some sort of half-assed allegiance to a monarch who wasn't much more than the mayor of Paris. Never fear: The court had a solution. They too could breed like rabbits. Or more accurately, *with* killer rabbits. Also known as Austrian Hapsburgs.

By dalliances and alliances, Paris reinvented itself as a centralized bureaucracy with a snarling army commanded by the in-laws. The French court then got the various princes, dukes, and numbskulls together, left the fops in charge in Paris (*encore*?), and marched on Brugges, where they conquered the excellent trade routes up north, by which the Flemish had stabilized their economy. Paris could now feed itself copiously without having to negotiate port fees. Yes, fruits and vegetables could now be brought straight into the heart of Europe without attendant taxes or that horrid squishiness that came from a long voyage. Mostly, though, rot-prone meat got to Paris more quickly and became "what's in," showing up for every high-end dinner.

The French were now in Europe's catbird seat. Trouble was, the mayors of Paris—a.k.a. the various monarchs—didn't have much of an indigenous culture. So they pulled in traditions wherever they could find them. Mostly from Russia. In came table service. Before the advent of "Russian service," the French did everything tableside. They carved and sauced at your seat. In Russian service, meat is sliced in the kitchen and presented in individual servings. Voilà, every restaurant you can name.

With Russian service saving French nobility from the Henry VIII moment of tearing into hunks of this or that and having the fat run down their chins at the table, meat could become the height of *elegance,* not just barbarism with jewelry. It could be an unshowy show of your wealth—prepared in the kitchen, out of sight, the big, costly joint of beef just the means to an end: a dainty serving on your plate. Even sauced and larded, it displayed your elegance—that is, your simplicity in the face of your opulence. Fruits and vegetables were occasional side dishes, mostly sugared or custarded, based on the dictates of the moment.

On it went. As the European (and American) middle class rose in the 18th and 19th centuries, it agreed wholeheartedly with these lessons in elegance. Rather simply adorned meat remained at the center of the plate. Big hunks of meat were discouraged in the face of dainty portions. (Think of the nervous giggles that go around the Thanksgiving table when you hand someone the whole leg from the bird.) Professional chefs might spend all day on sauces and garnishes, but these should disappear to reveal the steak or chop or fillet or what have you. Meat (and to a lesser extent, fish) was the thing, the most expensive single item among many, the height of elegance.

We dine in the ruins of the old empires. Despite its being a bit strange to consume most of our calories when the workday is finished, most of us eat fairly late—as the French established when they invented dinner. Side dishes are still perfunctory, sometimes just poured out of a bag and nuked.

In all this cultural folderol, whole grains suffered the most. Yes, they were once royal fare. Many preindustrial empires collected grains as tax payments and put them in imperial storehouses to open in the winter. But whole grains didn't fit into developing standards of elegance. They were too much on the plate, required too much chewing, were too inexpensive to show your true worth. And they, too, needed to be simplified—that is, refined down to their white endosperms: a hit of sweet, not stocked with competing flavors. Yes, removing the bran and germ made grains fit for longer storage. But doing so also kept them from being "rustic." They could now kowtow to the meat. White rice is never going to get in the way of a pork chop.

Thus this chapter is our attempt to redefine *elegance*. With the bran and the germ intact, whole grains command attention on their own. Sure, we want to balance them with other ingredients. Even hard-core whole-grainers don't yearn for a plate of unadorned wheat berries. But with more flavors in tow, whole grains can return to their central role without elitist notions of class-based simplicity mucking up a great dinner. They're a hearty hit of savory, some sour, and some moderately sweet flavors. What's more, a grain main isn't just elegant; it's satisfying, too. And that's pretty much the point of dinner.

BURGERS

When city friends show up for a long weekend, we serve at least one vegetarian meal. Apparently, it's a bit of a stretch for some people.

We had friends up to our New England home a while back. Manhattanites of the highest order, they come to our house once a year for the fresh air. Otherwise, they go to Central Park. "There are squirrels in the heart of the city," the wife once remarked, as if the wonders of nature undid her.

On Saturday, they sat down to lunch on our deck. We brought out a platter of grain burgers—which were admittedly unadorned, brown, round, and flat. They were decidedly not elegant.

Our friends backed up. "Why don't we go to that restaurant you like in Great Barrington?" the husband said. "Our treat."

We said that we'd talked about these burgers

the night before at dinner. They mumbled something about the wine.

They were saved further mumbling when we brought out a second platter of condiments and sides: a vinegary slaw, different kinds of mustards, pickles, some sliced tomatoes, a jar of purchased caponata.

"Ah," the wife said. "Embellishments."

Which is part of the point of grain burgers: Not only are the patties flavorful on their own, but they're also a palette for all those things that make any burger so darn irresistible. They can be drippy. They can be tarted up. They stand up to the folderol. With these caveats:

- Grain burgers are by and large more savory than beef or chicken burgers. They're even earthier. The sweet notes present in meat burgers are muted.

- Added spices sometimes come off duller, given the lack of inherent sweetness to sharpen them. Add more to compensate.

- Herbs carry forward more of their elemental flavors, not morphed and muted by animal fats.

- And a little salt goes a long way.

So go wild with the condiments. Look for sweet and/or spicy ones: chow-chow, caponata, honey mustard, and the like. But be careful of going too creamy: Mayonnaise can overwhelm the velvety texture of a whole-grain burger. When it's all said and done, you might even impress your friends. Ours had seconds.

BURGERS

Active time: 20 minutes

Total time: 1 hour 20 minutes, plus soaking the hull-less barley for at least 8 hours

Make ahead: Cooked burgers can be wrapped on a plate in the fridge and saved for up to 3 days; reheat (and recrunch) in a dry, nonstick skillet over medium heat for 2 or 3 minutes per side.

Save time: Use 2⅔ cups cooked hull-less barley and omit soaking and cooking the raw grains.

CHEF IT UP!

▐ Consider soaking the quartered figs in 2 tablespoons brandy before adding them to the food processor. Increase the bread crumbs in the recipe by 2 tablespoons.

TESTERS' NOTES

▐ These patties are ridiculously crunchy because they rely solely on barley for their binder. The grains are sticky enough that there's no need for an egg, which would increase their cakeyness.

▐ The figs are sensational against both the earthy, mellow barley and the nose of the dill. We used dried Calimyrna figs, but three dried Black Mission figs will work as well.

▐ These patties are rather sticky, so a nonstick skillet makes things go more smoothly. That said, you don't need to use a nonstick skillet; but if you don't, you should increase the oil by another tablespoon or so to keep the patties from sticking.

BARLEY AND PECAN BURGERS

1 cup hull-less barley

⅔ cup pecan pieces

2 dried figs, stemmed and quartered

½ cup whole wheat panko bread crumbs

2 tablespoons minced dill fronds or 1 tablespoon dried dillweed

1 teaspoon salt

3 tablespoons olive oil

1. Soak the hull-less barley in a big bowl of cool water for at least 8 and up to 16 hours. Drain in a fine-mesh sieve or small-holed colander set in the sink. Pour the barley into a large saucepan, fill it about two-thirds of the way with water, and bring to a boil over high heat. Reduce the heat to low and simmer until tender, about 55 minutes. Drain again in that sieve or colander, then run under cool water to stop the cooking. Drain thoroughly.

2. Scatter the pecan pieces in a large, dry skillet and set it over medium-low heat. Stir them around occasionally, just until they begin to brown a little and turn fragrant, maybe 4 minutes.

3. Scrape the cooked barley into a large food processor. Add the toasted pecan pieces, as well as the figs, panko, dill, and salt. Process into a thick paste, scraping down the inside of the bowl once or twice. Clean off and remove the blade from the food processor. (Busy bees can make the recipe up to this point in advance; store the batter, covered, in a bowl in the fridge for up to 2 days.)

4. Heat a large nonstick skillet over medium heat. Add the oil. Use dampened hands to form the batter into 6 patties. Slip these into the skillet and cook until browned and crisp, about 4 minutes. Flip them and continue cooking until set and browned on the other side, about 4 more minutes. If your skillet is not large enough to accommodate all 6 patties, work in batches, half at a time, using half the olive oil for each.

BUCKWHEAT AND CASHEW BURGERS

1½ cups water

¾ cup buckwheat groats (do not use toasted buckwheat—a.k.a. kasha)

4 tablespoons olive oil, divided

1 small yellow onion, chopped

1 carrot, shredded through the large holes of a box grater

1 tablespoon minced fresh ginger

1 garlic clove, minced

1 teaspoon ground cumin

½ teaspoon ground cinnamon

½ teaspoon ground coriander

½ teaspoon salt

⅓ cup cashew butter

1. In a large saucepan, bring the water up to a full boil over high heat. Slowly pour in the buckwheat groats, stirring constantly to try to avoid a foam volcano. Cover, reduce the heat to low, and simmer slowly until the groats have sucked up all the water and are tender, about 10 minutes, stirring occasionally to forestall any more foam and also to make sure the groats don't glom into quicksand. Scrape the cooked groats into a large food processor and let cool for a few minutes while you go on to the next step.

2. Heat a large skillet over medium heat. Pour in 1 tablespoon of the oil, tilt the skillet to slick it with the oil, then plop in the onion and carrot. Cook, stirring often, until somewhat tender, about 3 minutes. Stir in the ginger and garlic; cook for 1 minute, stirring a few times. Stir in the cumin, cinnamon, coriander, and salt. Scrape every speck into the food processor with the groats.

3. Add the cashew butter to the food processor. (You're going to need to use your finger or a rubber spatula to get the sticky stuff out of the measuring cup; and you're going to lick either clean. That's why people cook: for the perks.) Pulse to form a thick, pastelike batter, scraping down the inside of the bowl once or twice to make sure everything gets mushed together. Clean off and remove the center blade.

SERVES 4

Active time: 20 minutes
Total time: 40 minutes

Make ahead: Once cooked, the burgers can be cooled to room temperature, wrapped in plastic, and refrigerated for up to 3 days; reheat in a dry skillet over medium heat for 3 to 5 minutes, turning once, or on a baking sheet in a preheated 325°F oven for about 10 minutes.

Save time: Use 1½ cups cooked buckwheat groats and omit soaking and cooking the raw grains.

CHEF IT UP!

■ Make your own cashew butter by toasting 3 cups raw cashews on a large rimmed baking sheet in a preheated 325°F oven for about 8 minutes, stirring once or twice to prevent scorching. Cool at least 5 minutes on the baking sheet, then pour them into a large food processor. Add ¼ cup vegetable oil, 1 tablespoon sugar, and 1 teaspoon salt. Process until the cashews break down into a creamy butter, maybe 5 minutes, maybe a little longer depending on their residual moisture content. This'll make more than you need here—scrape the rest into a plastic or glass container, seal, and store in the pantry for up to 2 weeks. Also, get ready for some cashew-butter-and-jelly sandwiches for lunch.

4. Clean and dry the skillet, then set it back over medium heat. Pour in the remaining 3 tablespoons oil. Dampen your hands, then form the batter into 4 round, sticky patties. Slip the patties into the skillet and fry until crisp and brown on one side, 3 to 4 minutes. Flip them and continue cooking until well browned on the other side, 3 to 4 more minutes.

TESTERS' NOTES

▪ By taking advantage of the natural stickiness in buckwheat and cashew butter, these patties can forego any binder like an added egg yet still hold their shape.

▪ The crisper, the better. Don't be afraid to let them go for awhile over the heat before turning.

▪ In these burgers, kasha—a.k.a. toasted buckwheat groats—would offer a taste too pronounced, almost bitter.

▪ Serve the burgers in whole wheat pita pockets with shredded lettuce, chopped tomatoes, and a little purchased chutney.

BLACK QUINOA AND BLACK BEAN BURGERS

⅔ cup black quinoa

1 (15 ounces) can black beans, drained and rinsed

⅔ cup old-fashioned rolled oats (do not use quick-cooking or steel-cut)

3 tablespoons barbecue sauce

Up to 2 tablespoons pickled jalapeño rings

1 tablespoon Worcestershire sauce

1 tablespoon sweet smoked paprika

1 tablespoon chile powder

1 teaspoon ground cumin

3 tablespoons nut oil, such as walnut, pecan, pistachio, or hazelnut

1. Fill a large saucepan about halfway with water, pour in the quinoa, and bring it to a boil over high heat. Reduce the heat to low and simmer until the grains have developed their halos and are tender, about 10 minutes. Drain in a fine-mesh sieve or a lined colander set in the sink.

2. Scrape the quinoa into a large food processor. (Believe it or not, this is the hardest part of this entire recipe: getting all those grains out of a sieve.) Then add the black beans, oats, barbecue sauce, jalapeños, Worcestershire sauce, smoked paprika, chile powder, and cumin. Process to make a pastelike batter, scraping down the inside of the bowl once or twice. Scrape down and remove the chopping blade.

3. Heat a large skillet over medium heat and swirl in the oil. Use dampened hands to form the batter into 6 even, round, fairly flat patties. Slip these into the skillet and cook until deeply browned, about 4 minutes. Flip them and continue cooking until well browned and a little crisp on the other side, about 4 more minutes. (If your skillet is not large enough to accommodate all the patties at once, fry them in two batches, using half the oil for each batch.)

SERVES 6

Active time: 15 minutes
Total time: 40 minutes

Make ahead: Cooked burgers can be stored on a covered plate in the fridge and reheated on a baking sheet in a preheated 325°F oven for 5 to 10 minutes.

Save time: Use 2⅓ cups cooked quinoa and omit soaking and cooking the raw grains.

Make It Vegan: Use vegan-friendly Worcestershire sauce.

CHEF IT UP!

- Toast the quinoa grains for a few minutes in a dry skillet over medium heat to bring out more of their nutty flavor.

TESTERS' NOTES

- Hearty and rich, with that nice hit of barbecue sauce, these may be the best grain burgers for the plain ol' lettuce-and-tomato-on-a-bun application.

- The beans and oats are fairly sticky—and thus, you don't need any binders here like eggs, despite the inherent dryness of quinoa.

- For the best taste, look for a barbecue sauce without artificial flavors or corn syrup.

- Standard chili powder is actually a blend of ground dried chiles, ground cumin, and ground oregano, sometimes with salt in the mix. So-called "pure" chile powder is made from a single dried chile (chipotle, for example) without the other additives. Use either here.

KAMUT BURGERS WITH SHALLOTS, PECANS, AND LEMON ZEST

⅔ cup Kamut

4 tablespoons olive oil, divided

1 medium shallot, minced

¼ cup pecan pieces

1 tablespoon minced fresh sage leaves or 2 teaspoons dried sage

2 teaspoons finely grated lemon zest

2 teaspoons fresh thyme leaves or 1 teaspoon dried thyme

½ teaspoon salt

½ teaspoon ground black pepper

1 (15 ounces) can white beans, drained and rinsed

1 large egg

1. Fill a large saucepan about halfway with water and bring it to a good boil over high heat. Stir in the Kamut, reduce the heat to low, and cook until the grains are tender, about 1 hour, maybe a little longer. Drain in a fine-mesh sieve or a colander lined with a large coffee filter or paper towels.

2. Heat a large skillet over medium heat. Add 1 tablespoon of the oil, then the shallot and pecan pieces. Cook, stirring often, until the shallot starts to turn translucent, about 2 minutes. Add the sage, lemon zest, thyme, salt, and pepper. Set the skillet off the heat as the Kamut continues to cook.

3. Place the cooked Kamut in a food processor. Scrape the contents of the skillet into the food processor. Add the white beans and egg. Process to form a somewhat grainy, pastelike, thick batter, scraping down the sides of the bowl once or twice to make sure all the Kamut hits the blades. Scrape down and remove the cutting blade.

4. Wash and dry the skillet; set it over medium heat for a couple of minutes. Swirl in the remaining 3 tablespoons oil. With dampened hands, form the batter into 6 round, fairly flat patties. Slip these patties into the skillet and cook until browned and a little crisp on one side, about 4 minutes. Turn the patties and continue cooking until set throughout and browned on the other side, about 4 more minutes. If your skillet is not large enough to hold all 6 patties without crowding, work in two batches, using 1½ tablespoons olive oil for each batch.

FALAFEL BURGERS WITH ALMOND HARISSA

Harissa

8 dried New Mexican red chiles

¼ cup olive oil

2 tablespoons whole almonds

1 teaspoon caraway seeds

1 teaspoon cumin seeds

1 teaspoon coriander seeds

Burgers

1 cup water

1 cup quick-cooking whole-grain bulgur

1¾ cups canned chickpeas, drained and rinsed

3 tablespoons minced scallions

3 tablespoons minced fresh parsley leaves

2 tablespoons fresh lemon juice

1 large egg

1 garlic clove, quartered

1 teaspoon ground cumin

1 teaspoon mild paprika

1 teaspoon baking powder

¼ teaspoon cayenne pepper

¼ cup olive oil

SERVES 6

Active time: 25 minutes
Total time: 2 hours 20 minutes

Make ahead: The almond harissa can be made in advance and stored, covered, in the refrigerator for up to 4 days. Once cooked, the burgers can be cooled to room temperature, wrapped in plastic, and refrigerated for up to 3 days; reheat in a dry skillet over medium heat for 3 to 5 minutes, turning once, or on a baking sheet in a preheated 325°F oven for about 10 minutes.

Save time: Use 2½ cups cooked bulgur and omit soaking and cooking the raw grains.

CHEF IT UP!

■ Once the almond harissa has a slightly grainy consistency, put it through a food mill for a smoother, more luxurious texture.

1. To make the harissa: Stem the chiles, tear them open, and scrape out the seeds and the white membranes inside. Tear the remaining flesh into pieces, set them in a large heatproof bowl, and cover with boiling water. Set aside to soak for 20 minutes. Then go wash your hands—because they've got capsaicin on them, the hot stuff that makes eyes, lips, and other sensitive bits sting. And by the way, capsaicin isn't water-soluble. It's fat-soluble. So pour a little oil in your hands, then rub them around before washing them with soap and warm water.

2. Drain the chiles in a colander set over a big bowl, thereby catching and reserving the soaking water. Put the chiles, oil, almonds, caraway seeds, cumin seeds, and coriander seeds in a blender or a mini food processor. Add 3 tablespoons soaking liquid from the chiles. Blend to a slightly grainy sauce. You may need to add more of the soaking liquid to get a fairly smooth consistency—but don't add too much or the sauce will get watery. Scrape the harissa into a glass, plastic, or stainless steel bowl (it can react with certain pottery glazes and other metals).

(continued)

3. To make the burgers: Bring the water to a boil in a small saucepan over high heat. Stir in the bulgur, cover, and set aside off the heat for 1 hour, until the grains have sopped up all the water.

4. Fluff the bulgur with a fork and scrape it into a large food processor. Add the chickpeas, scallions, parsley, lemon juice, egg, garlic, cumin, paprika, baking powder, and cayenne. Pulse until the mixture forms a thick paste, scraping down the sides of the bowl once or twice. Scrape down and remove the chopping blade; cover the bowl and refrigerate for at least 30 minutes or up to 4 hours. This part is crucial. The ground bulgur must continue to hydrate until smooth.

5. Use dampened hands to form the mixture into 6 smooth, flat, round patties. Heat a large skillet over medium heat. Pour in the oil and add the patties. Cook until browned and crisp, about 4 minutes. Flip the patties and continue cooking until browned and crisp on the other side, about 4 more minutes. If your skillet is not large enough to hold all 6 patties at once, work in batches, using half the olive oil for each batch. To serve, smear the burgers with the harissa—or drizzle it over them on a platter.

TESTERS' NOTES

▥ These grain burgers replicate the taste of falafel but have a slightly softer texture, more in keeping with meat patties, thanks to the beans.

▥ Harissa is a spicy, North African condiment, often served with lamb or goat. This is a non-traditional interpretation. The almonds give it a somewhat sweet, European twist, a great match to the lemon and parsley in the burgers.

▥ Serve alongside a chopped salad of romaine, bell peppers, tomatoes, and cucumbers dressed with a creamy vinaigrette.

MILLET BURGERS WITH OLIVES, SUN-DRIED TOMATOES, AND PECORINO

SERVES 6

Active time: 15 minutes
Total time: 55 minutes

Save time: Use 2⅓ cups millet cooked until the grains are creamy like a porridge and omit cooking the raw grains.

MAKE IT EASIER!

⬛ In truth, these millet burgers can be made with lots of the ingredients found on your supermarket's salad bar: olives of all sorts, roasted red peppers, and the like. Just keep in mind an Italian antipasto flavor palette to create your own version.

3 cups water

1 cup millet

10 chopped dry-pack sun-dried tomatoes

1 garlic clove

¼ cup pine nuts

⅓ cup pitted green olives, chopped

¼ cup packed grated Pecorino Romano or Parmigiano-Reggiano

4 large jarred caper berries, minced

2 teaspoons minced fresh oregano leaves or 1 teaspoon dried oregano

2 teaspoons minced fresh marjoram leaves or 1 teaspoon dried marjoram

2 tablespoons unsalted butter

2 tablespoons olive oil

1. Combine the 3 cups water and the millet in a medium saucepan and bring to a boil over high heat. Cover, reduce the heat to low, and simmer slowly until it's like a thick, coarse, hot breakfast cereal, about 30 minutes. Uncover and stir well to incorporate any last bits of water. Scrape the millet into a large bowl and cool for 10 minutes.

2. Meanwhile, put the sun-dried tomatoes and garlic in a small heat-proof bowl. Cover with boiling water and steep for 10 minutes.

3. Place the pine nuts in a dry medium skillet set over medium-low heat. Toast until lightly browned and fragrant, about 5 minutes, stirring often. Pour them into the bowl with the millet.

4. Drain the sun-dried tomatoes and garlic in a fine-mesh sieve and add them to the bowl with the millet. Add the olives, cheese, caper berries, oregano, and marjoram. Stir well, mashing the ingredients together. You want texture here, bits of this and that scattered throughout the burgers, not a baby-food puree. Use dampened hands to form the mixture into 6 round, even patties.

(continued)

5. Melt the butter in the olive oil over medium heat in a large skillet, preferably nonstick. Slip the patties into the skillet and cook until mottled brown and somewhat crisp, about 4 minutes. Flip them and continue cooking until set throughout, mottled brown on the other side, and now nicely crisp, about 4 more minutes. If your skillet isn't large enough to hold all 6 patties at once, work in two batches, using 1 tablespoon olive oil and 1 tablespoon unsalted butter for each batch.

TESTERS' NOTES

▪ Here, we've used an Italian palette to balance the aromatic millet. Note that the recipe calls for the larger, oblong caper berries, not capers.

▪ The timing for cooked millet is a bit dodgy since the grains are notorious for picking up and holding ambient humidity—as well as releasing it in a dry environment. Don't stand on ceremony: Lift the lid and check the millet as it cooks, adding more water as necessary. You're looking for a crunchy texture that's nonetheless tender to the bite.

▪ These patties would be a treat on whole wheat buns with a little purchased caponata as well as thinly sliced red onion and crunchy lettuce. You could also slice the cooked patties into bite-sized bits and toss them in a large, Italian-style, chopped salad, dressed with a creamy vinaigrette.

▪ These patties don't reheat as well as some of the others, although they do make great late-night snacks right from the fridge, cut into small pieces and dipped in deli mustard.

SOUPS AND STEWS

Homemade soups and stews are not for the impatient. Most take time over the heat. Fortunately, so do whole grains like wheat berries and sorghum. Still, our Honest-to-Goodness Posole Verde (page 150) is probably the most labor-intensive recipe in this book.

Sure, there are whole grains that can mitigate soup's commitment to the clock: corn, for one, as well as whole-grain, quick-cooking bulgur, and even millet, a natural thickener. But the task is the same, no matter if it's an hours-long simmer for Kamut and Beef Chili (page 142) or a much quicker recipe for a Turkish favorite of red lentils and bulgur (page 149): You have to watch that pot.

In a soup, you want enough liquid so the ingredients dance in a slow simmer. If not, add a little more liquid and turn down the heat. In a stew like our Veal and Farro Stew (page 144), you need far less liquid—which means you have to pay more attention to the pot, making sure the ingredients don't scorch and turning the heat way down so you don't have to souse your meal with extra liquid.

That all said, if you find you're adding more liquid on a regular basis, check out your cookware. The problem is usually the result of an ill-fitting lid, not tight enough to hold in every drop of steam. Pots and lids can go out of kilter over the years, bashed together in cabinets until a secure seal is no longer possible. Maybe now's the time to buy heavier, more efficient cookware. Those droplets are bursts of flavor. You don't want to waste a one.

But there's a part of a soup or stew recipe that's even more important than proper equipment. No amount of fancy, French, enameled cast-iron cookware can mitigate the taste of insipid broth. Of course, homemade is best; but few of us have the time to make it. But if you do want to spend a weekend afternoon taking your cooking to new levels, consider a pot or two of stock on the back of the stove while you go about your weekend business around the house. (There's a simple recipe for chicken stock on page 153.) Strain the stock and store it in the freezer in sealable containers in 1- or 2-cup increments. Even a cup of your homemade stock added to canned broth will make a world of difference.

If you (like us) do use a lot of canned broth, do yourself a favor and have a taste-testing event one day with several brands. It'll be the best 20 bucks you ever spent. Heat them up and sip them without other adornment. One will be too salty; another, too oniony; but a third, exactly to your taste. And it may not be the most expensive one. Because of that simple taste-test, you'll have an opportunity to use the best broth you can comfortably afford. What's more, your soups and stews will be at their best. And your friends and family will thank you.

All that's left is the time you invest, that most precious commodity. But your reward will be a warming pot of lemony Avgolemono Soup with Corn Grits Dumplings (page 140) or a comforting, creamy stew with whole-grain farro (page 144). And these days, there are few surer returns on an investment.

SOUPS AND STEWS

ROASTED CORN SOUP
WITH ONION CONFIT

4 medium yellow onions

2 tablespoons olive oil

6 ears of corn, husked

3 tablespoons unsalted butter

1 yellow bell pepper, seeded and chopped

3 celery stalks, sliced lengthwise into three parts, then minced

2 teaspoons minced fresh oregano leaves or 1 teaspoon dried oregano

2 teaspoons fresh thyme leaves or 1 teaspoon dried thyme

1 teaspoon salt

½ teaspoon ground black pepper

½ cup dry white wine or dry vermouth

4 cups reduced-sodium vegetable broth

½ cup heavy cream, half-and-half, or whole milk

SERVES 6

Active time: 45 minutes
Total time: 1 hour 30 minutes

Make ahead: Roast the onions in advance and store them in their sealed packet in the fridge for 2 days; reheat in the oven before serving.

MAKE IT EASIER!

- You can use 2 bags (10 ounces each) of frozen corn kernels. However, you do want some of the roasted taste on the kernels so they're not too sweet. Spread them on a large rimmed baking sheet and broil 4 to 6 inches from a preheated element until lightly browned, 1 to 2 minutes.

1. Position the rack in the center of the oven and preheat to 300°F. Peel 3 of the onions and halve them through their root ends. Lay them on a large sheet of foil and drizzle with the oil. Seal the foil into a tight packet around the onions, place it on a rimmed baking sheet, and bake for 1 hour 30 minutes.

2. Meanwhile, wrap 3 ears of the corn in a double-thick packet of foil. Repeat with the remaining 3 ears. Set the packets over open, medium gas flames on your stovetop; cook for 8 minutes, turning the packets once with long-handled tongs. (Don't have open gas flames? Skip the foil packets and cook the husked ears over direct, high heat on a grill—or broil them on a rimmed baking sheet, 4 to 6 inches from the heat source, until lightly browned on all sides, turning often.) In any event, cool the ears in their packets or on the baking sheet for 10 minutes.

3. Get the corn ears out of the packets (if you've used them) and cut one end off each ear so it'll stand up on its end. Stand them up thusly and slice down the cobs, removing the kernels without taking off too much of the pale-white inner bits.

4. Chop the remaining onion into small bits. Melt the butter in a large saucepan over medium heat. Dump in the chopped onion, bell pepper, and celery. Cook, stirring often, until the onion begins to turn translucent, about 5 minutes. Stir in the oregano, thyme, salt, and black pepper, as well as all those corn kernels. Stir over the heat for 1 minute to render the herbs aromatic.

5. Pour in the wine or vermouth, crank the heat up to high, and bring the liquid to a boil, scraping up any browned bits in the pot with a wooden spoon. Cook for 1 minute. Pour in the broth and bring back to a simmer. Cover, reduce the heat to very low, and simmer for 45 minutes, stirring once in a while.

6. Working in batches, puree the soup in a large blender, adding cream, half-and-half, or milk to each batch. Make sure you take the center knob out of the blender's lid; otherwise, pressure can build up with hot liquids and the thing can spew them all over the kitchen. (Ugh.) But cover that opening with a clean kitchen towel to prevent overflows. Pour the pureed batches into a large bowl as they're pureed, then put everything back in the original pot and return it to a slow simmer over medium heat, just to take the edge off the raw dairy taste.

7. Unwrap the onions that have been roasting in their packet. Set one onion half in each bowl. Ladle the soup on top. Dig in.

TESTERS' NOTES

▪ Although this is a fairly complicated soup, the flavors are elemental enough to highlight the natural sweetness of corn. We kept the herbs to a minimum so the taste is more straightforward. The roasted onions and the slow-cooked corn are the point— although a little browning gives them both some extra notes. Still, you don't want to go too far. The soup shouldn't turn muddy.

▪ If you've got an immersion or stick blender, you can add the dairy and blend the soup right in the pot.

However, you'll never get the soup as creamy as you will in the narrow container of a blender canister. Still, cleanup will be so much easier. You pick your battles where you will. Bring the pureed soup back to a low simmer before moving on to the next step.

▪ Confit usually means that the item has been poached in fat at a low temperature—preserved in fat, as it were. These onions are not a true confit but get soft and luxurious like, say, duck confit.

AVGOLEMONO SOUP WITH CORN GRITS DUMPLINGS

SERVES 4

Active time: 25 minutes
Total time: 1 hour 25 minutes

Make It Vegetarian: Substitute reduced-sodium vegetable broth for the chicken broth.

Dumplings

½ cup whole-grain, medium- or fine-ground corn grits

½ cup whole wheat pastry flour (do not use whole wheat flour)

1 teaspoon baking powder

1 teaspoon salt

½ teaspoon mustard powder

¼ teaspoon grated nutmeg

1 large egg, at room temperature

2 tablespoons almond or vegetable oil

Soup

¼ cup olive oil

2 medium yellow onions, chopped

4 cups chopped, stemmed, washed kale

8 cups fat-free, reduced-sodium chicken broth

2 large eggs

⅓ cup fresh lemon juice

2 tablespoons minced dill fronds or 1 tablespoon dried dillweed

CHEF IT UP!

■ Substitute toasted almond oil for the vegetable oil in the dumplings.

TESTERS' NOTES

■ This is a storied, Greek soup to which we've added corn dumplings made from whole-grain grits. The technique for making them is modeled on that for making matzo balls.

■ If you can't find whole-grain corn grits, you can grind coarse, whole-grain polenta in a blender until it's the consistency of cornmeal.

■ The egg-and-lemon thickener must be whisked into the soup with abandon to keep from making threads of scrambled eggs. For the best results, use a large balloon whisk, not a small, prissy one.

■ Depending on the exact grind of the grits you're using, the dumplings may be quite firm—or actually a little delicate, prone to sharding. Finer grits yield firmer dumplings. It's all a matter of choice and taste, but take extra care with dumplings made with coarser grits. Gently ladle the soup around them in the bowls so they don't fall apart.

1. To make the dumplings: Whisk the grits, flour, baking powder, salt, mustard, and nutmeg in a large bowl. Stir in the egg and oil until the mixture forms a soft, fairly loose dough. Form this mixture into 8 balls. They'll be quite delicate. Set them on a large rimmed baking sheet or in a baking dish, cover with plastic wrap, and refrigerate for at least 20 minutes or up to 1 hour.

2. Meanwhile, make the soup: Heat a Dutch oven over low heat. Swirl in the oil and add the onions. Cook slowly, stirring once in a while, until soft and golden, about 15 minutes.

3. Raise the heat to medium, stir in the kale, and stir over the heat until the greens wilt, about 2 minutes. Pour in the broth, crank the heat up, and bring to a full simmer. Then drop the heat to low again—the barest bubble—and use a slotted spoon to lower the dumplings into the soup. Cover and simmer slowly for 20 minutes.

4. Use that slotted spoon to remove the dumplings to serving bowls. Whisk the 2 eggs, lemon juice, and dill in a small bowl until creamy. Whisk 1 cup of the hot soup into the bowl with the egg mixture until creamy. Remove the pot from the heat and whisk the egg mixture into the soup. Whisk constantly for 1 minute off the heat. Divide the soup among the serving bowls, slathering the delicate dumplings.

KAMUT AND BEEF CHILI

2 cups Kamut

10 dried chiles, preferably a mix
   of hot and mild—like 5 hot
   New Mexican and 5 mild
   New Mexican, or anchos and
   pasillas, or hot New
   Mexicans and guajillos

4 garlic cloves, quartered

2 tablespoons packed fresh
   oregano leaves

1½ teaspoons cumin seeds

1 teaspoon salt

½ teaspoon ground cinnamon

2 tablespoons peanut oil

1 medium yellow onion,
   chopped

2 small cubanelle peppers,
   chopped

2 pounds beef top or bottom
   round, cut into ½-inch cubes

1 bottle (12 ounces) dark beer

2½ cups fat-free, reduced-
   sodium beef broth

SERVES 6

Active time: 35 minutes
Total time: 3 hours, plus soaking the Kamut for at least 8 hours

Make ahead: Store in a covered container in the fridge for a couple of days—or in the freezer for a couple of months.

CHEF IT UP!

- Gussy up the bowls with dollops of sour cream and a sprinkling of minced scallions.

GRAIN SWAPS

- Substitute 2 cups spelt berries or hard red wheat berries for the Kamut.

1. Soak the Kamut in a big bowl of cool water for at least 8 and up to 16 hours.

2. Stem the dried chiles, then open them up and tear out all the seeds and white membranes inside. Tear the skin into small pieces, then set these in a large, dry skillet over medium heat. Toast them, stirring occasionally, until very fragrant, about 2 minutes. Scrape the pieces into a big bowl and cover them with boiling water. Set aside to soak for 20 minutes.

3. Scoop out ½ cup of the soaking water and set it aside. Drain the chiles in a colander set in the sink. Pour them into a food processor. Add the garlic, oregano, cumin seeds, salt, cinnamon, and 2 tablespoons of the reserved soaking liquid. Process to a coarse paste, scraping down the sides of the bowl once in a while to make sure everything takes a spin on the blades. If the mixture is too thick, add more of the reserved soaking liquid until you can get it to blend properly without becoming watery.

4. Heat a large Dutch oven over medium heat. Add the oil, then the onion and cubanelle peppers. Cook, stirring often, until the onion begins to turn translucent, about 4 minutes.

5. Scrape all the chile paste out of the food processor and into the pot. Stir it around over the heat to toast it and develop the flavors for 2 minutes, then stir in the beef. Continue cooking, stirring often, until the beef is browned, about 5 minutes.

6. Pour in the beer. Stir down the foam, also scraping up any browned bits in the pot's interior. Pour in the broth, raise the heat, and bring the mélange to a full simmer.

7. Drain the Kamut in a fine-mesh sieve or small-holed colander set in the sink, then stir the grains into the pot. Bring back to a full simmer. Cover, reduce the heat to low, and cook until the beef and Kamut are tender, about 2 hours. Before serving, set the pot off the heat, covered, for 10 minutes to meld and intensify the flavors.

TESTERS' NOTES

■ There are mavens who claim chili never has beans and those who claim it does. Nobody claims it has Kamut. Which is too bad, because this chewy, hearty grain offers newfangled texture and flavor to the pot.

■ If you've never made your own chile paste for chili, this will start you on the right road. You won't look back. The flavors are so much more intense than those in a bottle of run-of-the-mill powdered chili seasonings.

■ Don't used a flavored dark beer or a bock beer here. You want a somewhat sweet beer like Negro Modelo, Newcastle Brown Ale, or even Guinness Stout.

VEAL AND FARRO STEW

⅔ cup whole-grain farro

3 tablespoons unsalted butter

1 large yellow onion, halved through the root, then cut into thin half-moons

2 pounds boneless veal stew meat, cut into 1-inch cubes

2 teaspoons dried thyme

2 teaspoons dried sage

½ teaspoon salt

½ teaspoon ground black pepper

2 tablespoons whole wheat flour or whole wheat pastry flour

1 cup dry white wine or dry vermouth

1 cup fat-free, reduced-sodium chicken broth

¼ cup low-fat milk, whole milk, half-and-half, or heavy cream

1. Soak the farro in a big bowl of cool water for at least 8 and up to 16 hours. Drain the farro in a fine-mesh sieve or small-holed colander set in the sink. Pour the farro into a large saucepan, fill it about two-thirds of the way with water, and bring to a boil over high heat. Reduce the heat to low and simmer until almost tender, with some chew to each grain, about 1 hour. Drain again in that sieve or colander, then run under cool water until the grains are room temperature. Drain thoroughly.

2. While the farro is cooking, melt the butter in a large pot set over low heat. Add the onion and cook slowly, stirring often, until golden and soft, quite sweet smelling and irresistible, about 7 minutes.

3. Add the veal. Continue cooking, stirring often, until the pieces lose any raw, pink color, about 10 minutes. Raise the heat to medium and stir in the thyme, sage, salt, and pepper. Stir over the heat a few seconds, then add the flour. Stir over the heat until the onion and meat are well coated in the flour and it has just begun to brown in places, about 2 minutes.

SERVES 4

Active time: 40 minutes
Total time: 2 hours 15 minutes, plus soaking the farro for at least 8 hours

Make ahead: Store in a covered container in the fridge for a couple of days—or in the freezer for a couple of months.

Save time: Use 1⅔ cups cooked whole-grain farro and omit soaking and cooking the raw grains.

CHEF IT UP!

▪ Use 4 pounds bone-in veal shoulder chops, cut into 3-inch pieces. Complete the recipe as directed until you're ready to add the cooked farro. At this point, take the pot off the heat and transfer the veal chunks to a cutting board with a slotted spoon. After they've cooled a few minutes, debone the meat and cut it into smaller bits, discarding any bone and cartilage along the way. Strain what's in the pot, catching the liquid in a bowl. Discard all the solids in the strainer (the onion has given up its flavor anyway), then pour the strained liquid back into the pot and add the chunks of veal meat. Bring the mixture back to a simmer over medium heat, then finish the recipe by adding the cooked farro and milk or cream, and simmering the stew for the final few minutes as directed.

4. Stirring all the while, pour in the wine in a slow, steady stream. As it comes back to a simmer, stir well to dissolve the flour and get any of the flavorful, browned bits up off the bottom of the pot. Stir in the broth and bring back to a full simmer.

5. Cover and reduce the heat to low. Simmer slowly until the veal is quite tender, about 1 hour 30 minutes, stirring occasionally to make sure no flour has fallen out of suspension and is burning on the bottom of the pot. If so, reduce the heat further and stir more often.

6. Stir in the drained farro and the dairy product of your choice, depending on how much you intend to hit the gym this week. Raise the heat to medium and bring the mixture back to a full simmer. Cook, uncovered, stirring quite often, until luscious, about 15 minutes.

TESTERS' NOTES

▥ We debated this one: How can a whole-grain book include veal? Seems like matter and anti-matter—or good food politics and bad—all mixed up. In truth, there's lots of humanely raised, local veal out there. We buy ours from a producer at our local farmers' market in Norfolk, Connecticut. The first day we walked up to his table, he seemed relieved. "I never know if people are going to yell at me," he said. There's no debating that much of the veal sold is produced under intolerable circumstances; but there's a renaissance among local producers who are more savvy about their ethics.

▥ Why dried herbs in some recipes and fresh in others? First, it's all about taste. Dried herbs have a more subtle but also more pungent, slightly more bitter taste—and so are balanced by sweet ingredients like the veal in this recipe. Fresh herbs, while more present, are also sweeter, more floral—and so are often balanced by vinegar and the like. Second, it's all about stamina. Dried herbs stand up to long stewing (as here) far better than fresh herbs. Of course, in some cases, because of cooking techniques or more assertive flavors in the mix, the difference between the dried and fresh is rendered negligible; so you're free to choose between them.

SORGHUM SOUP WITH CHILES AND SWEET POTATOES

SERVES 4

Active time: 20 minutes
Total time: 2 hours and 10 minutes, plus soaking the sorghum for at least 8 hours

¾ cup sorghum

2 tablespoons peanut oil

1 medium yellow onion, chopped

2 tablespoons minced fresh ginger

2 jalapeño chiles, seeded and minced

3 Roma (plum) tomatoes, finely chopped

4 cups reduced-sodium vegetable broth

1 sweet potato (10 ounces), peeled and diced

3 tablespoons natural peanut butter

½ teaspoon ground allspice

½ teaspoon salt

¼ teaspoon cayenne pepper

TESTERS' NOTE

■ This stew is based on a central African stew called *ma'afe*, usually made with peanuts and sweet potatoes. Sorghum stands in for a protein, offering its own dry texture and slightly sweet flavor.

1. Soak the sorghum in a big bowl of cool water for at least 8 and up to 16 hours.

2. Heat a large pot over medium heat. Swirl in the peanut oil, then add the onion. Cook, stirring often, until softened, about 5 minutes. Stir in the ginger and jalapeños; cook for 1 minute, stirring most of the time, until ridiculously fragrant.

3. Drop in the tomatoes and cook until they begin to break down, about 3 minutes, stirring quite a bit. Drain the sorghum in a fine-mesh sieve or small-holed colander set in the sink; stir the grains into the pot.

4. Now dump in everything else: the broth, sweet potato, peanut butter, allspice, salt, and cayenne. Bring it to a boil, stirring a lot so that nothing sticks. Cover the pot, drop the heat to low, and simmer very slowly, just a few bubbles at a time, until the sorghum is tender, stirring occasionally, about 1 hour 45 minutes. Watch the liquid level in the pot. If yours is losing too much due to evaporation and a poor-fitting lid, drop the heat as low as you can and add a little more broth.

MILLET, BARLEY, AND SPLIT PEA SOUP WITH COCONUT AND GINGER

Active time: 20 minutes
Total time: 1 hour 20 minutes

CHEF IT UP!

■ Use ghee (clarified butter) instead of unsalted butter.

■ Substitute tamarind concentrate for the lemon juice.

■ Drizzle the bowls of soup with a little basil oil.

TESTERS' NOTES

■ This soup is hearty and filling yet surprisingly light because of the way the millet thickens the broth without weighing it down.

■ The whole spices add lots of complexity to the flavor. No need to remove them from the soup—they'll soften until they're edible. However, if you insist on not having a pop of aromatics in some spoonfuls, seal the cumin seeds, mustard seeds, and crushed cardamom pods in a large tea ball so they can be removed after cooking. Because liquid circulation is impeded by the ball, consider adding a few extra seeds to the mix.

■ The hull-less barley is added to the soup without presoaking so that it will break down a bit during the cooking and offer a luxurious silkiness.

2 tablespoons unsalted butter	½ teaspoon salt
1 small red onion, chopped	¼ teaspoon cayenne pepper
1 tablespoon minced fresh ginger	6 cups reduced-sodium vegetable broth
4 garlic cloves, minced	2 Roma (plum) tomatoes, chopped
¼ cup millet	
1 teaspoon cumin seeds	½ cup yellow split peas
1 teaspoon mustard seeds	½ cup old-fashioned rolled oats (do not use quick-cooking or steel-cut oats)
3 green cardamom pods, crushed into tiny bits in a mortar with a pestle or under a small saucepan on a cutting board	¼ cup hull-less barley
	¾ cup coconut milk (regular or "lite")
½ teaspoon turmeric	1 teaspoon fresh lemon juice

1. Melt the butter in a large pot over medium heat. Dump in the onion and cook, stirring often, until softened, about 4 minutes. Stir in the ginger and garlic and cook for 20 seconds, just until aromatic.

2. Dump in the millet, cumin seeds, mustard seeds, crushed cardamom pods, turmeric, salt, and cayenne. Stir over the heat for 1 minute. Pour in the broth and stir occasionally as it comes up to a full simmer.

3. Stir in the tomatoes, split peas, oats, and barley. Bring back to a full simmer, stirring once in a while. Then cover, reduce the heat to low, and simmer slowly for 45 minutes.

4. Stir in the coconut milk and lemon juice. Cover and continue simmering very slowly until the oats and barley are tender, about 15 minutes.

TURKISH RED LENTIL AND BULGUR SOUP

SERVES 4

Active time: 15 minutes
Total time: 55 minutes

Make ahead: Store in the fridge for up to 3 days—or in the freezer for several months. When you reheat it, if it's too pasty, thin it out with extra broth.

CHEF IT UP!

■ Search out dark, smoky, Turkish black pepper, a decidedly nosy hit.

TESTERS' NOTES

■ This is one of the easiest and most satisfying whole-grain main courses in the book.

■ This classic has as many interpretations as there are Turkish grandmothers. Some say it should include fresh mint; others, dried. Some say it should be spicy; others, not so much. In the end, we felt the mint was a bit overpowering and went with dill for a more savory aroma.

■ Because the bulgur will continue to absorb liquids, you may need to thin the soup out with extra broth when you reheat any leftovers.

2 tablespoon unsalted butter

6 scallions, thinly sliced

½ cup red lentils

½ cup quick-cooking, whole-grain bulgur

4 cups reduced-sodium vegetable broth

½ cup water

2 tablespoons minced dill fronds

1½ tablespoons no-salt-added tomato paste

2 teaspoons fresh thyme leaves or 1 teaspoon dried thyme

1 teaspoon ground black pepper

½ teaspoon salt

1 bay leaf

1. Melt the butter in a large pot. Add the scallions and stir them around until wilted, about 1 minute. Pour in the lentils and bulgur. Stir over the heat for another minute.

2. Add everything else: the broth, water, dill, tomato paste, thyme, pepper, salt, and bay leaf. Bring to a full simmer.

3. Cover, reduce the heat to low, and simmer slowly until somewhat thickened and concentrated, about 40 minutes, stirring occasionally to make sure nothing's sticking. Fish out and discard the bay leaf before serving.

HONEST-TO-GOODNESS POSOLE VERDE

SERVES 6

Active time: 45 minutes
Total time: 21 hours

10 cups water

⅓ cup food-grade pickling lime

1½ cups dried hominy

3 tablespoons olive oil

2¼ pounds bone-in pork stew meat or bone-in pork shoulder, cut into 3- to 4-inch chunks

1 medium yellow onion, chopped

2 poblano chiles, seeded and chopped

3 garlic cloves, minced

1½ pounds fresh tomatillos, husked and chopped

4 cups fat-free, reduced-sodium chicken broth

Up to ½ cup minced fresh cilantro

1 tablespoon minced fresh oregano leaves or 2 teaspoons dried oregano

1½ teaspoons ground cumin

1 teaspoon salt

Juice of 1 lime

MAKE IT EASIER!

- Omit the whole complicated process of making the hominy. Instead, use 3 cups canned hominy, drained and rinsed; start the soup by cooking the onion and carry on from there, adding the canned hominy where you would have added the home-cooked version.

CHEF IT UP!

- Use lard or rendered duck fat, rather than olive oil.

- Use unsmoked pork hocks or shanks for the meat. Since the bones are bigger in these cuts, you might want to use a little more— say 2¾ pounds.

1. Combine the water and pickling lime in a large stockpot and stir over high heat until the lime dissolves. Bring the mixture to a full boil, then cover and let it stand off the heat for 4 hours. Set a fine-mesh sieve or a colander lined with a large coffee filter over a big bowl; slowly pour in the contents of the pot to strain out the scum—however, stop pouring when you reach the white grainy sludge in the bottom of the pot. Discard what's in both the strainer and the pot. Wash the pot. Pour the strained liquid back into the pot.

2. Add the hominy and bring it all to a full boil over high heat. Turn off the heat, cover the pot, and set it aside for at least 12 and up to 18 hours.

3. Bring it back to a boil and simmer until the hominy is tender, 2 hours 30 minutes to 3 hours. Drain in a colander set in the sink and rinse under cold water. As the water runs over the hominy kernels, rub them between your hands to get rid of the little bits of translucent outer hull, about like tiny insect wings. Rinse the hominy well to get rid of any residual pickling lime; set aside. The brown germ on the kernels should be kept—it's delicious!

(continued)

4. Wash and dry the stockpot, then set it back over medium heat. Add the oil, then the meat. Brown the meat on all sides, taking care to turn the pieces with long-handled tongs so as not to break them up or tear them too much. It'll take 8 to 10 minutes to get the meat well browned on all sides. Transfer the pieces to a large plate.

5. Add the onion to the pot and cook, stirring often, until softened somewhat, about 4 minutes. Add the chiles and garlic; stir over the heat about 1 minute—then dump in all the tomatillos. Continue stirring over the heat until they soften and begin to break down, about 8 minutes.

6. Pour in the broth. Stir in the drained hominy and the browned meat, as well as any accumulated juices on that plate, plus the cilantro, oregano, cumin, and salt. Bring to a full simmer, stirring occasionally. Cover, reduce the heat to low, and simmer slowly until the meat is falling off the bone, up to 3 hours.

7. Fish the meat out of the pot with a slotted spoon. Cool for a few minutes, then remove the bones and chop up the remaining meat. Stir this back into the pot with the lime juice. As the pot comes back up to a good simmer just before you ladle it up, check to see if it needs additional salt—or pass more on the side at the table.

TESTERS' NOTES

▥ This is the real deal, no half-hearted effort: soaking dried field corn (or hominy), then softening it, cooking it, and turning it into a rich soup. Yep, it takes forever—which is why we call dishes like this "bubbe meals." Or in this case, "abuela meals." As we've said, some recipes should be aspirational; but we do hope you'll give this one a try sometime when you want to be very creative in the kitchen. Your reward will be a hearty rib-sticker that's sure to please just about everyone.

▥ Pickling lime—a.k.a. powdered calcium hydroxide or sometimes called "slaked lime"—is an inorganic compound long used in food production. It is used to make the Norwegian "delicacy" lutefisk and sometimes used in home canning to preserve pickles (hence, the name). You can find food-grade pickling lime at most high-end cookware stores and from many suppliers online.

▥ You can substitute skinless, bone-in chicken thighs for the pork; just cook them for about 2 hours instead of 3. No need to cut the thighs into smaller chunks, but do remove the meat from the bones at the end of cooking to make it more a soup suitable for spoons only.

▥ Homemade posole is a great holiday feast with tortillas and lots of garnishes: fresh tomato salsa, diced avocados, thinly sliced scallions, chopped radishes, sour cream, and grated cheese.

Active time: 20 minutes
Total time: 1 hour 30 minutes

Make It Vegan: Substitute reduced-sodium vegetable broth for the chicken broth.

CHEF IT UP!

▦ Use rendered chicken fat (a.k.a schmaltz) instead of the peanut oil.

▦ Of course, any grandmother worth her salt would make her own stock for this soup. If you want to have a go at it, cut up a whole chicken and put it in a pot with a couple of quartered onions, a few celery stalks, and a few black peppercorns. Fill the pot with water, then bring it to a boil over high heat. Reduce the heat so the water simmers very slowly—slowly enough, in fact, that you can count the bubbles as they form—and cook until reduced by one-third, about 3 hours. Strain out and discard all the chicken, vegetables, and peppercorns. Voilà: chicken stock.

TESTERS' NOTES

▦ Kasha varnishkes are a deli favorite: buckwheat pasta, toasted buckwheat groats (kasha), and caramelized onions. Here, we morphed it into a main-course soup.

▦ If you don't have kasha on hand, or if you can't find it at a kosher market or a high-end supermarket, toast regular buckwheat groats in a dry skillet over medium-low heat, stirring often, until golden and fragrant.

KASHA VARNISHKES SOUP

2 tablespoons peanut oil

2 large yellow onions, chopped

2 medium parsnips, peeled and diced

2 cups coarse kasha or toasted buckwheat groats

3 garlic cloves, minced

1 tablespoon fresh thyme leaves or 1½ teaspoons dried thyme

1 tablespoon minced fresh sage leaves

½ teaspoon ground allspice

½ cup dry sherry

8 cups fat-free, reduced-sodium chicken broth

4 ounces dried whole wheat farfalle (that is, bow-tie) pasta

½ teaspoon salt

½ teaspoon ground black pepper

1. Heat a large Dutch oven or soup pot over very low heat. Add the oil, then the onions and parsnips. Cook very slowly, stirring often, until the onions are gold and quite soft, caramelized and sweet, about 40 minutes. If they begin to brown too much or even singe, drop the heat even further.

2. Raise the heat to medium and pour in the kasha. Stir as the pot heats up to a good sizzle, then stir in the garlic, thyme, sage, and allspice. Cook, stirring all the while, about 30 seconds.

3. Stir in the sherry; scrape up any browned, tasty bits inside the pot. Pour in the broth, raise the heat to medium-high, and bring the soup to a full simmer. Cover, reduce the heat back to low, and simmer slowly for 30 minutes.

4. Stir in the pasta and cook until tender but with a little chew at the center of each piece, 7 to 8 minutes. Stir in the salt and pepper just before serving.

CASSEROLE COMFORT

Trends may come and go; the one about comfort food has been around for a while. We should know. We penned our first magazine article in early March, 2000. Since magazines work at least 6 months in advance, the article was all about leftover turkey: what to do with it after the holiday feast. We submitted 30 or so recipe concepts to our editor. Mind you, this was a high-end magazine. We were sure she'd want some Thai dishes, some Brazilian preparations.

"Think mac-and-cheese with turkey," she replied. "Chicken soup, too. But make it turkey soup. With rice."

We were a little surprised. Those old ideas?

But the dot-com bubble was just starting to burst. "Let's give them comfort food," she said.

We did. And do we need to remind you of what's happened since? More stock market woes, 9/11, several wars, a housing crash, crushing unemployment. Suffice it to say, comfort food isn't going anywhere.

But what is it exactly? Most of us would say "gooey." Maybe "cheesy." Probably baked. Most likely in a casserole dish. Big tastes. Rich. And nostalgic.

Whole grains sure fit this bill. They absorb big flavors like sponges, muting and morphing them into a more tantalizing balance. You might not think of gooey cheese and whole grains together—but in that case, you'd have missed something quite astounding. Whole grains mellow the cheese's acidity, balancing it without overpowering it. You probably already know what a pat of butter can do for a bowl of brown rice or a pile of spelt berries. With cheese, you're working with the flavors of dairy squared—or cubed.

And that's not all. Whole grains are also robust. Substantial, too. You get a lot of comfort for your money.

It's too bad that so many comfort foods are made with refined grains: regular spaghetti or white rice. It's as if the old recipes went part of the way, then stopped. They should have pressed on—because as you now know, whole grains are the original comfort food. When you try the Baked Wheat Berries, Barley, and Cheese casserole (page 163), the Teff Gnocchi in a Cheddar Sauce (page 164), or the Celery Root and Sorghum Gratin (page 157), you'll understand why whole grains should never have become the forgotten ingredient.

That said, we do have one caution before you get started. Some grain casseroles don't make great leftover fare. They absorb too much moisture, even after cooking. Teff, millet, and amaranth do so rather famously. These can render a casserole dry the next day—or even a few hours after it comes out of the oven. Best then to eat these dishes piping hot.

Or squirrel away individual servings in the freezer to be reheated some time in the future. The deep chill will slow down that moisture absorption so the dish will be tastier in the long run. And add a little more liquid when you reheat portions in the oven or the microwave.

There's no use fighting the inevitable. You might as well compensate for it and have a better meal.

Maybe some day we can even enjoy comfort food without needing the comfort. We can make no promises that any of us will be doing that any time in the future. But we can always hope.

CASSEROLE COMFORT

JAPANESE-INSPIRED BROWN RICE AND MILLET CASSEROLE

3 tablespoons toasted sesame oil

5 ounces shiitake mushrooms, stems discarded, caps thinly sliced

1 medium shallot, chopped

1 tablespoon minced fresh ginger

2 garlic cloves, minced

1 cup medium-grain brown rice

½ cup millet

¼ cup soy sauce (regular or reduced-sodium)

¼ cup mirin

3 cups reduced-sodium vegetable broth

1 sweet potato (10 ounces), peeled and diced into 1-inch bits

1½ cups shelled edamame (no need to thaw if frozen)

1½ cups jarred peeled chestnuts

1. Position the rack in the center of the oven and preheat to 350°F. One warning: You'll need to make this dish in a 2½- to 3-quart flameproof casserole or a large Dutch oven (or French oven). Those latter pots, when covered, may well be too big to sit on your oven rack without lid decapitation. Make any necessary adjustments but be sure the rack is situated as close to the center of the oven as possible while leaving a couple of inches of air space over the top of the pot.

2. Heat whichever pot you choose over medium heat, then swirl in the sesame oil. Add the mushrooms and shallot. Stir these around just until they start to soften, about 2 minutes. Add the ginger and garlic; continue stirring until aromatic, maybe 30 seconds or so.

3. Dump in the brown rice and millet. Stir over the heat to get the grains coated in the fat and liquids. Pour in the soy sauce and mirin. As they come to a full bubble, scrape up any browned bits that have glommed onto the pot's interior bottom.

4. Pour in the broth, then stir in the sweet potato, edamame, and chestnuts. Crank up the heat and bring to a simmer, stirring every once in a while to make sure the millet doesn't stick.

5. Cover the pot and slide it into the oven. Bake until the liquid has been absorbed and the rice is tender, about 1 hour. Turn the oven off and leave the covered pot in there to steam for 15 minutes (or up to 1 hour if the timing for your dinner has not been impeccable).

SERVES 6

Active time: 20 minutes
Total time: 1 hour 40 minutes

Make ahead: Store, covered, in the fridge for up to a day or two. Scoop out and reheat individual servings with a little added vegetable broth in the microwave.

TESTERS' NOTES

▥ Every autumn, many Japanese cooks celebrate the first of the *shinmai* (新米 or "new rice") with a comfort-food mash-up of rice, shiitakes, sweet potatoes, and chestnuts. The traditional dish can be cloyingly sweet since the chestnuts are often soaked in a teeth-aching sugar syrup. We've morphed this Japanese standard into a more savory casserole. We've also added edamame because they lighten the dish considerably, both in color and taste.

▥ Mirin is a sweetened Japanese rice wine. You can find it in the Asian aisle of almost any supermarket—and certainly in any Asian grocery store. If possible, avoid bottlings laced with corn syrup and monosodium glutamate, both used to mask the off notes of inferior bottlings.

CELERY ROOT AND SORGHUM GRATIN

SERVES 6

Active time: 45 minutes

Total time: 3 hours, plus soaking the sorghum for at least 8 hours

Make ahead: Individual servings freeze beautifully for a couple of months.

Save time: Use 1 cup cooked sorghum and omit the soaking and cooking of the raw grains.

CHEF IT UP!

- Stir up to 2 tablespoons minced tarragon into the milky sauce.

- Substitute shredded Comté or raclette for the Gruyère.

TESTERS' NOTES

- Sliced celery root offers a more aromatic balance to the starchy, mellow sorghum in this otherwise classic gratin.

- Have a crunchy salad on the side, but avoid any creamy dressings so that there's no competition with this ooey-gooey main course.

½ cup sorghum

1 (2-pound) celery root

2 tablespoons unsalted butter, plus more for greasing the pan

6 scallions, white and light green parts only, minced

2 tablespoons whole wheat flour or whole wheat pastry flour

1½ cups milk (whole, 2%, 1%, or even fat-free), divided

½ cup dry white wine or dry vermouth

2 ounces Gruyère, shredded

1 teaspoon ground black pepper

1. Soak the sorghum in a big bowl of cool water for at least 8 and up to 16 hours. Drain it in a fine-mesh sieve or small-holed colander set in the sink. Pour the grains into a large saucepan, swamp it with plenty of water, and bring to a boil over high heat. Reduce the heat to low and cook until fairly tender, about 1 hour 45 minutes. Sorghum will retain a grainy, starchy texture, even when fully cooked; however, the individual grains should still be tender to the bite.

2. Meanwhile, peel the celery root. Sounds easy but isn't. Use a vegetable peeler to get off some of the tough, outside bits, then switch to a paring knife to get off the last of the peel as well as any hairy roots in the pits and cracks. Cut the big knob into quarters, then cut these into ⅛-inch-thick slices. You can do that in several ways: with a food processor and a ⅛-inch slicing blade, with a mandoline set for ⅛-inch slices, or with a very sharp chef's knife.

3. Bring a second large saucepan of water to a boil over high heat. Add the celery root slices and blanch them for 5 minutes. (Don't want to dirty another pot? You can add them to the bubbling water in the sorghum pot, but you'll have to work in batches and you'll need a slotted spoon to get them out without disturbing the cooking grains. Maybe two pots isn't so much trouble after all.) Drain the celery root slices in a colander set in the sink; run under cool water.

(continued)

4. Dump the celery root slices out of the colander and onto a cutting board, then drain the sorghum in that colander set in the sink. Now you're ready to make the gratin.

5. Position the rack in the center of the oven and preheat to 400°F. Lightly butter a 9 × 13-inch baking dish.

6. Melt 2 tablespoons butter in a large skillet over medium heat, then add the scallions. Cook just until wilted a bit, about 1 minute, stirring all the while. Stir in the flour, coating the scallions as they continue to cook.

7. Whisk in 1 cup of the milk in a slow, steady stream. Since you're working with whole wheat flour, you'll need to pour the milk in more slowly and whisk more in line with the courage of your whole-grain convictions. Continue whisking until thickened and bubbling, then whisk in the wine or vermouth as well as the Gruyère. Remove the skillet from the heat.

8. Layer one-third of the celery root pieces in the prepared baking dish, overlapping the slices as necessary to make sure the bottom is fully covered. Spread one-third of the sauce over these slices, then sprinkle with half the sorghum. Now repeat the layering: half the remaining celery root slices, half the remaining sauce, and all of the remaining sorghum. Finally, layer the remaining celery root slices on top and shellac the whole thing with the remaining sauce. Pour the remaining ½ cup milk over the casserole and sprinkle it with the pepper.

9. Bake until golden brown and bubbling at the edges, about 45 minutes. Cool on a rack for 10 minutes before cutting the casserole into gooey squares or rectangles to serve.

WILD RICE AND VEGETABLE BIRYANI

2 cups wild rice

2 tablespoons ghee or clarified butter

1 medium yellow onion, chopped

2 red bell peppers, seeded and chopped

Up to 2 tablespoons minced fresh ginger

2 garlic cloves, minced

1 pound cauliflower florets

1 pound sliced okra (no need to thaw if frozen)

1 eggplant (12 ounces), diced

2 tablespoons curry powder

1 tablespoon garam masala

½ teaspoon salt

½ teaspoon ground black pepper

1 cup reduced-sodium vegetable broth

½ cup plain yogurt (whole-milk or low-fat)

2 tablespoons fresh lime juice

½ cup chopped fresh cilantro

½ cup chopped pecans

1. Rinse the wild rice thoroughly in a sieve, then pour it into a large saucepan. Add lots of water, covering the wild rice by at least 3 inches. Bring it all to a boil over high heat. Reduce the heat and simmer steadily until the grains are tender without splitting open, about 50 minutes. Drain in a small-holed colander set in the sink.

2. Position the rack in the center of the oven and preheat to 375°F.

3. Melt the ghee or butter in a large saucepan over medium heat. Add the onion, bell peppers, ginger, and garlic. Cook, stirring almost constantly so the ginger and garlic don't singe, until the onion softens a bit, about 5 minutes.

4. Stir in the cauliflower, okra, and eggplant. Toss over the heat for a couple of minutes.

SERVES 8

Active time: 40 minutes
Total time: 2 hours 40 minutes

Make ahead: Store the cooled casserole, covered, in the fridge for up to 3 days.

Save time: Use 7 cups cooked wild rice and omit soaking and cooking the raw grains.

CHEF IT UP!

- After baking, remove the casserole from the oven and set the rack 4 to 6 inches from the broiler heat source. Preheat the broiler. Brush the top of the casserole with about 2 tablespoons melted ghee, then place it under the broiler to crisp the top, about 4 minutes. One warning: To do this, the baking pan must be broilerproof. And don't turn the casserole upside down on a platter if you've gone to the trouble of creating a crunchy top.

- Omit the curry powder and garam masala; instead, use 1 tablespoon ground coriander, 1½ teaspoons ground turmeric, 1 teaspoon ground cumin, 1 teaspoon mild paprika, 1 teaspoon fennel seeds, ¾ teaspoon ground cinnamon, ½ teaspoon ground allspice, and ¼ teaspoon cayenne.

5. Mix in the curry powder, garam masala, salt, and black pepper. Stir a few times before adding the broth, yogurt, and lime juice. Stir well; bring the whole mélange to a simmer. Cover the pot, reduce the heat to low, and simmer slowly until the vegetables are quite tender, about 20 minutes, stirring once in a while. Stir in the cilantro and pecans.

6. Spread one-third of the cooked wild rice in the bottom of a 9 × 13-inch baking dish. Spoon and spread half the veggie mixture over the rice, taking care not to displace the grains. Top the veggies with half the remaining wild rice, smoothing it out to make an even layer, then top that with all the remaining vegetable mixture, again creating an even layer without disturbing those below. Finally, spread the remaining wild rice over the top of the dish.

7. Cover with parchment paper, then foil, and bake until hot, steaming, and bubbling at the edges of the pan, about 45 minutes. Uncover and let stand at room temperature for 5 minutes before either dishing it up into bowls with a big spoon or (the more traditional way) turning the whole thing upside down onto a large platter to scoop up servings at the table.

TESTERS' NOTES

▦ Wild rice offers more complex flavors than white rice—nutty, even grassy undertones—so the vegetables and spices need to be pumped to balance the dish.

▦ If you can't find ghee or clarified butter, use unsalted butter but reduce the heat under the saucepan a tad to make sure the butter doesn't burn.

▦ Because of the acid in the dish—the yogurt and lime juice, particularly—you shouldn't let the foil touch the casserole directly. A sheet of parchment paper on top will put a barrier between the two—and you'll still be able to seal the casserole tightly with the foil. When you lift the foil and parchment to check on the casserole, make sure you seal it all tightly again if the dish needs further cooking.

BAKED RED RICE CASSEROLE WITH AN EGG-AND-CHEESE CRUST

2 tablespoons olive oil

1 yellow onion (8 to 10 ounces), chopped

1 can (28 ounces) no-salt-added diced tomatoes, drained

1 garlic clove, minced

2 tablespoons minced fresh dill or 1 tablespoon dried dillweed

½ teaspoon ground cinnamon

1 cup long-grain red rice, such as Camargue red rice

2 cups reduced-sodium vegetable broth

½ teaspoon salt

1 package (10 ounces) frozen chopped spinach, thawed and squeezed in handfuls over the sink to remove excess water

4 large eggs, at room temperature

2 ounces Parmigiano-Reggiano, finely grated

1. Position the rack in the center of the oven and preheat to 350°F.

2. Heat a 10-inch round covered cast iron skillet or covered 3-quart flameproof casserole (neither with a cover right now) over medium-low heat. Swirl in the oil, reduce the heat to low, and add the onion. Cook, stirring often, until lightly browned and sweet smelling, about 10 minutes.

3. Raise the heat to medium and stir in the tomatoes, garlic, dill, and cinnamon. Stir over the heat until the tomatoes begin to break down a bit, about 3 minutes.

4. Add the rice and stir for 1 minute. Add the broth and salt. Raise the heat to medium-high and bring to a full simmer. Sprinkle the spinach over the top but do not stir it in. Cover the pan, place it in the oven, and bake until the liquid has been absorbed and the rice is tender, about 45 minutes.

5. Meanwhile, whisk the eggs and cheese in a large bowl until creamy. When the rice is ready, uncover the skillet or the casserole and pour this egg mixture evenly all over the top.

6. Continue baking, uncovered this time, until the eggs are set and even lightly browned in spots, about 8 minutes. Cool on a rack for a couple of minutes before dishing it up by the spoonful.

SERVES 4

Active time: 30 minutes
Total time: 1 hour 20 minutes

GRAIN SWAPS

▪ Substitute wild rice for the red rice; increase the broth to 2½ cups and the cooking time to about 55 minutes.

TESTERS' NOTES

▪ The egg crust sets up over the rice, sort of like an omelet over its filling. You might also consider this the perfect dish for a weekend brunch.

▪ Consider serving this Mediterranean-ish casserole with peeled, sliced oranges, drizzled with balsamic and sprinkled with crunchy salt.

SERVES 6

Active time: 20 minutes
Total time: 2 hours, plus soaking the grains for at least 8 hours

Make ahead: Cover the casserole and squirrel it in the fridge for up to 4 days.

TESTERS' NOTES

■ Consider this a whole-grains version of mac-and-cheese.

■ Because barley gets gummy as it cooks, make sure you've got plenty of water in the saucepan with the wheat berries to avoid any sticking. If you notice the water getting too low or the grains beginning to glom together, add more water and bring it back to a full boil over high heat before reducing the heat to low for a slow simmer again.

■ Don't stop working that whisk—the flour must dissolve to avoid lumps.

BAKED WHEAT BERRIES, BARLEY, AND CHEESE

½ cup wheat berries, preferably soft white wheat berries

¼ cup hull-less barley

2 tablespoons unsalted butter, plus more for greasing the baking dish

1 medium yellow onion, chopped

2 tablespoons whole wheat flour or whole wheat pastry flour

2 cups milk (whole, 2%, 1%, or fat-free)

3 ounces shredded Cheddar, divided

1½ ounces finely grated Parmigiano-Reggiano, divided

2 teaspoons minced fresh tarragon leaves or 1 teaspoon dried tarragon

1 teaspoon Dijon mustard

½ teaspoon ground black pepper

1. Soak the wheat berries and barley together in a big bowl of cool water for at least 8 and up to 16 hours. Drain the grains in a fine-mesh sieve or small-holed colander set in the sink. Pour the grains into a large saucepan, fill it about three-quarters of the way with water, and bring to a boil over high heat. Reduce the heat to low and simmer until tender but with a little chew in the bite, about 55 minutes. Drain again in that sieve or colander.

2. Position the rack in the center of the oven and preheat to 350°F. Lightly butter a 9-inch square baking dish.

3. Melt 2 tablespoons butter in a large saucepan over medium heat. Add the onion; soften, stirring often, for about 5 minutes.

4. Whisk in the flour until it coats the onion pieces; cook for 30 seconds. Then whisk in the milk in a thin stream. Once all the milk is in the pan, keep cooking, whisking almost constantly, until the mixture bubbles and thickens, about 3 minutes.

5. Whisk in 2½ ounces Cheddar, 1 ounce Parmigiano-Reggiano, the tarragon, Dijon mustard, and pepper until the cheese melts. Then whisk in the drained grains. Pour this mixture into the prepared pan. Top with the remaining Cheddar and Parmigiano-Reggiano, sprinkling both evenly over the casserole.

6. Bake until bubbling and irresistible, about 30 minutes. Cool on a wire rack for 10 minutes before serving.

TEFF GNOCCHI IN A CHEDDAR SAUCE

Gnocchi

¾ pound russet potatoes (about 2 medium)

1⅓ cups water

⅓ cup teff, preferably brown teff

1 cup whole wheat flour, plus a little more for dusting the work surface (do not use whole wheat pastry flour)

2 large egg yolks, at room temperature

Unsalted butter for greasing the baking dish

Sauce

2 tablespoons unsalted butter

2 tablespoons whole wheat flour

1 cup milk (whole, 2%, or 1%)

¾ cup dry white wine or dry vermouth

½ cup reduced-sodium vegetable broth

2 teaspoons Dijon mustard

2 teaspoons Worcestershire sauce

1 tablespoon minced fresh tarragon leaves or 2 teaspoons dried tarragon

¼ teaspoon grated nutmeg

4 ounces Cheddar, finely grated

SERVES 4

Active time: 1 hour
Total time: 3 hours

Make ahead: Make the entire recipe start to finish, then cover it and freeze the dish for a couple of months. After thawing in the fridge for a day or two, pour extra broth in the pan to a depth of an inch or so, cover the casserole, and rewarm it in a preheated 325°F oven for 15 to 20 minutes.

Make It Vegetarian: Use vegan-friendly Worcestershire sauce.

CHEF IT UP!

■ Search for aged white Cheddar, less oily and more grainy, with a bit of a sour kick in its flavor profile. Or try an aged goat Gouda instead of the Cheddar.

TESTERS' NOTES

▥ Only russet potatoes have the right starch/moisture balance to make soft, pillowy dumplings.

▥ Teff is a notorious moisture vacuum. Because of that, these little dumplings cannot be made in advance but need to be cooked fairly quickly.

1. To make the gnocchi: Position the rack in the center of the oven and preheat to 400°F. Place the potatoes directly on the baking rack and bake until soft to the touch, between 1 hour and 1 hour 15 minutes.

2. Meanwhile, bring the water to a boil in a small saucepan over high heat. Stir in the teff, reduce the heat to low, and simmer until thickened and almost all the water has been absorbed, about 10 minutes, stirring almost constantly. Cover the saucepan and set it aside while the potatoes continue to bake.

3. Once they're ready, cool the potatoes just until you can handle them. (Leave the oven on.) Halve the potatoes lengthwise. You can either scoop the flesh into a potato ricer and press it through the holes into a large bowl or put it into a fine-mesh sieve and press it through the mesh with the back of a wooden spoon.

(continued)

4. Stir in the cooked teff, the flour, and egg yolks to form a fairly stiff dough. Knead it a few times in the bowl, adding just a touch more flour if you find it's too sticky.

5. Sprinkle more flour on a clean, dry work surface. Break off a piece of the dough about the size of a large egg. Roll it in the flour until it's a log about ½ inch in diameter and 6 to 8 inches long. Sprinkle with more flour to make sure nothing's sticky. Cut the log into 1-inch pieces and place them on a flour-dusted baking sheet. Repeat this process until you've used up all the dough.

6. Bring a large pot of water to a boil over high heat. Meanwhile, lightly butter a 9 × 13-inch baking dish or 10-inch oval gratin dish.

7. Reduce the heat so the water simmers gently and stir in half the teff gnocchi. Stir gently in the pot until they all float, maybe 1 to 2 minutes—then simmer for 1 more minute. Drain with a slotted spoon and transfer to the prepared baking dish. Repeat, cooking the remaining gnocchi and adding them to the baking dish. Make sure you end up with a single layer of gnocchi in the dish.

8. To make the sauce: Melt the butter in a medium saucepan over medium heat. Whisk in the flour, cook for 30 seconds, and then whisk in the milk in a slow, steady stream to make sure the flour dissolves. Whisk in the wine and broth. Continue whisking over the heat until the mixture thickens somewhat.

9. Whisk in the mustard, Worcestershire sauce, tarragon, nutmeg, and all but about ¼ cup of the Cheddar. Continue whisking until the cheese melts, just a few seconds. Pour the sauce over the gnocchi in the baking dish. Sprinkle the reserved cheese on top.

10. Bake until bubbling and lightly browned, about 20 minutes. Cool on a rack for 5 minutes before dishing up.

MILLET AND SPINACH CASSEROLE

Active time: 30 minutes
Total time: 1 hour 50 minutes

Make ahead: Store, covered, in the fridge for up to 3 days. Reheat slices in the microwave or serve them cold.

TESTERS' NOTE

This dish is a millet reinterpretation of spanakopita, the Greek savory pie of spinach, feta, and other aromatics, baked under a flaky crust. In this case, the millet on top will dry out and form a crust, a lot of crunch to offset the soft spinach inside.

1 cup millet

1 tablespoon minced dill fronds

½ teaspoon salt

½ teaspoon ground black pepper

2 tablespoons olive oil, plus more for greasing the baking dish

3 garlic cloves, slivered

½ teaspoon red pepper flakes

1 pound fresh spinach, stemmed, washed, but not dried

1 large egg, separated, plus 1 large egg yolk

2 ounces feta

½ cup parsley leaves

¼ cup unseasoned dried whole wheat bread crumbs

1 tablespoon packed fresh oregano leaves

¼ teaspoon grated nutmeg

1. Place the millet in a large saucepan and fill it about halfway with water. Bring to a boil over high heat, then reduce the heat and cook until the grains are tender but still a little chewy, about 12 minutes. Drain in a fine-mesh sieve or a colander lined with a coffee filter, paper towels, or cheesecloth. Return the millet to the pan; stir in the dill, salt, and black pepper. Set aside.

2. Heat a large pot over medium heat. Swirl in the 2 tablespoons oil, then add the garlic and red pepper flakes. Stir over the heat just until the garlic begins to brown at the edges, about 2 minutes.

3. Add all the spinach. Wilt it over the heat, stirring often, about 2 minutes, until fairly soft. Set the pot off the heat and cool for a minute or so.

4. Use tongs to pick up small clumps of the spinach and squeeze dry, letting the liquid fall back into the pot, transferring the spinach to a food processor as you work. When all the spinach has been squeezed dry, fish out any red pepper flakes and garlic left in the pot and add these to the food processor as well.

(continued)

5. Bring the liquid remaining in the pot to a boil over high heat. Continue boiling until it reduces to a concentrated glaze, a couple of minutes, maybe a few more, depending on how much liquid you started out with. Pour this glaze into the food processor. Cool for 15 minutes.

6. Meanwhile, position the rack in the center of the oven and preheat to 350°F. Grease a 9-inch square baking dish with a little olive oil on a wadded-up paper towel.

7. Add the 2 egg yolks, the feta, parsley, bread crumbs, oregano, and nutmeg to the food processor. Process until well blended but not a smooth puree, more like a coarse pesto.

8. Mix the egg white into the millet mixture in the pan. Spoon and spread half this millet mélange into the prepared baking dish. Top with all the spinach mixture, making a flat, even layer. Spoon and spread the rest of the millet on top, sealing it to the edges.

9. Bake until lightly browned, about 45 minutes. Cool on a rack for 10 minutes before serving.

Active time: 25 minutes
Total time: 1 hour 35 minutes

Make ahead: Freeze individual servings in small, sealable containers that can be microwaved for lunch.

TESTERS' NOTES

▪ Talk about winter comfort food: a fairly traditional corn pudding with ham in the mix. We felt it needed the jalapeños to balance all the creaminess, but you can leave them out if you're too Protestant for the heat or want a thoroughly unctuous meal.

▪ Buy one big chunk of smoked ham from the deli, not slices. That way, you can dice it into small cubes at home, each about the same size as a kernel of corn.

▪ When you're buying smoked ham, remember that no part of a pig looks like a football. If the ham at the deli counter does, it was processed and extruded. Go for the roasted smoked ham, the one that looks like the back end of a pig. Otherwise, find another supermarket where they offer a better deli selection.

HAM AND CORN PUDDING

6 ears of corn, husked

6 tablespoons unsalted butter, plus more for greasing the baking dish

6 medium shallots, minced

1 or 2 jalapeño chiles, seeded and minced

½ teaspoon cumin seeds

½ pound smoked ham, chopped

5 large eggs, beaten in a small bowl until smooth

2 cups milk (whole, 2%, 1%, or fat-free)

8 ounces ricotta (whole-milk or part-skim)

½ cup finely ground whole-grain cornmeal

12 fresh basil leaves, minced

2 ounces Parmigiano-Reggiano, finely grated

1. Cook the corn in a grill pan over medium-high heat or on a baking sheet 4 to 6 inches from a preheated broiler, turning occasionally, until lightly browned, about 5 minutes. Cool a few minutes, then slice off one end of each ear so it will stand up straight on a cutting board. Run a sharp knife down the ears to remove the kernels. Discard the cobs.

2. Position the rack in the center of the oven and preheat to 375°F. Grease a 9-inch square baking pan with a little butter on a wadded-up paper towel or piece of wax paper.

3. Melt the 6 tablespoons butter in a large skillet over medium heat. Add the shallots, jalapeño(s), and cumin seeds. Cook, stirring often, until the shallots begin to soften, about 5 minutes.

4. Stir in the ham and toss about 2 minutes over the heat to warm it up. Stir in the corn, then dump and scrape everything into a big bowl. Cool for 10 minutes.

5. Stir the beaten eggs, milk, ricotta, cornmeal, and basil into the corn mixture. Blend it all together, then pour it into the prepared pan. Top with the Parmigiano-Reggiano and bake until set and lightly browned, 40 to 45 minutes. Cool on a rack for a few minutes before serving it up by the big spoonfuls.

SERVES 8

Active time: 30 minutes
Total time: 1 hour 20 minutes

Make ahead: Freeze individual servings for up to 3 months.

MAKE IT EASIER!

▧ Forego the topping altogether and use frozen puff pastry dough, available in boxes at your supermarket. Thaw a sheet as directed on the package, then roll it on a lightly floured surface to smooth it out and make it slightly thinner. Cut it into shapes to fit as a mosaic across the top of the casserole.

CHEF IT UP!

▧ You can use a mix of fairly quick cooking, springtime vegetables, rather than the frozen ones. You'll need 2 pounds diced onions, bell peppers, asparagus, green beans, broccoli florets, cauliflower florets, and/or sugar snap peas. For even cooking, make sure you cut even the florets into very small pieces.

VEGETABLE AND GRITS POT PIE

Filling

Unsalted butter for greasing the baking dish

3½ cups reduced-sodium vegetable broth

2 teaspoons fresh thyme leaves or 1 teaspoon dried thyme

1 teaspoon minced fresh marjoram leaves or ½ teaspoon dried marjoram

½ teaspoon salt

½ teaspoon ground black pepper

½ cup amaranth

¼ cup millet grits

20 ounces frozen mixed vegetables, thawed

¼ cup light or heavy cream

Biscuit topping

1½ cups whole wheat pastry flour, plus more for dusting a work surface (do not use whole wheat flour)

3 tablespoons finely grated Parmigiano-Reggiano

2 teaspoons baking powder

¼ teaspoon grated nutmeg

6 tablespoons light or heavy cream, plus more for brushing the biscuits

6 tablespoons unsalted butter, melted and cooled to room temperature

1. Position the rack in the center of the oven and preheat to 375°F. Lightly grease a 9 × 13-inch baking dish with a little butter on a wadded-up paper towel or piece of wax paper. Make sure you get into the corners and along the seams.

2. To make the filling: Combine the broth, thyme, marjoram, salt, and pepper in a large saucepan and bring to a full simmer over high heat. Stir in the amaranth and millet grits. Cover, reduce the heat to low, and simmer, stirring often, for 10 minutes. Stir in the vegetables and cream and return to a simmer; then pour into the prepared baking dish.

3. To make the biscuit topping: Stir the whole wheat flour, Parmigiano-Reggiano, baking powder, and nutmeg in a large bowl until the baking powder and nutmeg are evenly distributed throughout. Stir in the cream and melted butter to make a fairly stiff dough.

(continued)

4. Dust a clean, dry work surface with a little whole wheat flour, then turn the dough out onto it. Dust the top of the dough with a little more flour and roll it out, without pressing down too hard, until it's an 8 × 10-inch rectangle. Cut this rectangle into squares, smaller rectangles, and/or triangles. Collage the biscuits over the filling in the baking dish. Use a pastry brush to smear the top of each with a little cream.

5. Bake until the filling is bubbling and the biscuits have set on top, about 40 minutes. Cool on a rack for 5 minutes before spooning it up into bowls.

TESTERS' NOTES

▓ You can use most blends of frozen mixed vegetables for this good ol' casserole, although it's best with the fairly standard mixing of corn, peas, and green beans. Avoid Asian vegetable mixes, which are best for stir-fries.

▓ Amaranth and millet grits function as the thickeners. They will also dry the casserole out. Best to freeze individual servings right after dinner, rather than leaving them in the fridge for a couple of days.

▓ The topping is a whole wheat biscuit dough that is still flaky and irresistible, but with a little more tooth than the standard fare.

▓ Millet grits are a finely ground form of hulled millet. They are sometimes called "millet meal." If you can't find millet grits, grind hulled millet in a food processor with a few quick pulses, just to get it to the consistency of course sand.

CHEF IT UP!

▥ For more chicken-y flavor, use boneless, skinless chicken thighs, rather than breasts.

▥ Or substitute skinless pheasant breasts for the chicken breasts.

TESTERS' NOTES

▥ This dish is really arroz con pollo with wild rice. Wild arroz con pollo? Arroz salvaje con pollo? It doesn't make linguistic sense, but the dish is a complex meal, thanks especially to the wild rice.

▥ You really have to get rid of the excess moisture in those artichoke hearts. Don't squeeze them until they break apart, but try to get them as dry as possible.

SPANISH-INSPIRED WILD RICE, CHICKEN, AND CHORIZO CASSEROLE

1 tablespoon olive oil

1 pound dried chorizo, cut into 1-inch pieces

1 pound boneless, skinless chicken breasts, cut into strips about 1-inch wide

1 medium yellow onion, chopped

1 green bell pepper, seeded and chopped

2 teaspoons dried thyme

1 teaspoon dried oregano

1 teaspoon sweet smoked paprika

½ teaspoon salt

½ teaspoon ground black pepper

¼ teaspoon saffron

1 bottle (12 ounces) dark beer, such as Negro Modelo or Newcastle Brown Ale

1 can (28 ounces) no-salt-added diced tomatoes

1 package (9 ounces) frozen artichoke hearts, thawed and gently squeezed to remove excess moisture

1 cup green peas (no need to thaw if frozen)

2 tablespoons sherry vinegar

1½ cups wild rice

1. Since you'll be making this in a large Dutch oven, preferably one with a very heavy, tight-fitting lid, you'll need to figure out how it'll fit in your oven. Position the rack so that the covered pot sits as close to the center of the oven as possible with a couple of inches of air space above the lid. Preheat the oven to 350°F—without the pot in there!

2. Set the pot over medium heat on the stovetop and get it warmed up. Pour in the oil, then add the chorizo pieces. Brown them well on all sides, maybe 4 or 5 minutes, turning often. Transfer to a plate.

3. Add the chicken strips and brown them, taking care to stir occasionally so they don't stick, about 4 minutes as well. Transfer to the plate with the sausage pieces.

(continued)

4. Pour off all but 2 tablespoons fat from the pot, then add the onion and bell pepper. Cook, stirring often, until softened somewhat, about 4 minutes.

5. Stir in the thyme, oregano, smoked paprika, salt, black pepper, and saffron until very aromatic, maybe 30 seconds. Pour in the beer; as the foaming subsides, stir to scrape up any browned bits in the pot.

6. Stir in the canned tomatoes and their juice, the artichoke hearts, peas, and vinegar. Jack up the heat and bring the mixture to a full simmer.

7. Stir in the wild rice, then nestle the sausage and chicken strips into the pot. Once the sauce is back at a simmer, cover the pot and slide it into the oven. Bake until the rice is tender and most of the liquid has been absorbed, between 40 and 50 minutes, depending on the moisture content of the wild rice. Set outside the oven, covered, for 10 minutes to steam and meld the flavors before serving.

CLASSICS, WHOLE-GRAINED

Here's a collection of warm dishes that sets out to reimagine standard recipes with whole grains in the mix. In other words, these dishes have been tweaked to include whole grains—like Stir-Fried Buckwheat (page 197), a way to bring one of the most ancient grains of China up into a modern technique; or Louisiana-Inspired Red Beans and Kamut (page 188), a twist on the classic Creole dish with the chewy, substantial, but still sweet, whole grain standing in for the blander white rice.

When we set out to develop these recipes, we imagined they'd be among the easiest in the book: recipes that we knew well from years in the food business, that we'd made many a time both at home and for work, now with a whole grain.

How wrong we were! Take the Lamb and Triticale Tagine (page 192), a glorious twist on a North African classic. We knew we wanted to put the more aggressive, slightly sweet/sour flavors of triticale berries into the highly flavored, aromatic stew. However, we soon discovered that the whole grain required more adjustments than we'd first thought. We had to "rearrange" the spice blend several times, settling on a fuller palette of "warm" spices like cinnamon, cloves, and cumin to balance the grain's flavors. We discovered that the grain's sweetness meant we needed far less honey than we'd been putting in

tagines for years. And we played around with the fat quite a bit before landing on the slightly nutty, silky finish of almond oil.

All that's par for the course when developing recipes, of course, but we were still surprised when it came to these classics. And it was the same story time and again. The baked beans with barley (page 183) required a more commanding mix of molasses and vinegar; our well-stocked couscous (page 184) required a good punch of cayenne and cilantro to balance the barley, probably the original grain used to create this North African classic.

All of which has led us to believe that some of these standard recipes have dialed down their flavors over the years to compensate for their dependence on refined grains. With white rice or refined-wheat couscous, a dish's essential flavors have dulled to a vague sweetness—and the other enhancements have been toned down to harmonize better. You can't toss a nice handful of cilantro into a bowl of white rice. The refined grain's going to come out the loser in that fight!

Which is too bad. We are hard-wired to relish big tastes. Bland dishes lead to mindless eating. Instead, we should demand the bolder flavors that bring more satisfaction in every bite. And we should savor them more slowly—which is what a whole grain allows. We chew, we slow down, we enjoy. That's the essence of a great meal.

CLASSICS, WHOLE-GRAINED

BROWN RICE AND BEANS

6 cups water

1 smoked pork hock

1 yellow onion (8 to 10 ounces), chopped

2 teaspoons fresh thyme leaves or 1 teaspoon dried thyme

½ teaspoon red pepper flakes

1 cup dried pink or Roman beans

1 cup long-grain brown rice, such as brown basmati rice

SERVES 4

Active time: 15 minutes
Total time: 4 hours

Make ahead: Store, covered, in the fridge for several days or in the freezer for several months.

CHEF IT UP!

- A finely minced tinned or jarred anchovy fillet, added with the onion, would give a sophisticated finish.

1. Combine the water, hock, onion, thyme, and red pepper flakes in a large pot. Bring to a simmer over high heat. Cover, reduce the heat to low, and simmer for 1 hour.

2. Add the beans, cover, and continue simmering until the beans are almost tender, about 2 hours.

3. Remove the hock from the pot, cool for a few minutes, then chop the meat off the bones. Stir the meat back into the pot with the rice. Raise the heat to high and bring the whole pot back to a full boil. Then reduce the heat to low, cover, and simmer until the rice is tender and most of the water has been absorbed, about 45 minutes. If necessary, uncover, turn the heat to medium, and stir until the liquid is absorbed and the whole thing is sort of like a very creamy risotto with beans.

TESTERS' NOTES

- Nothing could be simpler; all you need is time—which is why this might be the perfect grain main to make on a Sunday afternoon midwinter.

- It needs a vinaigrette-dressed tossed green salad on the side—or even simpler, a nice range of sweet, spicy, and sour pickles.

- The dried beans are not presoaked so they'll stand up to the longer cooking as the flavors meld—and then break down a bit in the final presentation.

- There's no salt in this recipe because the smoked hock will add lots of sodium to the dish. Almost all hocks are cured in a brine before they're smoked. That said, there are some small, artisanal producers that cold-smoke

hocks without first curing them. If you find yourself with one of these hocks, by all means stir 1 teaspoon salt into the dish after it's finished cooking—and pass more at the table for those who like a saltier dish (and puffier ankles).

- Hocks are often cured with nitrates or nitrites, which keep the meat pink through the cooking process. Unfortunately, these chemicals are known carcinogens—and your intake of them should be strictly limited. A quick Internet search will bring you to producers curing hocks without the chemical fandango; some of these products are available in almost all high-end supermarkets and many neighborhood grocery stores.

Active time: 25 minutes
Total time: 3 hours 45 minutes

CHEF IT UP!

■ Substitute thawed frozen shelled edamame for the peas.

TESTERS' NOTES

■ There's not much to this one except the long simmer, until the beef and brown rice are meltingly tender.

■ A favorite among Syrian Jews, this dish is traditionally made with white rice, not brown. We feel the dish gets far more punch from the brown—and needs lots of sweet leeks as a balance.

■ Short ribs are sold in one of two ways. First, there's the English cut, which is a single rib bone with a mound of meat on it. That's not what you need here. Instead, this recipe calls for the other cut, most often called "cross-cut short ribs" (or sometimes, in old-world-style butcher shops, *"flanken"*)—that is, a slice taken across the rib bones. Each piece of meat will have several small bits of rib bone in it. Cross-cut short ribs can be fairly thick, up to a couple of inches. Look for cuts that are thinner, perhaps only ½ inch thick, sometimes called "Korean-style cross-cut short ribs."

■ Serve this stew with just a green salad dressed with a lemony vinaigrette.

BIZEH B'JURAH (SYRIAN-STYLE RICE AND SHORT RIBS)

1 tablespoon olive oil

2 pounds flanken or Korean-style cross-cut beef short ribs, each piece between ½ and 1 inch thick

3 medium leeks, white and pale green parts only, halved lengthwise, well washed, and sliced crosswise into thin half-moons

2 cups reduced-sodium beef broth

1 cup dry white wine or dry vermouth

1 cup long-grain brown rice

1 cup fresh or thawed frozen green peas

1 teaspoon ground black pepper

½ teaspoon coriander seeds

½ teaspoon salt

¼ teaspoon ground cinnamon

2 bay leaves

1. Heat a large Dutch oven over medium heat. Swirl in the oil, then add the short ribs, working in batches so as not to crowd the pan. Brown them all over, on all sides, and really well, about 10 minutes. Transfer to a large bowl and continue browning the next batch. At the end of the whole process, drain off all but 2 tablespoons of the hot fat in the pan.

2. Add the leeks and cook, stirring often, until softened, about 2 minutes.

3. Pour in the broth and wine. As the liquid comes to a boil, scrape up any browned bits on the bottom or sides of the pan.

4. Return the browned short ribs to the pan. Cover, reduce the heat to low, and simmer slowly until the meat is about to fall off the bones, about 1 hour 30 minutes.

5. Stir in the rice, peas, pepper, coriander seeds, salt, cinnamon, and bay leaves. Cover and continue simmering slowly until the rice is tender and the liquid has been absorbed, about 50 minutes. Remove the bay leaves before serving.

BROWN RICE–STUFFED CABBAGE

SERVES 6

Active time: 40 minutes
Total time: 3 hours 30 minutes

Make ahead: Store, covered, in the fridge for up to 4 days. The teff may absorb quite a bit of internal moisture, so consider serving the leftovers slathered with some heated tomato sauce.

2½ cups water

¾ cup short-grain brown rice

½ cup teff

2 celery stalks, minced

1 carrot, finely shredded through the large holes of a box grater

½ cup chopped toasted walnuts

1 tablespoon fresh thyme leaves or 2 teaspoons dried thyme

1 tablespoon minced fresh sage leaves or 1½ teaspoons dried sage

12 large Savoy cabbage leaves

3 cups reduced-sodium vegetable broth

1½ cups canned no-salt-added crushed tomatoes

2 tablespoons fresh lemon juice

2 tablespoons honey

½ teaspoon dried dillweed

½ teaspoon ground caraway

½ teaspoon salt

CHEF IT UP!

- Serve these stuffed cabbage rolls topped with a little sour cream—or even crème fraîche.

1. Combine the water, rice, and teff in a medium saucepan and bring to a boil over medium-high heat. Cover, reduce the heat to low, and simmer until thick and pasty, about 45 minutes. Scrape and dump the contents of the saucepan into a bowl to cool for 10 minutes.

2. Stir in the celery, carrots, walnuts, thyme, and sage. The final mixture will have a ground-meat texture.

3. Fill a large Dutch oven halfway with water and bring it to a boil over high heat. Add the Savoy cabbage leaves in batches, half at a time. Blanch for 5 minutes per batch, then rinse under cool water to stop the cooking. The leaves should not be the slightest bit warm when finished.

4. Pour the water out of the Dutch oven. Add the broth, tomatoes, lemon juice, honey, dill, caraway, and salt to the pot. Set aside.

5. Lay one of the cabbage leaves on a cutting board so that the leaf's raised veins are facing down. Cut out the thick stem at one end by cutting on either side of it about a third to halfway up the leaf, depending on how tough and thick the stem is. Put about ¼ cup

(continued)

of the rice filling in the center of the leaf and seal it by folding the sides over the filling and then roll-ing the leaf closed. Set it seam side down in the pot with the tomato mixture. Continue making stuffed cabbage leaves with the remaining leaves.

6. Cover the pot and bring the liquid to a simmer over medium heat. Reduce the heat to very low and simmer slowly for 1 hour and 20 minutes. Let the pot sit off the heat, covered, for 10 minutes before scooping them out to serve.

TESTERS' NOTES

■ It wasn't enough to just swap brown rice for white in this classic. We also added teff, which gives a toothsome, chewy filling to the rolls. With the rice, it's a nice mix of earthy and sweet flavors, too.

■ To keep the rolls together as they cook, they should be tightly rolled and placed seam down in the pot. Use a pot in which they fit fairly snugly together.

Active time: 20 minutes

Total time: 3 hours 15 minutes, plus soaking the barley for at least 8 hours

Make ahead: Store, covered, in the fridge for up to 3 days or in the freezer for up to 3 months.

Save time: Use 2⅔ cups cooked hull-less barley and omit soaking and cooking the raw grains.

CHEF IT UP!

■ Add up to 1 tablespoon fresh thyme leaves, minced fresh oregano leaves, and/or minced fresh parsley leaves.

TESTERS' NOTES

■ Although this tweaked campfire favorite takes a long while to make, nothing could be easier—just an occasional stir in the oven. The sweet-and-sour sauce built in the pot is a better foil to the barley than the more standard bottle of barbecue sauce.

■ For a less-sweet sauce, you can reduce the maple syrup to 2 tablespoons. For more sweet-and-sour pop, you can also increase the cider vinegar to 3 tablespoons.

■ Almost all Dutch ovens are ovensafe—with the exception of those with wooden handles, which can burn in the oven. If yours has such handles, cover them tightly with foil before putting the pot in the oven.

BAKED BARLEY, BEANS, AND BACON

1 cup hull-less barley

½ pound slab bacon, diced

1 medium yellow onion, chopped

1 can (15 ounces) black beans, drained and rinsed

1 can (15 ounces) posole or white hominy, drained and rinsed

1 can (14 ounces) no-salt-added diced tomatoes

½ cup fat-free, reduced-sodium chicken broth

3 tablespoons packed dark brown sugar

3 tablespoons molasses

3 tablespoons maple syrup

2 tablespoons cider vinegar

2 tablespoons Worcestershire sauce

Up to 4 pickled jalapeño rings, minced

1 tablespoon mustard powder

1. Soak the barley in a big bowl of cool water for at least 8 and up to 16 hours. Drain the barley in a fine-mesh sieve or small-holed colander set in the sink. Pour and scrape the grains into a large Dutch oven and fill it about halfway with water. Bring to a boil over high heat. Reduce the heat to low and simmer until the grains are tender, about 55 minutes. Drain the cooked barley in that sieve or colander.

2. Meanwhile, position the rack in your oven so that the Dutch oven can fit as near the middle as possible and still have at least 2 inches headspace when the lid is on. Preheat the oven to 325°F.

3. Pour the cooked barley into the Dutch oven. Mix in everything else: the bacon, onion, black beans, posole or hominy, tomatoes, broth, brown sugar, molasses, maple syrup, vinegar, Worcestershire sauce, jalapeños, and mustard. Bring to a boil over high heat.

4. Cover, slip into the oven, and bake until the barley is thick and bubbling, the sauce has reduced, and the tomatoes have broken down, about 1 hour 30 minutes, stirring occasionally at the start and then more often toward the end of cooking.

MOROCCAN-INSPIRED BARLEY COUSCOUS

2 tablespoons olive oil

1 whole chicken (4 pounds), cut into 8 or 9 pieces; then cut each breast half crosswise into 2 pieces (for a total of 4 breast pieces)

1 large yellow onion, chopped

24 large green olives, pitted and halved

2 to 3 tablespoons minced fresh ginger

1 tablespoon ground cumin

1½ teaspoons ground cinnamon

½ teaspoon coriander seeds

½ teaspoon saffron

½ teaspoon cayenne pepper

½ lemon, seeded and chopped

4 cups fat-free, reduced-sodium chicken broth

½ cup chopped fresh cilantro

2½ cups whole-grain barley couscous

SERVES 6

Active time: 30 minutes
Total time: 2 hours 15 minutes

CHEF IT UP!

■ After browning, set the chicken breast pieces aside on a plate and refrigerate. Add them to the pot after the other pieces have simmered for 40 minutes. They'll have a better chance of being tender without being overcooked.

1. Heat a large Dutch oven over medium heat. Pour in the oil, let it coat the bottom of the pot, and add the chicken. Brown it on both sides, about 10 minutes. Don't cheat. The best way to keep chicken from sticking is to leave it be for a while. The natural sugars need to caramelize, fuse to the pan, and then release. Start it skin side down, then flip it over, rather than giving the skin the second go-round once there's already stuff stuck in the pot. Transfer the chicken pieces to a large plate.

2. Drain off all but 2 tablespoons of the fat in the pot, then add the onion. Cook, stirring often, just until the onions begin to soften at the edges, about 2 minutes.

3. Dump in the olives, ginger, cumin, cinnamon, coriander seeds, saffron, and cayenne. Stir it around just until very aromatic, then add the chopped lemon. Again, stir it around just a bit, maybe 1 minute.

4. Pour in the broth and bring the mixture to a full simmer, scraping up any browned bits in the pot. Stir in the cilantro, then all the chicken pieces and any juices on their plate. Bring to a full simmer again; then cover, reduce the heat to low, and simmer for 1 hour 30 minutes.

5. Use long-handled tongs to remove the chicken pieces from the pot, then stir in the couscous. Set the chicken back into the pot, cover it, and set it off the heat for 10 minutes, until almost all the liquid has been absorbed.

TESTERS' NOTES

▥ Barley couscous is rather traditional in Moroccan dishes, a slightly more assertive flavor than the wheat couscous. Look for whole-grain versions at Middle Eastern markets or from online retailers.

▥ If you buy a standard, cut-up chicken at the supermarket, you'll find 8 or 9 pieces, with 2 larger breast pieces in the mix. You'll need to cut each of these in half crosswise (the short way). Although there's not much meat on the back, add it to dish for the flavor it will impart. Even the neck, if it's in the package, can add lots of flavor. However, do not add the giblets: the liver, heart, and gizzard.

▥ There's a range of ginger here, so the couscous can be tailored to your personal taste. We liked the larger amount; some testers thought it overwhelmed the other spices.

▥ You can make the dish more healthful by removing the chicken skin from the pieces before they get nestled back into the pot. You can also make it easier for little hands at the table if you skin and debone the meat, chopping it into small bits that are then stirred into the pot with the couscous before it all gets set aside to rest.

TURKEY KIBBEH LOAF WITH TZATZIKI SAUCE

Kibbeh loaf

1 cup whole-grain quick-cooking bulgur, ground in a food processor or large blender for 2 minutes until the consistency of dry sand

1½ cups water, brought to a boil over high heat

1 teaspoon dried sage

1 teaspoon ground allspice

1 teaspoon ground coriander

1 teaspoon ground cumin

1 teaspoon salt

½ teaspoon freshly ground black pepper

2½ pounds ground turkey, preferably a mix of white and dark meat without skin or cartilage in the mix

1 large yellow onion, chopped

2 tablespoons olive oil, plus more for oiling the loaf pan and loaf

¼ cup pine nuts

2 teaspoons ground oregano

1 tablespoon pomegranate molasses

Tzatziki sauce

Half a small cucumber, peeled, cut lengthwise, seeded, and minced

⅓ cup Greek yogurt

1 tablespoon tahini

1 tablespoon lemon juice

1 small garlic clove, finely minced or put through a garlic press

¼ teaspoon salt

¼ teaspoon freshly ground pepper

1. To make the kibbeh loaf: Put the bulgur in a large heatproof bowl, pour in the boiling water, and soak for 1 hour. Meanwhile, mix the sage, allspice, coriander, cumin, salt, and black pepper in a small bowl.

2. Fluff the bulgur with a fork. Now you need to grind the bulgur with 2 pounds of the ground turkey, all of that spice mixture you just made, and half the chopped onions. Here's how: In a food processor, working in 2 or 3 batches, add some of the bulgur, some of the 2 pounds of turkey, half or a third of the spice mixture, and some of the chopped onion. Process to make a pasty

Active time: 50 minutes
Total time: 3 hours

Make ahead: The tzatziki sauce can be made up to 2 days in advance; store, covered, in the fridge. The cooked kibbeh loaf can be covered and stored in the refrigerator for 2 or 3 days. Reheat individual slices with a little oil in a skillet over medium heat—or on a baking sheet under a preheated broiler for a couple of minutes.

TESTERS' NOTES

- Traditional Middle Eastern kibbeh is made from both spiced ground meat and a "dough" made from more pureed ground meat. Here, the two are mixed together and shaped into a loaf, then baked and sliced for more homey fare. Think of it as Middle Eastern meatloaf.

- Pomegranate molasses is a Middle Eastern condiment made by boiling down the juice of a particularly sour variety of pomegranate. It can be found in most supermarkets and certainly all Middle Eastern markets, as well as from suppliers online.

- Don't forget sandwiches the next day. Place leftover slices of the meatloaf inside whole wheat pita pockets with shredded lettuce and some of the sauce.

dough, scraping down the sides of the processor bowl once or twice. Scrape this mixture into a bowl and continue making more of this "dough" until you've used all the requisite ingredients.

3. Heat a large skillet over medium heat. Swirl in the 2 tablespoons oil, then add the remaining chopped onion. Cook, stirring frequently, until softened, about 3 minutes. Add the remaining ½ pound ground turkey. Stir over the heat about 5 minutes, browning the turkey thoroughly as you break it up. Stir in the pine nuts, oregano, and pomegranate molasses.

4. Position the rack in the center of the oven and preheat the oven to 350°F.

5. Now you're ready to build the loaf. Lightly grease a 9 × 5-inch loaf pan with a little olive oil on a wadded-up paper towel. Divide the "dough" into 4 pieces. Using dampened hands, press one piece into the bottom of the loaf pan. Spread one-third of the pine nut mixture over the top. Press another piece of the dough on top, sealing it to the edges of the loaf pan. Sprinkle half the remaining pine nut mixture over the top. Add another piece of dough, spread it out, and seal it again to the sides of the pan. Top with the remaining pine nut mixture, then the final piece of dough, again spreading it out to the edges. Keep wetting your hands as necessary to make sure the dough 1) doesn't stick to *you* and 2) *does* stick to the pan. Press down to compact. Brush some olive oil over the top of the loaf, then bake until an instant-read thermometer inserted into the center of the loaf registers 165°F, about 1 hour. Let the loaf cool in the pan on a rack for 10 minutes.

6. Meanwhile, make the tzatziki sauce: Whisk together the cucumber, yogurt, tahini, lemon juice, garlic, salt, and pepper in a small bowl.

7. Turn the loaf over in its pan and unmold it onto a cutting board. Set it top side up again and cut it into slices. Serve dolloped with tzatziki.

LOUISIANA-INSPIRED
RED BEANS AND KAMUT

1 cup Kamut

1 cup dried red beans

2 tablespoons peanut oil

1¼ pounds smoked sausage
(preferably a beef or pork
sausage like smoked kielbasa,
Spanish chorizo, or even a
spicy smoked Cajun sausage),
cut into 1-inch pieces

1 large yellow onion
(12 ounces), chopped

1 large green bell pepper,
seeded and chopped

3 celery stalks, chopped

3 garlic cloves, minced

2 teaspoons dried thyme

1 teaspoon dried sage

½ teaspoon ground allspice

½ teaspoon cayenne pepper

2 bay leaves

1 tablespoon cider vinegar

1 tablespoon Worcestershire
sauce

4 cups fat-free, reduced-sodium,
chicken broth

SERVES 4

Active time: 25 minutes
Total time: 2 hours 30 minutes, plus
soaking the beans and Kamut for at
least 8 hours

MAKE IT EASIER!

▤ Use 2½ cups canned red beans,
drained and rinsed. Let the Kamut
and sausage cook in the stew for
1½ hours, then stir in the canned
beans for the last 30 minutes of
covered cooking.

CHEF IT UP!

▤ Search out heirloom red beans,
like Good Mother Stallard beans,
Jacob's Cattle beans, or Rio Zape
beans.

GRAIN SWAPS

▤ Substitute 1 cup hard red wheat
berries for the Kamut.

TESTERS' NOTES

▤ Hearty, comforting, and warm—
this dish was made for a winter
night.

▤ The Kamut will never be as soft as,
say, farro; it will instead offer a
decidedly satisfying chew to
complement the softer beans.

1. Soak the Kamut and beans in 2 separate bowls of cool water for at least 8 and up to 16 hours. If possible, change the water in the beans at least once during soaking.

2. Heat a large Dutch oven over medium heat. Swirl in the oil. Working in 2 batches, brown the sausage all sides, maybe 4 or 5 minutes. Use a slotted spoon to transfer them to a plate and add the remaining sausage. Why not just dump in all the sausage? Because it can release too much liquid all at once, liquid that won't then boil off quickly enough, thus causing the sausage to braise rather than brown. By working in batches, you're giving the smaller amount of released liquid time to boil off before adding more to the pot.

3. Here's a choice: Drain off all the fat in the pot except about 2 tablespoons, or leave it in the pot and work out on the treadmill an extra 20 minutes. Add the onion, bell pepper, and celery. Stir over the heat until the onion softens somewhat, about 4 minutes.

4. Stir in the garlic, then all the herbs and spices: the thyme, sage, allspice, cayenne, and bay leaves. Keep stirring for maybe 30 seconds, then pour in the vinegar and Worcestershire. They'll almost instantly boil—but keep stirring for 30 seconds, about as long as it takes to sing "Happy Birthday" twice. Pour in the broth and bring it to a full simmer, scraping up any browned bits in the pot.

5. Return the sausage pieces and any accumulated juices on their plate to the pot. Drain the Kamut in a small-holed colander set in the sink and stir it into the pot. Bring it all back to a full simmer; then reduce the heat to low, cover the pot, and simmer slowly for 30 minutes.

6. Drain the beans and add them to the pot. Cover and continue simmering slowly, stirring every once in a while, until the Kamut and beans are tender, about 1 hour 30 minutes.

7. Uncover the pot and raise the heat to medium-high, bringing the stew to a full boil. Reduce what's in the pot until it's the consistency you like. It should be like a thick stew, definitely not a soup. We prefer a wetter texture, one that requires a bowl rather than a plate. However, you can dry it out to become plate-food—if so, you've got to stir all the time to keep everything from sticking. Check for salt and discard the bay leaves before serving.

RYE BERRIES STEWED WITH SAUERKRAUT AND PORK

SERVES 4 TO 6

Active time: 40 minutes
Total time: 3 hours 45 minutes

Make ahead: Freeze individual servings; thaw in the fridge and microwave on high for 5 minutes to reheat.

1 tablespoon olive oil

2¼ pounds bone-in pork stew meat, such as bone-in shoulder chops, neck bones, skinned shanks, or country-style pork ribs

1 medium red onion, chopped

⅔ cup chopped dried apple

1 tablespoon juniper berries

1 teaspoon caraway seeds

½ teaspoon dried dillweed

½ teaspoon ground black pepper

2 bay leaves

1 cup dry white wine or dry vermouth

2 pounds packaged sauerkraut, rinsed in a colander and squeezed dry by the handfuls

1 cup rye berries

2 cups fat-free, reduced-sodium chicken broth

1. Position the rack in your oven so that a large Dutch oven can fit as near the middle as possible and still have at least 2 inches head-space when the lid is on. Preheat the oven to 350°F.

2. While the oven preheats, set the Dutch oven over medium heat and leave it there a couple of minutes, then swirl in the oil. Add the pork in batches and brown it on all sides, working really hard to splatter your stove into oblivion, about 10 minutes. Transfer the pork to a plate.

3. Drain off all but 2 tablespoons fat from the pot, then add the onion and dried apple. Cook, stirring often, until the onion soft-ens a bit, about 3 minutes. Stir in the juniper berries, caraway seeds, dill, pepper, and bay leaves.

4. Pour in the wine or vermouth. As it comes to a simmer, scrape up any browned bits in the pot. Then stir in the sauerkraut, rye berries, and broth. Nestle the pork back into the pot and bring it all to a boil.

5. Cover and slip the pot into the oven where everything can braise until the rye berries are tender but have a distinct chew and the pork is falling-off-the-bone tender, about 3 hours.

6. Set the pot back on top of the stove—careful, it's hot—and use a slotted spoon to transfer the pork hunks to a big cutting board. They're very fragile and will fall apart. Don't carry them across open flooring, and put the dog outside. As the meat cools a few minutes, forage through the pot for the bay leaves and toss them out. You might also want to check the juniper berries—they are generally in shards and pieces at this point, but you don't want a big chunk in a single bite. Toss out any of those big pieces or whole berries as well.

7. After a few more minutes, debone the meat and cut it into bite-size bits. Stir these back into the pot and bring the whole thing back up to a simmer so it's good and hot when you ladle it up.

TESTERS' NOTES

It's too bad rye berries are such a forgotten grain. They have great texture, plus an herbaceous, slightly sour, but pleasantly sweet taste, like a floral white wine. Here, they're given the full Wagnerian treatment with pork and sauerkraut, a meal that'll help you stave off whatever comes, even Valkyries.

You can also use an unsmoked pork hock for some of the pork in the stew. However, since its taste will be more pronounced, a bit more like organ meat, don't use only unsmoked hocks as the meat here. Rather, mix a hock with bone-in pork stew meat.

No need to soak the rye berries first. They'll have plenty of time over the heat. And they'll get a little mushier, a better contrast to the sauerkraut.

LAMB AND TRITICALE TAGINE

1 cup triticale berries

2 teaspoons ground coriander

1 teaspoon ground ginger

1 teaspoon ground cinnamon

½ teaspoon ground cloves

½ teaspoon ground cumin

½ teaspoon cayenne pepper

¼ teaspoon saffron

1½ pounds boneless lamb shoulder meat, cut into 1-inch cubes

2 tablespoons almond oil

3 small yellow onions, halved and then sliced into thin half-rings

¾ cup pitted oil-cured olives

¼ cup whole almonds

2 very small preserved lemons, seeded and chopped (about ⅓ cup)

1½ teaspoons honey

1 cup fat-free, reduced-sodium chicken broth

1 cup dry white wine or dry vermouth

1. Soak the triticale berries in a big bowl of cool water for at least 8 and up to 16 hours.

2. Meanwhile, mix the coriander, ground ginger, cinnamon, cloves, cumin, cayenne, and saffron in a big bowl. Pour in the lamb hunks and stir it all up until they're coated with the spice mixture. Cover and set in the fridge for 8 to 12 hours.

3. Heat the bottom of a large (2-quart) flameproof tagine oven over medium heat. Swirl in the oil, then add all the onions. Stir until somewhat softened, about 5 minutes. Pour in the meat and all its spices, scraping down the bowl to get every last drop into the pan. Cook, stirring and tossing fairly often, until the meat has browned, about 5 minutes.

4. Drain the triticale berries in a fine-mesh sieve or small-holed colander set in the sink and stir them into the pan along with the olives, almonds, preserved lemons, and honey. Stir it all around until everything's mixed up, then pour in the broth and wine.

(continued)

SERVES 6

Active time: 30 minutes
Total time: 2 hours 30 minutes, plus soaking the triticale for at least 8 hours

Make ahead: Freeze the entire thing or individual servings for up to 3 months. Reheat with additional broth to moisten the stew.

MAKE IT EASIER!

- Use a large Dutch oven, rather than a tagine. Check the stew regularly, especially if your pot's lid is not heavy and tight-fitting.

CHEF IT UP!

- Substitute ground Aleppo pepper, a smoky, spicy hit, for the cayenne.

- Substitute boneless goat shoulder meat for the lamb.

- Use a half-and-half mixture of unsalted butter and almond oil.

- Use a very aromatic honey, such as oak, pine, or even eucalyptus honey.

GRAIN SWAPS

- Substitute 1 cup rye berries for the triticale berries.

5. Bring the contents of the pan to a good, steady simmer; then set the tagine lid in place, reduce the heat to low, and simmer slowly until the lamb and triticale berries are tender but still have a bit of chew for texture, about 2 hours. Although you want to lift the lid off as few times as possible, you also want to watch the tagine carefully during the last 30 minutes or so to make sure it doesn't scorch. Add more broth if necessary.

TESTERS' NOTES

▪ The spice blend used in this tagine is so flavorful, you might consider doubling or tripling the amount you need, then saving the rest in a jar in your spice cabinet. It's a great addition to rich, dark beef or pork stews—and when mixed with a little almond or walnut oil, makes a rub for steaks on the grill.

▪ Although there are many makes of North African tagines—those conical-lidded, shallow pans designed to soak the stew in a continue drizzle of condensed steam—search out flameproof ones *without* a hole in the lid. The hole simply lets too much of the precious steam escape. If yours has that dreaded hole, seal it with a paste of all-purpose flour and water. You're also going to have to check the stew as it simmers slowly, adding more broth as needed to create a somewhat dry, thick stew that never sticks. You want those flavors to meld over the heat for a good long time.

BUCKWHEAT HASH

1 cup buckwheat groats

1 large egg, lightly beaten

2 cups water

1 pound very small yellow potatoes

4 tablespoons unsalted butter, cut into small chunks

1 large yellow onion, chopped

2 garlic cloves, minced

1 teaspoon minced fresh oregano leaves or ½ teaspoon dried oregano

½ teaspoon celery seeds

½ teaspoon salt

⅔ cup fat-free, reduced-sodium chicken broth

1 tablespoon cider vinegar

½ teaspoon ground black pepper

1. Position the rack in the center of the oven and preheat to 350°F. Spread the buckwheat groats on a large rimmed baking sheet. Roast until toasted and a little browned, about 15 minutes, stirring occasionally. Cool to room temperature, about 30 minutes.

2. Pour the toasted groats (now "kasha") in a bowl and add the egg. Stir to coat and separate the groats.

3. Heat a large saucepan over medium heat. Add the groats and stir for 2 minutes to set the egg, keeping the grains separate. Pour in the water and bring to a boil over high heat. Cover, reduce the heat to low, and simmer slowly until all the water has been absorbed and the groats are tender, about 15 minutes. Spread them on a large baking sheet and cool, about 30 minutes.

4. Meanwhile, dice the potatoes and place them in a vegetable steamer; cover and steam until tender when pierced with a fork, about 10 minutes. Set aside off the heat.

5. Melt the butter in a large skillet over medium heat. Add the onion and cook, stirring often, until softened, about 8 minutes.

6. Add the garlic, oregano, celery seeds, and salt. Stir over the heat about 1 minute, then add the potatoes and buckwheat groats. Spread them all out into one layer as well as you can, then pour in the broth. Cook until the broth is absorbed, about 5 minutes.

7. Use a wide, flat spatula to turn the potatoes in chunks and groups. Cooking until well browned and heated through, about 5 more minutes. Sprinkle with vinegar and pepper before serving.

SERVES 4

Active time: 25 minutes
Total time: 2 hours 20 minutes

Save time: Use 1 cup raw kasha (toasted buckwheat groats) and omit roasting the raw grains.

Make It Vegetarian: Substitute reduced-sodium vegetable broth for the chicken broth.

CHEF IT UP!

▥ Rather than using water, substitute 2 cups chicken or vegetable broth for cooking the egg-coated kasha.

▥ Add up to 8 ounces chopped, smoked brisket, smoked chicken, or smoked ham after the onions have softened. Cook about 2 minutes before continuing with the recipe.

TESTERS' NOTES

▥ The chicken broth adds some silky body to this wintry hash, a good mix of grains and potatoes. Because the buckwheat can get gummy in the skillet, have some extra broth on hand to use if you notice any pronounced sticking.

▥ Don't rush the potatoes—let them brown!

▥ If you use a nonstick skillet for this dish, make sure you use only a spatula approved for its surface so you don't nick it as you try to turn the potatoes.

STIR-FRIED BUCKWHEAT

SERVES 4

Active time: 15 minutes
Total time: 40 minutes

Make ahead: Prepare the buckwheat in advance, through drying the grains on a baking sheet: Cover the cooked, separate groats on their baking sheet and store in the fridge for up to 2 days.

GRAIN SWAPS

▦ Substitute 2 cups *cooked* long-grain brown rice for the buckwheat and omit all the buckwheat cooking steps.

TESTERS' NOTES

▦ Buckwheat is sticky, so this very old-fashioned preparation (coating the groats in egg and then boiling them) keeps them separate—at which point they can be stir-fried, just like fried rice.

▦ In truth, you can substitute buckwheat groats cooked in this manner for the rice in any fried rice stir-fry. We thought we'd offer a fairly straightforward preparation here to get you thinking about more uses for these tasty, nutty groats.

1 cup buckwheat groats

1 large egg, lightly beaten

2 cups reduced-sodium vegetable broth

2 tablespoons soy sauce (regular or reduced-sodium)

2 tablespoons unseasoned rice vinegar (page 97)

1 teaspoon Asian chile paste or sambal

1 teaspoon sugar

2 tablespoons toasted sesame oil

6 scallions, thinly sliced

2 garlic cloves, minced

1 tablespoon minced fresh ginger

2 large carrots, shredded through the large holes of a box grater

1 red bell pepper, seeded and chopped

½ pound green beans, cut into ½-inch pieces

1. Pour the buckwheat groats into a large bowl and mix in the egg until they are well coated, all the grains separated from one another.

2. Heat a large, dry saucepan over medium heat. Pour in the coated groats and stir over the heat for 2 minutes to set the egg. The groats should still be separate from each other.

3. Pour in the broth and increase the heat to high. Bring to a boil. Cover, reduce the heat to low, and simmer until the liquid has been absorbed and the groats are tender, about 15 minutes.

4. Spread the buckwheat on a large rimmed baking sheet and cool for 10 minutes to make sure the grains stay separate, rather than glomming onto each other.

5. Meanwhile, whisk the soy sauce, vinegar, chile paste, and sugar in a small bowl.

6. Heat a large wok over medium-high heat. Swirl in the oil, then add the scallions, garlic, and ginger. Stir-fry for 30 seconds.

7. Add the carrots, bell pepper, and green beans. Stir-fry until crisp-tender, about 2 minutes. Add all the buckwheat. Continue stir-frying for 1 minute. Pour in the soy sauce mixture and bring to a simmer, tossing and stirring for 1 more minute.

UNEXPECTED ELEGANCE

You'll know grains have broken the final barrier when they become part of your dinner-party repertoire. And yes, you should have a dinner-party repertoire—mostly because there are few better ways to experience the comfort of friends and family than around the table. We designed these last dishes as fare fit for those evenings.

One of the reasons we moved to rural New England is so we could have a dining room. In Manhattan, space was at a premium. What we had resembled what Lucy and Ricky had: We would pull the couch away and move the dining table into position. One Thanksgiving, when 14 descended on our apartment, we actually moved most of the furniture into the bedroom.

Out in the country, we've got the space for dinner parties. Which are events at our house. Eight is the perfect number: the two of us and six guests. More and it turns into an extravaganza. We do plated courses, one after another, over several hours. We drink a lot of wine, eat a lot of food, and all end up in a sort of buzzed euphoria. The conversation rolls on past midnight. Friends say "We've got to go" and stay another hour.

More and more, we're serving whole-grain dishes like these. They pace the courses better. Over the years we've witnessed what can only be called "the meat coma." People start to flag on the third course. And it's not just the hard hit of protein. The flavor palette among the meat dishes starts to flatten out, meld, and lose vibrancy.

Not so with whole grains. Their appearance makes everyone pause, sit up, and take notice. Plus, they subtly alter even the undertones of the accompanying dishes. Stocked with polyunsaturated fats—which are more like reverb than volume when it comes to the way flavors orchestrate together—the grains carry forward tasty notes and aromas that would be left in the dust in a big hunk of roasted meat.

In fact, the very first recipe we tested for this book was the Pumpkin-Quinoa Soufflé (page 207). It came out as the first course of a dinner party on a winter evening—and set the tone for the night: gentle, quiet conversations about life's foibles and fears. We're not saying that the soufflé caused all that. But it somehow contributed to the general mood, as would any of these dishes, from the simple Triticale with Olive Oil, Garlic, and Anchovies (page 200), a riff on a Roman pasta dish, to the elegant Seared Tuna and Brown Rice Chirashi (page 212), a welcome first course to a larger meal—or a fine dinner-party dish on its own with some crunchy Japanese pickled vegetables on the side.

In the end, as we've said all along, food is far more than sustenance. It's not only a primary pleasure vehicle for our bodies; it's also a way to nurture the relationships in our lives, to treat people well, to show them that we love them. No single food group can do that as well as whole grains, with their long history of nurturing human community. So have some friends over and try out the Trout Stuffed with Wild Rice (page 209) or the Black Rice Paella (page 210). A whole-grain meal with the people you love: What could be more satisfying?

UNEXPECTED ELEGANCE

TRITICALE WITH OLIVE OIL, GARLIC, AND ANCHOVIES

1 cup triticale berries

⅓ cup olive oil

6 garlic cloves, slivered

6 tinned or jarred anchovy fillets, minced

½ teaspoon red pepper flakes

1½ tablespoons fresh lemon juice

2 ounces Parmigiano-Reggiano, finely grated

SERVES 4

Active time: 10 minutes
Total time: 1 hour 10 minutes, plus soaking the triticale berries for at least 8 hours

Save time: Use 2⅔ cups cooked triticale berries and omit soaking and cooking the raw grains.

1. Soak the triticale berries in a big bowl of cool water for at least 8 and up to 16 hours. Drain the triticale berries in a fine-mesh sieve or small-holed colander set in the sink. Pour the grains into a large saucepan, fill it about halfway with water, and bring to a boil over high heat. Reduce the heat to low and simmer until tender with some bite left at the center of the grains, 50 to 55 minutes. Drain again in that sieve or colander, then run under cool water. Drain thoroughly, shaking the sieve or colander repeatedly over the sink.

2. Pour the oil into a large skillet and add the garlic, anchovies, and red pepper flakes. Set the skillet over very low heat and leave it undisturbed until the anchovy bits begin to melt and the garlic begins to turn light brown at its edges, 4 to 5 minutes.

3. Pour in the cooked triticale berries. Raise the heat to medium-high and stir constantly for 1 minute over the heat. Pour in the lemon juice, add the Parmigiano-Reggiano, and toss for a few seconds over the heat. Serve at once.

CHEF IT UP!

■ All tinned or jarred anchovies are not created equal. Those in the supermarket can be far too salty and ridiculously fishy, not much flavor besides a slap in the ol' pucker. If you've got access to an Italian supermarket, search out *alici salata*, fat whole anchovies packed in salt. They're so large, you'll only need 3 or 4 for this dish. You'll also need to bone them by splitting them lengthwise and pulling out the long spine. Scrape out the guts and take off the tiny tail. But all this effort will be rewarded by a more complex taste, briny as well as bright.

TESTERS' NOTES

■ This is a take on a Roman dish, a simple supper, only in need of some crunchy bread to fall in the sauce completely by accident.

■ Triticale berries offer a complex, slightly musky taste with sour notes and sweet undertones. In other words, they're way more complex than the run-of-the-mill pasta usually used—and so stand up much better to the anchovies and garlic without being overwhelmed.

BARLEY, MUSHROOMS, AND PEAS

SERVES 4

Active time: 35 minutes

Total time: 1 hour 35 minutes, plus soaking the barley for at least 8 hours

Save time: Use 2⅔ cups cooked hull-less barley and omit soaking and cooking the raw grains.

CHEF IT UP!

▦ Substitute 2 teaspoons dukkah (a dried Egyptian spice mixture) or dried za'atar (an Arabic spice mixture) for the thyme.

▦ Substitute a bolder, dry, aged cheese for the Parm—like aged Asiago or a pecorino.

TESTERS' NOTES

▦ This is a fairly simple dish, the better to let the elemental flavors of the barley and mushrooms come through.

▦ Although the stems of white button or cremini mushrooms are edible, those of shiitake mushrooms are not, even when very fresh. They're too fibrous and have a rather unpleasant, silage aftertaste.

1 cup hull-less barley

¼ cup olive oil

2 medium yellow onions, chopped

8 ounces sliced cremini or brown button mushrooms

6 ounces shiitake mushrooms, stems discarded, caps thinly sliced

2 garlic cloves, minced

½ pound shelled fresh or thawed frozen green peas

2 tablespoons white wine vinegar

1 tablespoon fresh thyme leaves or 2 teaspoons dried thyme

½ teaspoon salt

½ teaspoon ground black pepper

2 ounces Parmigiano-Reggiano, finely grated

1. Soak the barley in a big bowl of cool water for at least 8 and up to 16 hours. Drain the barley in a fine-mesh sieve or small-holed colander set in the sink. Pour the barley into a medium saucepan, fill it about two-thirds of the way with water, and bring to a boil over high heat. Reduce the heat to low and simmer until tender with still some texture in the grains, about 55 minutes. Drain again in that sieve or colander, then run under cool water until the grains are room temperature. Drain thoroughly.

2. Heat a large high-sided sauté pan or a wok over medium heat. Pour in the oil, then add the onions. Drop the heat to low and cook, stirring once in a while, until the onions are golden and exceptionally sweet, about 10 minutes.

3. Stir in both kinds of mushroom and the garlic. Cook until the mushrooms give off their liquid and it reduces to a glaze, about 5 minutes, stirring occasionally.

4. Stir in the barley, peas, vinegar, thyme, salt, and pepper. Toss and stir over the heat for 2 minutes. Remove from the heat and stir in the Parmigiano-Reggiano until melted.

BARLEY RISOTTO WITH MUSHROOMS AND LEEKS

4 cups fat-free, reduced-sodium chicken broth

½ teaspoon saffron

2 tablespoons unsalted butter

2 small leeks, white and pale green parts only, halved lengthwise, well washed, and cut crosswise into very thin half-moons

1 pound thinly sliced cremini or white button mushrooms

1 cup hull-less barley

1 tablespoon fresh thyme leaves

1 teaspoon ground black pepper

½ cup dry white wine or dry vermouth

1 cup fresh or frozen green peas (no need to thaw if frozen)

2 ounces Parmigiano-Reggiano, finely grated

1. Heat the broth and saffron in a large saucepan over medium-low heat just until steaming, just below the simmering point. Adjust the heat to maintain this temperature.

2. Melt the butter in a large high-sided sauté pan or risotto pan over medium heat. Add the leeks and cook, stirring occasionally, until somewhat softened, about 2 minutes.

3. Dump in the mushrooms and cook, stirring frequently, until they give off their liquid and it reduces to a glaze, about 5 minutes.

4. Add the barley, thyme, and pepper. Stir over the heat for 1 minute, then pour in the wine or vermouth. Raise the heat to medium-high. As the liquid comes up to a full simmer, scrape up any browned bits in the pan.

5. Pour in the saffron broth and bring to a full, rolling simmer. Cover, reduce the heat to very low, and simmer slowly for 1 hour.

6. Uncover and raise the heat back to medium. Stir until reduced and creamy, about 25 minutes. Stir in the peas and Parmigiano-Reggiano. Remove from the heat and let rest 5 minutes before serving.

SERVES 4

Active time: 20 minutes
Total time: 1 hour 50 minutes

Make It Vegetarian: Substitute reduced-sodium vegetable broth for the chicken broth. Because you'll be losing some of the broth's heft, consider adding more mushrooms, perhaps up to 4 ounces more.

MAKE IT EASIER!

▥ Barley risotto can be made in a slow cooker. Make the recipe up to and including pouring in the broth with its saffron. Dump the contents of the pan into a 5- to 6-quart slow cooker, set the lid in place, and cook on low for 7 to 8 hours, until the liquid has been mostly absorbed and the barley is tender. Stir in the peas and cheese, set the lid ajar over the slow cooker, and continue cooking 10 minutes to heat them through.

TESTERS' NOTES

▥ With hull-less barley, the Italian first course becomes a delicate, creamy main course. Yes, you must stir—but only for the last 25 minutes. If you're making this dish for a dinner party, have a glass of wine in hand and just continue talking to everybody. (They'll be gathered in the kitchen anyway.)

▥ You need a high-sided sauté pan or a risotto pan to make this dish. A standard skillet just won't cut it. Its sloping sides will speed up the evaporation of the liquids—and you'll end up running out before the barley is tender and the sauce has properly thickened with leached starches.

SOUTHWESTERN AMARANTH POLENTA

1 ounce dried shiitake mushrooms

2¾ cups boiling water

2 poblano chiles

1 tablespoon unsalted butter

½ teaspoon cumin seeds

8 scallions, thinly sliced

1½ cups amaranth

½ teaspoon salt

½ teaspoon ground black pepper

2 teaspoons minced fresh marjoram or 1 teaspoon dried marjoram

2 ounces queso fresco

1. Place the dried mushrooms in a large heatproof bowl and cover them with the boiling water. Set aside for 10 minutes.

2. Meanwhile, char the chiles by holding and turning them with flame-safe tongs over an open gas flame or placing them on a baking sheet 4 to 6 inches from a preheated broiler, turning occasionally. Place them in a bowl and cover tightly with plastic wrap—or put them in a paper bag and seal it shut. Set aside for 10 minutes.

3. Set a colander over a bowl and drain the mushrooms into the colander, thereby saving the soaking liquid. Remove and discard the mushroom stems. Chop the caps into small bits. Check the soaking liquid. If it's sandy, strain it through a large coffee filter.

4. Melt the butter in a large sauté pan or a large high-sided skillet over medium heat. Add the cumin seeds and cook for 30 seconds. Add the scallions and cook, stirring occasionally, for 1 minute.

5. Add the amaranth, salt, pepper, chopped mushrooms, and the mushroom soaking liquid. Bring the whole thing to a boil. Cover, reduce the heat to low, and simmer slowly for 15 minutes.

6. Meanwhile, remove the chiles from their bowl and stem them. Rub off most of their charred skins. Slice them open lengthwise and discard any white pith and seeds. Dice the flesh into bits.

7. After the amaranth has cooked for 15 minutes, stir in the marjoram and chopped chiles. Cover and continue simmering until the amaranth is tender, about 15 minutes. The consistency should be about like a hot breakfast cereal. Crumble the queso fresco on top, stir gently, cover, and set aside for 5 minutes to blend the flavors.

TESTERS' NOTES

- Of course, most people think of polenta as a side dish to a large meal. But if you pump up the flavors and use tiny, sticky, somewhat sweet, but decidedly grassy amaranth, the dish morphs into a main course. Best of all, there's very little stirring necessary!

- Queso fresco is a fresh, soft, unaged white cheese that originated in Spain and spread to Latin America. Look for it at the cheese counter of most high-end grocery stores and all Latin American or Mexican supermarkets. Queso fresco is often made from a combination of cow's and goat's milk; queso blanco, from only cow's milk. In truth, either will work here, although we like the slightly more assertive flavor of queso fresco as a balance to the poblano chiles.

ROASTED RATATOUILLE WITH JOB'S TEARS

SERVES 4

Active time: 25 minutes
Total time: 1 hour 30 minutes

MAKE IT EASIER!

- Look for cubed eggplant and chopped onions in the refrigerator case of your supermarket's produce section.

TESTERS' NOTES

- As we've noted before, Job's tears suck the moisture out of everything and go fairly stiff within a day, so you can't make this ahead or keep much of it for leftovers— not that any will last that long.

- Roasting the vegetables gives them a little more chew than in the standard, stewed version of ratatouille—and thus a better match to the grain.

1 cup Job's tears *(hato mugi)*, preferably dark *(yuuki hato mugi)*

2 eggplants (10 to 12 ounces each), cut into 1-inch cubes

1 large red onion, coarsely chopped

½ cup olive oil

1 pint cherry tomatoes, halved

½ cup chopped pitted black olives

1 tablespoon minced fresh rosemary leaves or 2 teaspoons dried rosemary

1 tablespoon fresh thyme leaves or 2 teaspoons dried thyme

1 teaspoon salt

½ teaspoon ground black pepper

½ cup dry white wine or dry vermouth

1. Place the Job's tears in a large saucepan and fill it about two-thirds of the way with water. Bring to a boil over high heat. Reduce the heat to low and simmer until tender to the bite, between 1 hour and 1 hour 15 minutes. Drain the Job's tears in a colander set in the sink. Run them under cool water to return them to room temperature.

2. Meanwhile, position the rack in the center of the oven and preheat to 400°F. Toss the eggplants, onion, and oil in a deep roasting pan. Roast until soft and irresistible, stirring once in a while, about 30 minutes.

3. Stir the tomatoes, olives, rosemary, thyme, salt, and pepper into the eggplant and onions. Continue roasting for 15 minutes, stirring once halfway through.

4. Stir in the cooked Job's tears and the wine or vermouth. Continue roasting for 5 minutes, tossing once or twice.

PUMPKIN-QUINOA SOUFFLÉ

Active time: 25 minutes
Total time: 1 hour 15 minutes

Save time: Use 1¾ cups cooked quinoa and omit soaking and cooking the raw grains.

TESTERS' NOTES

▥ A perfect soufflé is a work of art: puffed, light as air, but here made more far more healthy and hearty with featherweight quinoa in the mix. However, have everyone at the table, ready to eat. Soufflés begin to collapse the moment they leave the oven.

▥ There are a few secrets to a perfect soufflé: You need to make sure your oven is properly preheated, the eggs must be at room temperature, you must not skimp in beating the ingredients (you want as much air in the mix as possible before the soufflé starts to puff in the oven), and you must not open the oven door as the soufflé bakes.

▥ To get eggs to room temperature, leave them out on the counter for 15 to 20 minutes or submerge them in their shells in a bowl of warm tap water for 4 to 5 minutes.

▥ Make sure you use canned pumpkin puree, not pumpkin pie filling.

½ cup quinoa, preferably white quinoa

½ cup finely grated Parmigiano-Reggiano

6 large eggs, at room temperature and separated

4½ tablespoons unsalted butter, plus more for the soufflé dish

6 tablespoons whole wheat flour or quinoa flour

1 cup milk (whole, 2%, 1%, or fat-free)

½ cup dry white wine or dry vermouth

1½ cups canned pumpkin puree

½ teaspoon grated nutmeg

½ teaspoon ground sage

½ teaspoon salt

½ teaspoon ground black pepper

1. Fill a medium saucepan about halfway with water and bring it to a boil over high heat. Stir in the quinoa, reduce the heat to low, and cook until the grains have developed their halos and are tender, about 12 minutes. Drain in a fine-mesh sieve or a lined colander set in the sink. Cool the grains down under some running tap water. Drain thoroughly.

2. Position the rack in the center of the oven and preheat to 375°F. Lightly grease a 2-quart soufflé dish or round high-sided baking dish with a little butter on a wadded-up paper towel or piece of wax paper, making sure to get the butter down into the seam between the bottom and the sides. Coat the sides and bottom of the dish with the grated Parmigiano-Reggiano, turning the dish this way and that to make sure it's all nicely cheesed up.

3. Whisk the egg yolks in a small bowl until creamy and light.

4. Melt the butter in a large saucepan set over medium heat. Whisk in the flour. Cook for 30 seconds, whisking constantly.

5. Whisk in the milk in a slow, steady stream; then whisk in the wine, not as slowly, but certainly not all at once, in a heavier but controlled stream. Continue cooking, whisking almost the whole time, until thick and very creamy, about 2 minutes.

(continued)

6. Remove the pan from the heat and whisk in the cooked quinoa, beaten egg yolks, pumpkin puree, nutmeg, sage, salt, and pepper.

7. Use an electric mixer at high speed to beat the egg whites in a large bowl until they form droopy peaks when the turned-off beaters are dipped back in the mix. Use a flat, rubber spatula to fold half these beaten egg whites into the pumpkin mixture until no trace of white remains. Then fold in the remaining half very gently, stirring in wide arcs, until incorporated and even throughout but not dissolved. Scrape, pour, and spread this mixture into the prepared soufflé dish.

8. Bake until puffed and set, about 40 minutes. Bring it straight to the table and serve it up hot before it begins to deflate.

Active time: 30 minutes
Total time: 1 hour 15 minutes

Save time: Use 3½ cups cooked wild rice and omit soaking and cooking the raw grains.

CHEF IT UP!

▨ Drizzle each cooked trout with 2 teaspoons aged balsamic vinegar.

TESTERS' NOTES

▨ Figure on one trout per person—unless you have more courses or side dishes, at which point half a trout would do it.

▨ For the best texture and flavor, ask the butcher at your supermarket to slice prosciutto crudo into paper-thin strips for you, rather than buying the presliced prosciutto in the deli case. Keep the prosciutto crudo tightly sealed and refrigerated just until you're ready to use in this recipe.

▨ This filling would also be excellent stuffed into a flank steak or thick, bone-in pork chops. Ask the butcher at your supermarket to open pockets in these cuts of meat so you can stuff them at home.

TROUT STUFFED WITH WILD RICE

1 cup wild rice

¼ cup pine nuts

4 teaspoons finely grated lemon zest

4 teaspoons minced fresh rosemary leaves

1 garlic clove, minced

½ teaspoon salt

½ teaspoon ground black pepper

¼ pound thinly sliced prosciutto crudo

4 cleaned, scaled, and gutted trout

2 tablespoons olive oil

1. Pour the wild rice into a large saucepan and cover it with a generous amount of water. Bring to a boil over high heat. Reduce the heat a bit and simmer steadily until tender, between 30 and 55 minutes, depending on the varietal and the grains' residual moisture content. Check the package for more information. Drain in a fine-mesh sieve or a lined colander set in the sink. Pour the cooked wild rice into a bowl.

2. Toast the pine nuts in a skillet over medium-low heat until lightly browned, stirring often, about 5 minutes. Add them to the wild rice, and stir in the lemon zest, rosemary, garlic, salt, and pepper.

3. Position the rack in the center of the oven and preheat to 400°F.

4. Divide the prosciutto strips into 4 portions. Lay each portion on your work surface in overlapping strips so that you have 4 "beds" for the trout.

5. Stuff a quarter of the wild rice mixture into the body cavity of each trout. Lay each trout on top of a portion of overlapping prosciutto strips. Fold the prosciutto over so that it encircles the trout, holding the filling inside.

6. Heat a very large ovenproof skillet over medium heat. A cast iron skillet works best. Add the oil, swirl it around the skillet to coat, and set the 4 trout in the skillet, alternating directions if it helps them fit. Cook for 2 minutes, then use a large, wide metal spatula to flip them over one by one. Take care to keep the prosciutto intact and thus the wild rice stuffing inside.

7. Set the skillet in the oven and roast for 12 minutes. Cool in the skillet for a few minutes before transferring them to serving plates.

BLACK RICE PAELLA

SERVES 6

Active time: 25 minutes
Total time: 1 hour 15 minutes

4 cups reduced-sodium vegetable broth

¼ teaspoon saffron

2 tablespoons olive oil

1 large yellow onion, chopped

1 cup dry white wine or dry vermouth

1 can (14 ounces) no-salt-added diced tomatoes

2 teaspoons mild smoked paprika

1 tablespoon minced fresh oregano leaves or 2 teaspoons dried oregano

1 tablespoon fresh thyme leaves or 2 teaspoons dried thyme

2 cups black Italian rice, such as venere rice (do not use Forbidden rice or Thai black sticky rice)

½ pound cleaned squid, cut into rings and tentacles

½ pound sea scallops, each disk cut into two coins

½ pound shelled fresh or thawed frozen peas

1 pound large shrimp, peeled and deveined

2 lobster tails, halved lengthwise

12 littleneck clams or other small clams

CHEF IT UP!

▪ Omit the scallops. Use ½ pound cleaned baby octopus. In this case, put them in the broth with the saffron, bring it to a simmer, cover, reduce the heat to low, and simmer the octopus for 1 hour. Remove the octopuses and slice each in half. Reserve the octopuses to add with the other seafood; keep the broth warm until you're ready to use it.

TESTERS' NOTE

▪ The black rice will stain this all-seafood paella black. It's like making a squid-ink paella without ever using any squid ink! Have a side dish that's a color contrast—for example, roasted asparagus spears and cauliflower florets.

1. Place the broth and saffron in a large saucepan and bring to a low simmer over medium-high heat. Reduce the heat to very low, cover, and simmer very slowly while you prepare the paella.

2. Heat a 14-inch cast iron skillet or a 13-inch paella pan over medium heat. Dump in the oil, then add the onion. Cook, stirring often, until softened, about 4 minutes.

3. Stir in the wine or vermouth. Bring it to a boil and keep cooking until the liquid has reduced by half, about 3 minutes.

4. Stir in the tomatoes, smoked paprika, oregano, and thyme. Reduce the heat a bit but continue simmering until the tomatoes begin to break down, about 5 minutes, stirring occasionally.

5. Stir in the rice, pour in the warmed broth, stir well, and bring the mixture back to a simmer. Reduce the heat even more and simmer very slowly, stirring all the time, for 15 minutes. Don't stop. Keep stirring the whole time. At long last, cover the skillet or pan and continue simmering for 25 minutes. You may have to improvise a cover if you're working with a paella pan—use a large lid from another pan or cover tightly with foil.

6. Add the squid, scallops, and peas. Arrange the shrimp, lobster tail halves (meat side down), and clams (hinge down) over and in the rice mixture. Cover the skillet or pan again and continue cooking at a fairly low simmer until the clams open, about 10 minutes. If desired, remove the cover and boil off the excess liquid for a few minutes. However, the rice will also absorb more liquid as the dish sits off the heat for 5 minutes to blend and mellow the flavors.

SEARED TUNA AND BROWN RICE CHIRASHI

SERVES 4

Active time: 40 minutes
Total time: 1 hour 30 minutes

1½ cups water

1 cup short-grain brown rice

3 tablespoons rice vinegar
(page 97)

1 tablespoon soy sauce (regular
or reduced-sodium)

2 teaspoons sugar

¼ cup sesame seeds, preferably a
50/50 blend of black and
white sesame seeds

1 tuna steak (2 pounds)

1 tablespoon toasted sesame oil

2 teaspoons prepared wasabi
paste

One 8-inch piece of daikon,
sliced into paper-thin rings

TESTERS' NOTE

▪ Chirashi is traditionally made with seasoned white rice, on top of which is laid various sorts of sliced fish, mostly raw. Because brown rice has so much more flavor per spoonful, we've coated the tuna in sesame seeds and seared it to balance the dish more successfully.

1. Combine the water and rice in a medium saucepan and bring to a boil over high heat. Cover, reduce the heat to low, and cook until the rice is almost tender and the water has been absorbed, about 40 minutes. Set aside, covered, to steam for 10 minutes.

2. Meanwhile, whisk together the vinegar, soy sauce, and sugar in a small bowl until the sugar dissolves.

3. Spread the cooked rice into a 9 x 13-inch baking dish. Drizzle the vinegar mixture over the rice. Cool for 15 minutes, tossing every few minutes and spreading the rice out again.

4. Press the sesame seeds into the tuna steak on a cutting board. You may need to put some on one side, press them gently in place, then turn the tuna steak over and press down gently while adding more to the other side, repeating this until the thing is coated.

5. Heat a large skillet over medium heat. Swirl in the sesame oil, then slip the tuna steak into the pan. Cook for 3 minutes, then turn with a wide, flat spatula, keeping as many of the sesame seeds in place as possible. Continue cooking until rare, about 2 more minutes, or medium-rare, about 3 more minutes. Transfer the tuna steak to a cutting board and slice into thin strips.

6. Spoon the seasoned cooked rice into 4 individual serving bowls. Smear ½ teaspoon wasabi paste over the rice in each bowl. Top with tuna slices and daikon rings.

THAI-STYLE CORN AND PORK SKEWERS

4 ears of corn, husked and cut into 2-inch pieces

2 pounds center-cut boneless pork loin, cut into 2-inch cubes

2 tablespoons Thai yellow curry paste

¼ cup fresh lime juice

2 tablespoons Asian fish sauce

2 tablespoons packed dark brown sugar

Oil for greasing the grill grate or grill pan

1. Thread the corn and pork onto 4 long metal skewers or 8 shorter bamboo ones, alternating the grain and meat as you go.

2. Whisk the curry paste, lime juice, fish sauce, and brown sugar in a small bowl until the brown sugar dissolves. Brush this mixture onto the corn and pork on the skewers. Reserve the excess marinade and set aside the skewers at room temperature while you prepare the grill.

3. Set up a grill for direct high-heat cooking or heat a grill pan over medium-high heat. Dip a crumpled paper towel in some oil, grasp it with long-handled tongs, and rub it over the cooking grate or the grill pan.

4. Set the skewers on the cooking grill grate directly over the heat or in the grill pan. Brush with more of the marinade. Grill, turning occasionally to brown all sides and brushing often with the marinade, until an instant-read thermometer inserted into a pork cube without touching the skewer registers 150°F, about 12 minutes. Remove from the heat and let stand at room temperature for a few minutes before serving.

Active time: 30 minutes
Total time: 45 minutes

CHEF IT UP!

▓ Make your own Thai curry paste: Crush and then mince a 2-inch section of the white part of a lemongrass stalk. Place this in mortar or a mini food processor. Add 1 seeded and quartered serrano chile, 1 quartered garlic clove, 2 whole cloves, 1 tablespoon cumin seeds, 1 tablespoon turmeric, 1 teaspoon ground coriander, and 1 teaspoon ground cinnamon. Grind with the pestle into a grainy paste—or snap on the lid and pulse many times, scraping down the canister once or twice to make sure everything takes a spiral onto the blades. Scrape the paste into a small bowl, cover, and store in the fridge for up to 2 weeks.

TESTERS' NOTES

▓ This is fairly simple summer fare. Consider serving these on a bed of cooked brown rice, whole-grain farro, or black barley.

▓ Read the label before you buy a Thai yellow curry paste. Some can be incendiary. Check to see that several aromatics come in the list before the hot stuff.

SERVES 4

Active time: 45 minutes
Total time: 1 hour 20 minutes

Make ahead: The yellow pepper relish can be made in advance, covered, and stored in the refrigerator for up to 1 week.

TESTERS' NOTES

- The teff is not precooked but instead cooks via the heat and internal steam once the balls hit the oil.

- You can also substitute ¾ pound finely chopped, peeled and deveined, cooked shrimp for the crab.

- You can serve these as you would falafel. Make a chopped salad bed with chopped iceberg lettuce, diced red bell pepper, diced celery, diced red onion, and chopped tomatoes. Spread the salad on the plate, then top with the fried balls. Forego the pepper relish and drizzle them with Tzatziki Sauce (page 186).

FRIED TEFF AND CRAB BALLS WITH YELLOW PEPPER RELISH

Relish

2 yellow bell peppers, cut into quarters and seeded

1 small yellow onion

½ cup water

½ cup plus 2 tablespoons distilled white vinegar, divided

3 tablespoons sugar

¼ teaspoon salt

¼ teaspoon red pepper flakes

Teff balls

¾ cup whole-grain, finely ground, yellow cornmeal

¾ cup whole wheat pastry flour

¼ cup brown teff

¼ cup old-fashioned rolled oats (do not use quick-cooking or steel-cut)

1½ tablespoons sugar

2 teaspoons baking powder

1 teaspoon dried thyme

1 teaspoon dried marjoram

1 teaspoon onion powder

½ teaspoon cayenne pepper

½ teaspoon salt

¾ pound pasteurized crabmeat, picked over to remove bits of shell and cartilage

¼ cup milk (whole, 2%, 1%, or fat-free)

1 large egg plus 1 large egg white

2 tablespoons unsalted butter, melted and cooled

Peanut oil, for frying

1. To make the yellow pepper relish: Bring a large tea kettle of water to a boil over high heat. Shred the bell peppers and onion with the large holes of box grater or in a food processor fitted with shredding blade. Place in a large bowl, cover with the boiling water to a depth of 1 inch, and set aside for 5 minutes. Drain in a colander set in the sink.

2. Place the peppers and onion in a medium saucepan. Stir in the ½ cup cool water and ½ cup of the vinegar and bring to simmer over high heat. Remove from heat, cover, and let stand for 10 minutes. Drain in a colander set in the sink.

(continued)

3. Return the peppers and onion to the saucepan. Stir in the remaining 2 tablespoons vinegar, the sugar, salt, and red pepper flakes. Bring to a simmer over medium-high heat. Reduce the heat to low and simmer for 10 minutes, or until thickened like marmalade, stirring often. Set aside.

4. To make the teff balls: Mix the cornmeal, whole wheat pastry flour, teff, oats, sugar, baking powder, thyme, marjoram, onion powder, cayenne, and salt in a large bowl. Stir in the crabmeat, milk, whole egg, egg white, and melted butter to form a stiff but also sticky dough.

5. Pour enough oil into a large Dutch oven, a large high-sided skillet, or a large sauté pan so that it is about 2 inches deep in the pan. Clip a deep-frying thermometer to the inside of the pan and heat the oil over medium-high heat until between 325°F and 350°F.

6. Scoop up the dough in rounded, heaping tablespoonfuls. Slip these into the hot oil. Adjust the burner temperature so that the oil's heat remains fairly constant. Fry until browned and crisp, turning occasionally, 4 to 5 minutes. Transfer to a rack with paper towels under it to drain. Continue making more of the balls in batches. Serve with the relish as a condiment.

Active time: 35 minutes

Total time: 1 hour 20 minutes plus soaking the groats for at least 8 hours

Save time: Use 1⅓ cups cooked oat groats and omit soaking and cooking the raw grains.

GRAIN SWAPS

- Substitute ⅔ cup whole-grain farro for the oat groats and cook an extra 10 minutes to make sure it's soft enough to forestall a hard, nut-shell crunch in the pancakes.

OAT GROAT AND POTATO PANCAKES WITH SMOKED SALMON AND CRÈME FRAÎCHE

⅔ cup oat groats

3 medium russet potatoes (about 1¾ pounds)

1 small yellow onion, peeled

4 large eggs, well beaten in a small bowl

½ teaspoon caraway seeds

½ teaspoon salt

½ teaspoon ground black pepper

4 tablespoons olive oil, divided

8 thin slices smoked salmon

About ½ cup crème fraîche, sour cream (regular or low-fat), or Greek yogurt (whole-milk or 2%)

Minced scallions, for garnish

1. Soak the oat groats in a big bowl of cool water for at least 8 and up to 16 hours. Drain the groats in a fine-mesh sieve or small-holed colander set in the sink. Pour the groats into a large saucepan, fill it halfway with water, and bring to a boil over high heat. Reduce the heat to low and simmer until tender with a nutlike chew, about 45 minutes. Drain again in that sieve or colander. Run cool water over the groats to bring them to room temperature, stirring once in a while. Drain thoroughly.

2. Grate the potatoes and onion through the large holes of a box grater and into a large bowl. Pick the mixture up by handfuls and squeeze them almost dry over the sink. Put them all back in the bowl and stir in the drained groats, beaten eggs, caraway seeds, salt, and pepper.

(continued)

3. Heat a large skillet, preferably nonstick, over medium heat. Swirl in 2 tablespoons of the oil. Spoon up ½ cup of the oat groat mixture and slip it into the oil. Press down to create a pancake about 4 inches in diameter. Make 3 more pancakes in the skillet. Cook until crisp and well browned, 3 to 4 minutes. Flip the cakes and continue cooking until the other side is equally crisp and browned, 3 to 4 more minutes. Transfer the pancakes to a serving platter. Add the remaining 2 tablespoons oil to the skillet and use the remaining groat mixture to make 4 more pancakes. Once they're all on the platter, top each with some slices of smoked salmon and a small dollop of crème fraîche or one of its stand-ins. Garnish with minced scallions.

TESTERS' NOTES

Although we began this book by saying we weren't going to use a grain as a "bed" for anything—because it seemed a cheating way to turn a whole grain into a main course—we couldn't resist these crunchy, savory pancakes, perfect for a weeknight dinner (provided you've got cooked oat groats on hand) or a weekend brunch. Find a mild smoked salmon, nothing assertive, so the nutty taste of the oat groats won't be lost in the mêlée.

Don't use any other potato than a russet, the gold standard for baking potatoes. Russets have exactly the right amount of starch both to help the pancakes stay together and to get them crisp over the heat.

QUINOA CREPES WITH CORN, AVOCADO, AND MEXICAN CREMA

SERVES 4

Active time: 45 minutes
Total time: 1 hour 20 minutes

Make ahead: Prepare the corn filling up to 2 days in advance; however, omit the salt and add it only at the last minute.

Save time: Use 1¾ cups cooked quinoa and omit cooking the raw grains.

Filling

4 ears of corn, husked

2 large Hass avocados, diced

12 cherry tomatoes, quartered

2 tablespoons cider vinegar

2 tablespoons almond oil

2 teaspoons minced fresh oregano leaves or 1 teaspoon dried oregano

1 teaspoon ground cumin

½ teaspoon salt

½ teaspoon ground black pepper

Crepes

½ cup white or red quinoa

1½ cups milk (whole, 2%, 1%, or fat-free)

¼ cup almond oil, plus more for the skillet

1 tablespoon honey

1 large egg, at room temperature

1½ cups whole wheat pastry flour (do not use whole wheat flour)

1½ teaspoons baking powder

½ teaspoon salt

Garnish

Mexican crema or crème fraîche, thinned with a little white wine until pourable, for serving

MAKE IT EASIER!

- Skip boiling the whole ears; instead, use 2½ cups frozen corn kernels, thawed.

CHEF IT UP!

- Grill the corn—or follow the procedure for roasting the ears in a foil packet over an open flame on page 138.

1. To make the filling: Bring a large pot of water to a boil over high heat. Add the corn, cover, turn off the heat, and set aside for 10 minutes. Drain, then slice the kernels off the ears. Cool for 10 minutes.

2. Mix the corn with the rest of the filling ingredients in a large bowl: the avocados, tomatoes, vinegar, almond oil, oregano, cumin, salt, and pepper. Set aside.

3. To make the crepes: Fill a large saucepan halfway with water, add the quinoa, and bring it to a boil over high heat. Reduce the heat to low and cook until the grains have developed their halos and are tender, 10 to 12 minutes. Drain in a fine-mesh sieve or a lined colander set in the sink. Run under cool water until the grains are room temperature. Drain thoroughly.

4. Whisk the cooked quinoa in a large bowl with the milk, the ¼ cup almond oil, honey, and egg. Whisk in the whole wheat pastry flour, baking powder, and salt to make a batter.

5. Lightly grease a 12-inch nonstick skillet with some almond oil on a wadded-up paper towel. Heat over medium-low heat. Pour in a scant ½ cup batter all around the skillet, not in a lump in the center; quickly shake and swirl the skillet to thin the batter out into an even coating. Cook until the bottom is set and the batter has bubbles throughout, about 2 minutes. The top will already look dry. Loosen the crepe with a large spatula and flip it in the skillet. Cook about 30 seconds more, until set and lightly browned. Transfer to a large plate, oil the skillet again, and continue making more crepes until you have 8 or 9.

6. Set a crepe on a serving plate and spoon about ⅔ cup of the prepared corn filling into its center. Fold the edges over the filling and drizzle with a little Mexican crema or thinned-out crème fraîche. Add another crepe to the plate, fill it, drizzle on some crema. Keep working until you've made up 4 plates with 2 crepes each.

TESTERS' NOTES

▪ These crepes are not the delicate, wispy standards—they are thick and substantial, more in keeping with whole grains themselves.

▪ A 12-inch nonstick skillet is crucial to the success of the dish. If yours is smaller, you'll need to use much less batter to make a thin, even crepe—and end up making more crepes as well.

▪ The quinoa adds a lovely crunch and some savory notes to these gorgeous crepes, a worthy dish for any dinner party. A shrimp or fish ceviche would be the perfect first course—then follow up the crepes with some mango sorbet and crunchy cookies.

▪ Mexican crema is like sour cream or crème fraîche. It's actually a cultured sour cream and sometimes not quite as thick as crème fraîche. You can substitute crème fraîche for the Mexican crema in this recipe, but you may need to whisk a little milk into it to get it to the right, saucelike consistency.

ACKNOWLEDGMENTS

A cookbook is a work of friction: heat, time, and effort. After 20 or so, we've gotten used to the rub. It doesn't get easier, just better, especially when you've got people like these on your side.

What started out as a simple proposal morphed into an editorial relay match. Kudos and kisses to Pam Krauss for acquiring the work and believing in its possibilities, to Gena Smith for confidently shepherding the manuscript through all the permutations, and to Elissa Altman for calming our nerves and championing our book both in house and beyond.

This book was finessed by some of the finest copy editors, Kate Slate and Deri Reed: careful, considerate, exacting. We also couldn't have gotten this project aloft without Nancy Bailey who oversaw the production details, Jessica Lee who took on its marketing, Aly Mostel who pumped its publicity prospects, and Steven Perrine in the offing, who protected the book when the prospects looked grim.

As to the book's design, we give props to Chris Gaugler who oversaw the photo shoot and then designed a work of art. We adore Tina Rupp for her pitch-perfect eye as well as her protective but graceful assistant, Linda Pugliese. We set Tina the impossible task of finding a cross between downtown and the Hamptons—she got it spot on. Leslie Siegel is a terrific prop stylist: a clear aesthetic and no drama. We can't wait to work with her again! She had a tip-top team with Kate Parisian and Joshua Fennell. Finally, Matt Hill was a crackerjack chef, working in the kitchen with Bruce to create the food in the photographs.

Thanks to Jeffrey Elliot at Staub USA for outrageously flawless cookware, Krista Erickson with Zojirushi America Corp. for a decidedly fantastic rice cooker, and Laurie O'Hara at OXO for a gaggle of handy gadgets. With so many kitchen tools, we tested not only recipes but the patience of our friends, who endured meal after meal, particularly Richard Bradspies, Dore Everett, Fayette Reynolds, and Rich Rosenfeld. And many thanks to the book group at the Norfolk Library. We're just glad you didn't beat each other senseless getting to the bowls on the table.

Finally, the best for last. Much gratitude to Stacy Testa at Writers House, a reassuring voice; to Susan Ginsburg, the agent of any writer's dreams, who has overseen our tag-team, two-person career for almost fifteen years, surely a record in this world of words; and to Dreydl, because everyone needs a collie.

INDEX

Underscored page references indicate boxed text. **Boldfaced** page references indicate photographs.

Hominy. *See* Posole
Hypertension, 1

I

Italian-style dishes
    Barley Risotto with Mushrooms and Leeks, 202, **203**
    Italian-Style Black Quinoa and Spinach Summer Rolls, 118, **119**
    Sicilian-Inspired Wheat Berry and Tuna Salad, 68

J

Job's tears
    about, 18
    Asian Picadillo with Job's Tears, 110–11
    Job's Tears and Edamame in a Carrot Dressing, 109
    Roasted Ratatouille with Job's Tears, 205

K

Kale
    Avgolemono Soup with Corn Grits Dumplings, 140, **141**
Kamut
    about, 31
    Breakfast Polenta Cake with Kamut Crunch Topping, 59–60, **61**
    Deconstructed Kamut Caesar Salad, 80
    Kamut and Beef Chili, 142–43
    Kamut Burgers with Shallots, Pecans, and Lemon Zest, 129
    Kamut Salad with Cauliflower, Olives, and Raisins, **78**, 79
    Louisiana-Inspired Red Beans and Kamut, 188–89
    Way-More-Than-Just-Oats Granola, 38, **39**
Kasha
    Kasha Varnishkes Soup, 153

L

Lamb
    Lamb and Triticale Tagine, 192–94, **193**
Lemons
    Avgolemono Soup with Corn Grits Dumplings, 140, **141**
    Kamut Burgers with Shallots, Pecans, and Lemon Zest, 129
    Lamb and Triticale Tagine, 192–94, **193**
    Wheat Berry Salad with Zucchini, Boiled Lemon, and Almonds, 67
Lentils
    Red Rice and Lentils, 91
    Turkish Red Lentil and Bulgur Soup, **148**, 149
Lunch. *See also* Salads
    Italian-Style Black Quinoa and Spinach Summer Rolls, 118, **119**

Roasted Corn and Shrimp "Ceviche," 120
Sandwich Wrap with a Wheat Berry Spread, 117
Tomatoes Stuffed with Black Rice and Shrimp, 116

M

Meat. *See* Beef and veal; Lamb; Pork
Millet
    about, 22
    Groats and Grits Hot Cereal with Honey and Orange Zest, 42
    Japanese-Inspired Brown Rice and Millet Casserole, 156
    Millet, Barley, and Split Pea Soup with Coconut and Ginger, 147
    Millet and Spinach Casserole, 167–68
    Millet Burgers with Olives, Sun-Dried Tomatoes, and Pecorino, 133–35, **134**
    Millet Salad with Corn and Peanuts, 103
    Slow-Cooker Three-Grain Porridge with Dates and Honey, 44
    Vegetable and Grits Pot Pie, **170**, 171–72
Muffins
    Quinoa Cashew Muffins, 56–57
Mushrooms
    Asian-Inspired Quinoa with Canadian Bacon, 99
    Barley, Mushrooms, and Peas, 201
    Barley Risotto with Mushrooms and Leeks, 202, **203**
    Japanese-Inspired Brown Rice and Millet Casserole, 156
    Quinoa with Asparagus and Shiitakes, **100**, 101
    Southwestern Amaranth Polenta, 204

N

Nectarines
    Farro with Nectarines, Basil, and Toasted Pine Nuts, 74, **75**
Nuts. *See also* Almonds; Pecans; Pine nuts; Walnuts
    Buckwheat and Cashew Burgers, 126–27
    Japanese-Inspired Brown Rice and Millet Casserole, 156
    Millet Salad with Corn and Peanuts, 103
    Quinoa Cashew Muffins, 56–57
    Red Rice Romesco Salad, 90
    Spicy Brown Rice Salad with Chicken and Peanuts, 85–86, **87**
    Wild Rice Salad with Orange Supremes, Shaved Fennel, and Pistachios, 92, **93**

O

Oats
    about, 22–23
    Black Quinoa and Black Bean Burgers, 128
    Cornmeal and Oat Waffle Mix, 48, **49**